# Diverging Paths of Development in Central Asia



Newly gained sovereignty, uneven penetration of neo-liberal ideals and the growth of disparate capitalist markets have elicited varied responses in Central Asia. What does development mean for the political class and for ordinary citizens? What are the effects of new capitalist institutions and markets? What impact did western development blueprints and external donor engagement leave in the region?

This book illuminates the diverse realities of post-Soviet development in Central Asia through a multidisciplinary prism. The contributing articles are grounded in a range of social science disciplines including architecture, anthropology and geography. The analyses demonstrate how a synthesis of specialist knowledge from area studies and individual disciplinary methodologies can provide well-grounded critical positions on development. The book highlights the complexities of everyday routines of dispossession and coping strategies in the face of natural and manmade disasters. These experiences create deep moral anxieties under the debilitating effects of monetisation and marketisation of ordinary livelihoods, social ties and environmental resources. This book was originally published as a special issue of *Central Asian Survey*.

**Gül Berna Özcan** is Reader in International Business and Entrepreneurship at the School of Management, Royal Holloway, University of London, UK. She is the author of *Building States and Markets: Enterprise Development in Central Asia* (Palgrave, 2010).

## ThirdWorlds

Edited by
Shahid Qadir, *University of London, UK*

**ThirdWorlds** will focus on the political economy, development and cultures of those parts of the world that have experienced the most political, social, and economic upheaval, and which have faced the greatest challenges of the postcolonial world under globalisation: poverty, displacement and diaspora, environmental degradation, human and civil rights abuses, war, hunger, and disease.

**ThirdWorlds** serves as a signifier of oppositional emerging economies and cultures ranging from Africa, Asia, Latin America, Middle East, and even those 'Souths' within a larger perceived North, such as the U.S. South and Mediterranean Europe. The study of these otherwise disparate and discontinuous areas, known collectively as the Global South, demonstrates that as globalisation pervades the planet, the south, as a synonym for subalterity, also transcends geographical and ideological frontier.

For a complete list of titles in this series, please visit https://www.routledge.com/series/TWQ

**Recent titles in the series include:**

**Food Sovereignty**
Convergence and Contradictions, Condition and Challenges
*Edited by Eric Holt-Giménez, Alberto Alonso-Fradejas, Todd Holmes and Martha Jane Robbins*

**The International Politics of Ebola**
*Edited by Anne Roemer-Mahler and Simon Rushton*

**Rising Powers and South-South Cooperation**
*Edited by Kevin Gray and Barry K. Gills*

**The 'Local Turn' in Peacebuilding**
The Liberal Peace Challenged
*Edited by Joakim Öjendal, Isabell Schierenbeck and Caroline Hughes*

**China's Contingencies and Globalization**
*Edited by Changgang Guo, Liu Debin and Jan Nederveen Pieterse*

**The Power of Human Rights/The Human Rights of Power**
*Edited by Louiza Odysseos and Anna Selmeczi*

**Class Dynamics of Development**
*Edited by Jonathan Pattenden, Liam Campling, Satoshi Miyamura and Benjamin Selwyn*

**Offshore Central Asia**
*Edited by John Heathershaw and Alexander Cooley*

**Third World Approaches to International Law**
*Edited by Amar Bhatia, Usha Natarajan, John Reynolds and Sujith Xavier*

**Aid to Support Fragile States**
The Challenge of Chronic State Weakness
*Edited by Rachel M. Gisselquist*

# Diverging Paths of Development in Central Asia

## Market Adaptations, Interventions and Daily Experience

*Edited by*

**Gül Berna Özcan**

Routledge
Taylor & Francis Group
LONDON AND NEW YORK

First published 2017 by Routledge

2 Park Square, Milton Park, Abingdon, Oxfordshire OX14 4RN
52 Vanderbilt Avenue, New York, NY 10017

*Routledge is an imprint of the Taylor & Francis Group, an informa business*

First issued in paperback 2020



*British Library Cataloguing in Publication Data*
A catalogue record for this book is available from the British Library

ISBN 13: 978-1-138-73447-0 (hbk)
ISBN 13: 978-0-367-59507-4 (pbk)

Typeset in TimesNewRomanPS
by diacriTech, Chennai

**Publisher's Note**
The publisher accepts responsibility for any inconsistencies that may have arisen during the conversion of this book from journal articles to book chapters, namely the possible inclusion of journal terminology.

# Contents

# Citation Information

The chapters in this book were originally published in *Central Asian Survey*, volume 34, issue 4 (December 2015). When citing this material, please use the original page numbering for each article, as follows:

**Chapter 1**
*Introduction: market adaptations, interventions and daily experience*
Gül Berna Özcan
*Central Asian Survey*, volume 34, issue 4 (December 2015) pp. 409–417

**Chapter 2**
*Ideology in brick and tile: Timurid architecture of the 21st century*
Elena Paskaleva
*Central Asian Survey*, volume 34, issue 4 (December 2015) pp. 418–439

**Chapter 3**
*The ideology of development and legitimation: beyond 'Kazakhstan 2030'*
Diana T. Kudaibergenova
*Central Asian Survey*, volume 34, issue 4 (December 2015) pp. 440–455

**Chapter 4**
*Social, environmental and economic sustainability of Kazakhstan: a long-term perspective*
Marzhan Thomas
*Central Asian Survey*, volume 34, issue 4 (December 2015) pp. 456–483

**Chapter 5**
*Uzbekistan's 'spirit' of self-reliance and the logic of appropriateness: TAPOich and interaction with Russia*
Bernardo Teles Fazendeiro
*Central Asian Survey*, volume 34, issue 4 (December 2015) pp. 484–498

**Chapter 6**
*Promoting empowerment? The World Bank's Village Investment Project in Kyrgyzstan*
Babken Babajanian
*Central Asian Survey*, volume 34, issue 4 (December 2015) pp. 499–515

**Chapter 7**

*'Donors are not interested in reality': the interplay between international donors and local NGOs in Kyrgyzstan's HIV/AIDS sector*
Svetlana Ancker and Bernd Rechel
*Central Asian Survey*, volume 34, issue 4 (December 2015) pp. 516–530

**Chapter 8**

*The monetization of social celebrations in rural Kyrgyzstan: on the uses of hashish money*
Gulzat Botoeva
*Central Asian Survey*, volume 34, issue 4 (December 2015) pp. 531–548

**Chapter 9**

*Everyday disasters, stagnation and the normalcy of non-development: Roghun Dam, a flood, and campaigns of forced taxation in southern Tajikistan*
Diana Ibañez-Tirado
*Central Asian Survey*, volume 34, issue 4 (December 2015) pp. 549–563

# Notes on Contributors

**Svetlana Ancker** is a PhD graduate at the Department of Health Services Research and Policy of London School of Hygiene & Tropical Medicine, London, UK.

**Babken Babajanian** is an Associate Professorial Lecturer at the Institute of Public Affairs, London School of Economics and Political Science. He previously worked at the Overseas Development Institute, the Asian Development Bank, and the World Bank.

**Gulzat Botoeva** is a Lecturer in Social Sciences Department, University of Roehampton, London, UK.

**Diana Ibañez-Tirado** is a Research Fellow at the School of Global Studies (Anthropology), University of Sussex, Brighton, UK, and a Research Associate at the Centre of Contemporary Central Asia and the Caucasus, Department of Anthropology and Sociology, SOAS, University of London, London, UK.

**Diana T. Kudaibergenova** earned her PhD from the Department of Sociology, University of Cambridge, and she is currently a research fellow at the Centre of Development Studies, University of Cambridge, UK.

**Gül Berna Özcan** is Reader in International Business and Entrepreneurship at the School of Management, Royal Holloway, University of London, UK. She is the author of *Building States and Markets: Enterprise Development in Central Asia* (Palgrave, 2010).

**Elena Paskaleva** is a Lecturer at the Leiden University Institute for Area Studies, Leiden, the Netherlands.

**Bernd Rechel** is Researcher at the European Observatory on Health Systems and Policies, London School of Hygiene & Tropical Medicine, London, UK.

**Bernardo Teles Fazendeiro** is a teaching fellow at the School of International Relations at the University of St Andrews, Scotland, UK.

**Marzhan Thomas** is a chartered marine scientist (IMarEST) and earned her PhD from the Department of Geography, Environment and Envelopment Studies, Birkbeck, University of London, UK.

# Introduction: market adaptations, interventions and daily experience

Gül Berna Özcan

*School of Management, Royal Holloway University of London, Egham, Surrey, UK*

This special issue illuminates diverse realities of post-Soviet development in Central Asia through a multidisciplinary prism. The contributing articles are grounded in a range of social science disciplines including architecture, anthropology and geography, as well as drawing from mainstream social sciences. The analyses demonstrate how a synthesis of specialist knowledge from area studies and individual disciplinary methodologies can provide well-grounded critical positions on development.

Newly gained sovereignty, uneven penetration of neoliberal ideals, and the growth of disparate capitalist markets have elicited varied responses in Central Asia. The discourse of transition from communism to a free market economy and democracy has long disappeared from policy circles, replaced by growing anxiety about the future of insular economies such as Uzbekistan and the fragility of Kyrgyzstan and Tajikistan. The region is increasingly buffeted between the fickle interests of China and Russia, and security-conscious Western policy objectives. Deepening instability and radicalization in Pakistan and Afghanistan threaten even the modest achievements of post-Soviet states with the looming danger of Middle Eastern influences on regional politics which may lead to social fragmentation and the spread of radical jihadist movements.

The current literature does not fully capture the post-transition economic and social realities and development prospects of the region. What does development mean for the political class and for ordinary citizens? What are the effects of new capitalist institutions and markets? What impact did Western development blueprints and external donor engagement have in the region? Not only are these vast and difficult research problems, but they also present multiple challenges. The institutional interests of donors, corporations and security agencies skew research-area priorities and funding. The region's governments and ruling elite are hostile to academic scholarship that challenges their position and control. The cognitive distance between Western observers and Central Asians remains large, and only major disasters and violent conflicts attract significant attention.

This special issue illuminates diverse realities of post-Soviet development in Central Asia through a multidisciplinary prism.[1] The contributing articles are grounded in a range of social science disciplines including architecture, anthropology and geography, as well as drawing from mainstream social sciences. The analyses demonstrate how a synthesis of specialist knowledge from area studies and individual disciplinary methodologies can provide well-grounded critical positions on development. This sort of pluralistic, and somewhat eclectic, scholarship can best contribute to new perspectives on development philosophy and practice (Sen 1999; Pieterse 2010). Such an approach benefits, on the one hand, from dealing with features of contemporary capitalist processes and, on the other, from opening up new avenues of understanding and empowerment (Arsel and Dasgupta 2015).

The contributors to this volume present a wealth of positions and evidence. First, several articles illustrate how authoritarian regimes have diverted national resources towards the advancement of personalized power structures. This trajectory has emerged through highly opaque wealth allocation processes using disparate forms of market liberalization and taking advantage of newly acquired sovereignty. The choices and the interests of ruling elites and their legitimacy concerns have opportunistically shaped diverging forms of capitalism and governance structures in the region. Second, the uneven but steady penetration of foreign interests and external agencies reconfigures development rhetoric as they replace the once Moscow-driven Soviet mega-structure of re-allocation and distribution regimes. These external interventions bring about contestations over local power positions and development agendas. Finally, the issue highlights the complexities of everyday routines of dispossession and coping strategies in the face of natural and manmade disasters. These experiences create deep moral anxiety under the debilitating effects of monetization and marketization of ordinary livelihoods, social ties and environmental resources.

### *Development trajectories: adaptations, interventions and experience*

Development trajectories in the region are contextualized broadly in relation to capitalist adaptations, foreign interventions and the everyday struggle to hold on to livelihoods and subsistence.

*Capitalist adaptations.* Several essays show how capitalist development in Central Asia can be seen through the lens of the spread of neoliberalism and its institutionalization through policy templates by multilateral organizations, aid agencies and the global interdependencies of financial capital. Contrary to misleading perceptions of its economic isolation, Central Asia is not insulated from international capital movements. On the contrary, as the recent special issue of *Central Asian Survey* on 'Offshore Central Asia' (Heathershaw and Cooley 2015) illustrates, the region's economic assets and natural resources are increasingly integrated into global value networks. Offshore accounts and monetary transactions show a complex interplay among multiple actors involving the region's ruling elites, new business classes and Western financial and legal institutions across multiple geographical domains.

Central Asia's ruling elites attempt to legitimize their market dominance through political processes that lead to diverging outcomes. While Kazakhstan prefers a steady but controlled integration into world markets by allowing a degree of market participation through foreign direct investment in its rich energy reserves, Uzbekistan pursues an archaic model of import substitution and self-sufficiency to maintain narrow elite interests in the economy. These interlinkages are not unique to Central Asia, and the essays presented here fit into a broader puzzle around developing economies. Rather than a uniform, orderly process, evidence points to many customized neoliberal modes emerging with a range of paradoxes under diverse political ideologies (Özcan and Gündüz 2016). The contradictions of these adaptations are lucidly illustrated in a recent special issue of the *International Review of Political Economy* (Ban and Blyt 2013) on the BRIC nations (Brazil, Russia, India and China). Analyses show, for example, how the Chinese Communist Party pursues market liberalization and de facto privatization while legitimizing its stance by appeal to communist principles. Central Asia's ruling elites try to chart their own course in a piecemeal manner while taking advantage of market capitalism and private ownership, albeit on the basis of weak state formation (Hale 2014). The essays refer to such juxtapositions with evidence from urban aesthetics, industrial policies and features of local economies. One emerging form is the deepening authoritarianism with patrimonial leadership in countries such as Uzbekistan and Kazakhstan; another is the hazardous dismantling of the state apparatus in

Kyrgyzstan and Tajikistan by partisan interests. As shown by Kudaibergenova, President Nazarbayev's ideological strategy in Kazakhstan 2030 is primarily an exercise of control over regional economic and political elites and aims to guarantee legitimacy for the regime. The defensive position of Uzbekistan demonstrates the limits of protective policies in the context of trade liberalization (see Teles Fazendeiro in this volume).

*Foreign interventions.* There is a multiplicity of competing international agendas in Central Asia for the penetration of global actors through trade, civilian and military aid, and diplomatic cooperation. The relative retreat of direct Russian involvement is increasingly replaced by new political and military cooperation and a customs union under Russia's leadership. However, the region is no longer part of a tightly networked and self-sufficient realm as it was during the Soviet era. Nevertheless, the ruling elites' economic interests in key industries have shaped their external relations and their receptivity to aid (Junisbai 2010). China's steady penetration in energy markets and infrastructure investments, combined with the will of the EU and US to remain influential, lead to a messy brawl for influence through special deals and grants. China has also been pushing for alternative institutions, as a means of extending its growing economic power (Pirani 2011). Some evidence from Chinese involvement in Africa points to a new form of influence on a grand scale (Tan-Mullins, Giles, and Power 2010; Brautigam 2011).

Evidence points out that many aid programmes come at the expense of long-term sustained economic development because they have short-term horizons and conflict with local initiatives. Yet, while Russia's influence lacks economic vision, the achievements of Western assistance over the years have also been meagre. As identified by Babajanian and Ancker and Rechel in this volume, international aid has failed to enable state institutions and to create good governance for long-term sustainability. Kyrgyzstan is a case in point. While the country's political elite manipulated their image to appear progressive to secure access to donor resources, international actors wilfully ignored the most debilitating aspects of the state institutions: corruption and poor accountability. This led to false claims about the achievements of both parties. This is no surprise to many scholars who have long emphasized that aid is a mechanism for power building in global politics (Sinha 1974; Hattori 2001; Woods 2008).

*Everyday experience.* Development outcomes are essentially about human experience and cognition. The essays here illustrate the complexity of everyday experience and the debilitating nature of fragmentation, which inhibits the emergence of new social forces to shape better future prospects and visions for communities. At the micro level, poor developmental outcomes lead to a diversity of coping strategies through everyday responses for survival (see the contributions of Botoeva and Ibañez-Tirado in this volume). These responses generate their own institutional forms, which breed new patterns of inertia in the long run. Growing forms of illicit trade, the normalization of corruption, and lives divided across borders through seasonal migration leave millions to their own devices in isolated geographies. Norms evolve to accept fuzzy morals, while cynicism and loss of confidence in collective action bring about further hazards. Fading hope amongst the population for some form of equitable and just economic order is arguably the biggest hindrance to future development prospects in the region. This fragmentation leads to tolerance of morally dubious positions. In Uzbekistan, due to limited political participation, market players have no voice or power beyond the superficial consultation rounds managed by top-down state organs. The regime maintains control of markets through its coercive bureaucracy and affiliated oligarchic groups eager to eliminate their business competitors (Özcan 2010). Uzbekistan's economic management is best described by falsifications. Ordinary citizens are indoctrinated daily in an engineered history, official mottos and image making in a fashion similar to Soviet practices, generating a façade of uniformity and order. Paskaleva's analysis of the architectural representation of history illustrates the spatial reflection of this overbearing state.

Although the emphasis of this volume is on the post-Soviet experience with the region's diverse experiments in capitalism, legacy effects are persistent and interwoven within new institutional forms. Post-Soviet market development and new property ownership have been functions of Soviet-era endowments and institutional structures (Gleason 2003; Özcan 2010). Central Asia's transformation and transitional status present similarities with other parts of the globe where earlier post-colonial experiments with national development and more recently neoliberal policy templates brought about other forms of dependence at the expense of sovereignty. Therefore, the investigative frameworks and theoretical positions in this volume can usefully be applied to other sorts of local conditions elsewhere in the post-command economy (Kandiyoti 1996) and post-colonial world where the spread of neoliberal economic opportunism has shifted the boundaries of markets and states to a new level of uncertainty with deepening control of multinational enterprises. The key findings point out how development agendas and tools have been captured by powerful external agents and local power position holders, especially as far as organizing economic activities are concerned. This resonates with the cycles of power and repositioning of local rulers from the tsarist Russian Empire to the Soviet Union (Sabol 2003; Cummings and Hinnebusch 2011). The latter is significant not just as an example of modernizing affirmative empire (Martin 2001) but more so of imposing institutional hubris far beyond the reach of Central Asia's influence and resolve (Payne 2001; Khalid 2007; Cummings 2012). However, the fine line between newly gained post-Soviet sovereignty and market liberalism offers possibilities of choice for local actors in modifying allocation regimes and economic opportunities to opt for broader versus narrower participation. Thus, emerging differences between inclusive versus exclusive institutions for economic development, as shown by historical experiences around the world, generate starkly different outcomes (Acemoglu and Robinson 2012). If Kazakhstan manages to achieve this broader participation by widening economic opportunities to larger segments of societal actors on an equal footing, it may indeed become a development success story in the region for others to emulate.

### *Between pretence and reality*

The collection starts with Elena Paskaleva's analysis of the evolving relationship between aesthetics and politics in post-Soviet urban development in Uzbekistan. In addition to the commercialization of the historical past, the study shows how, throughout the two decades of Uzbek independence, key Timurid monuments have been considerably rebuilt to emphasize the symbolic legitimation of power maintenance (Cummings 2012). Restoration and the landscape manipulation of leading monuments frequently distort historical artefacts for the sake of a political ideology. Often these provide the public with messages about authoritarianism, as the Soviets once did for their own ideological advancement. Paskaleva contributes to critical heritage studies and urban development as a narrative of power making and relational space (Harvey 2009).

The next three articles tackle the state of development practice and prospects at the national level. Diana Kudaibergenova questions the ideology of development and legitimation in the Kazakhstan 2030 vision, while Marzhan Thomas examines legacy effects on the social, environmental and economic sustainability of Kazakhstan. According to the thesis of Bernardo Teles Fazendeiro, Uzbekistan's self-reliance shapes its relations with Russia and the future of its key industries, built during the Soviet Union. Kudaibergenova's textual analysis of the Kazakhstan 2030 strategy document and its origins points out that its seven tautological priorities form a substitution of ideology under the leadership of Kazakhstan's long-term president, Nursultan Nazarbayev. Its nationalizing mission seeks popular legitimation, while its critical support base rests on regional elites and interest-based clans for the creation of a stable sociopolitical and economic foundation. Regional alliances as well as clashes stem from the vested interests in exploitation of Kazakhstan's rich mineral and energy resources. This extractive industry and commodity-focused development trajectory lead to a path-dependent continuity under state-sponsored capitalism, with a new concentration of private wealth.

The study by Thomas puts prosperity into a historical perspective while providing a first comprehensive attempt to analyse sustainability in Kazakhstan through a longitudinal analysis. She shows that most regions but especially northern ones faced rapid environmental degradation and exploitation during the Soviet Union. One of the most striking figures is the 40-year (1917–1957) population depletion, mostly due to famine, war and forced migration. Her study points out that, despite improvements in income and prosperity, the transition to a market economy did not significantly diminish economic dependency on natural resources or regional inequalities in the country. However, in her final note Thomas provides some optimism for future growth potential in that the Kazakh economy has more room for manoeuvre than its highly constrained Central Asian neighbours such as Uzbekistan and surprisingly might even do better than Russia in the long run. However, this all depends on the sustainability of political institutions and management of resources.

Bernardo Teles Fazendeiro's analysis, based on a narrative developed through a 'logic of appropriateness', reveals how the Uzbek government under the authoritarian leadership of Islam Karimov followed a different trajectory from Kazakhstan's steady but cautious integration into the world economy. In managing their key economic assets and enterprises, Uzbek governments pursued self-reliance characterized by the rules of control and stability, self-sufficiency, the promotion of manufacturing, and the pursuit of economic growth via mercantilism. However, the strict adherence to these rules has produced economically damaging outcomes for the country as it narrowed the scope of business opportunities and enterprise development. Self-reliance shaped the negotiations between Tashkent and Moscow on the survival of the only aircraft production facility, which was located in Uzbekistan but connected to a range of suppliers in Russia. Uzbekistan would not compromise in its obsession with self-reliance, though Moscow held the major assets and research expertise; they found self-reliance incompatible with bilateral collaboration. In the end, Uzbeks had to relinquish aircraft production.

The next group of contributions question the efficacy and the impact of international aid on the region's development trajectories. Babken Babajanian provides a compelling assessment of the World Bank's Village Investment Projects, while Svetlana Ancker and Bernd Rechel examine the role of Western actors in HIV/AIDS policy in Kyrgyzstan. These essays highlight the ways in which Central Asia's small nations (such as Kyrgyzstan and Tajikistan) are vulnerable and the region's elites are dependent on major external donors to maintain a degree of economic and social provision. Babajanian's article, which is based on in-depth interviews and group discussions in 16 poor rural communities in the Chuy, Naryn, Issyk-Kyl and Osh regions, examines the extent to which Village Investment Projects enabled people to influence decision making about micro-project priorities and to exact accountability from their leaders. The evidence presented here sheds light on the limits of community participation and provides a contextual understanding of the barriers to empowerment and the deepening intra-communal mistrust in the use of funds. These findings challenge the managerial and performance indicators of the bank, which do not allow inference about how micro-projects affect social relations, power dynamics and institutional structures in local communities. The bottom-up development model was not sufficient to enable people to exercise power in the absence of effective horizontal accountability institutions within the state.

The analysis of Ancker and Rechel is equally critical of the managerial superficialities of global operations of international aid organizations. Despite significant transfers of know-how and funding in tackling HIV/AIDS, the interactions between donors and local recipient organizations have not been easy. Using 'soft' and 'hard' power through ideational influence and financial support, donors have been exerting pressure to adopt certain international policies and guidelines. They also focus on programmatic priorities and funding requirements, often at the expense of local stakeholders' authority and the country's real needs. High levels of international aid, coupled with the lack of transparency and accountability, created free riders disguised by glossy project templates and reporting systems. This has led to 'virtual realities' through which vested interest are maintained. These grim findings on the outcomes of Western development assistance should be compared to and contrasted with the growing and highly opaque presence of China in Central Asia.

Moving from this big picture to tangible consequences, the issue closes with two gripping studies of local realities and individual experiences of everyday life. Gulzat Botoeva shows that neoliberal ideas about individual freedoms have infused Kyrgyz society with the view that each individual is responsible and accountable for his or her own actions and well-being. The economic shock therapy of the World Bank and the International Monetary Fund created uneven but strong market economy effects that modified and commoditized the moral economy. Botoeva shows that money from hashish-growing plays an important role in sustaining reciprocal relationships between families and is intertwined with gift-giving practices, conditional relationships between well-off and poor families, and the monetization of social ties. These findings indicate that capitalist relations fundamentally alter individuals' social standing, moral values and the formation of social networks. The amount of money one can splash out in social ceremonies and gift-giving exchanges determines the size and strength of social ties. Those who cannot afford these simply get left out and end up with poorer networks. The article's findings contribute to theories of moral economy (Booth 1994; Browne and Milgram 2008), while also elaborating on how monetization of gift giving transforms social networks into more layered and stratified dependencies.

Finally, Diana Ibañez-Tirado's sobering account of the everyday life of ordinary people explores their harrowing experiences in a Tajik city, Kulob. Her analysis advances the notion of 'everyday disasters' to explain, first, the imprecise boundaries between catastrophic events and daily life as experienced by her informants and referred to by them as everlasting, yet 'normal' disasters; and second, these events' negative effects encompassing the course of their daily lives. Ibañez-Tirado demonstrates the importance that Kulob residents pay to joking and cunning as means of enduring and circumnavigating disastrous events towards everydayness. They avoid presenting themselves straightforwardly as amoral cheaters, pitiful victims of floods or of structural violence, or passive objects of economic crises that are beyond the scope of their agency. Through these acts of accommodation, individuals attempt to establish themselves as moral subjects rather than simple victims (Anderson 2013). Yet, while this coping strategy allows a dignified survival, it is also interwoven with a deepening cognitive stance that normalizes victimhood and helplessness.

### *Postscript*

Central Asia continues to pose many challenges for fieldwork-based research. Not only are Soviet-era statistics and official categories of very limited use, meanings and experiences are in constant flux. The contributors to this volume rely on mostly first-hand data. Fazendeiro and Thomas make good use of secondary material in different domains that can widen the scope of macro-level analysis in areas where there is little or no academic coverage. Thomas's work on long-term sustainability indicators, in particular, highlights the further possibilities of using national statistics, which enable longitudinal analyses to contextualize post-Soviet development trajectories with the Soviet past.

Most contributors' engagement with their research topics and methodologies is novel and essentially qualitative in nature, though sometimes supported with available statistics. The work involves risks and personal sacrifices that those of us who work and travel in the region know well. Their accounts are vivid and compelling. Babajanian's work captures the implementation of community-driven projects in the context of local power relations, which pervaded the micro-project processes and contributed to distrust and misunderstanding, in contrast to the metrics used by donors to show successful project completions. Ibañez-Tirado's persuasive account of the normalization of 'everyday disasters' and the lack of development illustrates the double-edged sword of normality that takes us into ordinary lives and her own experience of a devastating flood. Mingling among hashish farmers as a guest, Botoeva recounts how hashish money emerges as a justified moral means of survival. Her analysis is in an especially high-risk area that many scholars and institutions would choose to avoid. The years of conservation work and the encounters of Paskaleva in Uzbekistan provide a wealth of evidence on the changing meanings of space and architecture under redesigned power.

However, qualitative methodological perspectives have their own limits. The local context and the nature of access shape the contours of research encounters. Some information is collected through publicly available sources, but most is gathered through snowballing techniques and personal encounters over long periods of personal dedication and time commitment. The skill of the researcher, the level of receptivity of local communities, and local conditions circumscribe the boundaries of interaction and knowledge building.

Nevertheless, the empirical insights presented here are immensely valuable for a region where fieldwork access presents risks and is subject to suspicion and scrutiny. State officials hold non-technical social science in contempt. Even if they are persuaded, officials find it hard to appreciate the need for and utility of scholarly research. The combination of suspicion and lack of exposure to diverse research techniques may lead to awkward encounters. When I was carrying out a small business questionnaire to identify entrepreneurial development paths with the firms that benefitted from micro-credit lending run by the European Bank for Reconstruction and Development, I had to go through a money laundering and fraud check with a Kazakh bank official. At the end of a thorough interview, I also had to sign several dubious forms. The situation is most challenging in Turkmenistan and Uzbekistan. It is, therefore, no coincidence that, despite efforts and calls in diverse scholarly forums, we were not able to secure a contribution on Turkmenistan. Ordinary people are also weary of being questioned on issues that in the end do not contribute to their well-being. With some sympathy one can understand their frustration with unaccountable power games, poor economic outcomes and the growing sense of uncertainty of post-Soviet trajectories.

Authorities sometimes see researchers as outside agents with suspicious intentions.[2] There is also another worrying trend in the realm of creeping bureaucratization and regulation of scholarship in UK universities. The growing number of procedural barriers in the form of approval forms, ethical panels and layers of other research control mechanisms hamper imaginative and risk-taking approaches by aiming to formalize every iota of intellectual inquiry in a risk-averse manner. While funding for open-call fieldwork-driven research is diminishing, politicization of grant-giving priorities and selective judgments about the 'value for money' narrow the scope of possibilities. Area studies seem to be suffering most from these trends.

**Acknowledgements**

We are grateful to *Central Asian Survey*'s editor, Deniz Kandiyoti, who agreed to give our collective project a chance, and all anonymous reviewers for their insightful comments and suggestions. The issue has been made possible by the generous funding by Nurol Bank of annual doctoral workshop events since 2011. Alisher Khamidov kindly offered guidance in the development of several articles.

## Disclosure statement

No potential conflict of interest was reported by the author.

## Notes

1. The second Eurasian Studies Society Doctoral Workshop, in January 2014, which I organized along with Diana Kudaibergenova and Sevket Akyildiz at Senate House in London, and which focused on the theme of Social and Economic Development in Central Asia: Theory and Practice, prepared the ground for this collaborative project. All the articles presented here originate from recently completed doctoral theses or post-doctoral research projects. Since we began working on the issue, several contributing authors have successfully completed their PhD studies. Each article went through two stages of development. In the first stage, the authors read and discussed each other's work. Later, article submissions went through the external review process of *Central Asian Survey*. This production method enhanced the cross-disciplinary character and the originality of the volume.
2. The scholarly community was shocked by the news of a Tajik doctoral student's arrest in 2014. He had been carrying out interviews for an academic study funded by the Economic and Social Research Council of the UK. He was held in captivity for several weeks by Tajik security forces.

## References


Acemoglu, D., and J. Robinson. 2012. *Why Nations Fail: The Origins of Power, Prosperity, and Poverty*. New York: Crown Publishing.

Anderson, P. 2013. "The Politics of Scorn in Syria and The Agency of Narrated Involvement." *Journal of the Royal Anthropological Institute* 19 (3): 463–481. doi:10.1111/1467-9655.12045

Arsel, M., and A. Dasgupta. 2015. "Critique, Rediscovery and Revival in Development Studies." *Development and Change* 46: 644–665. doi:10.1111/dech.12183

Ban, C., and M. Blyt. 2013. "The BRICs and the Washington Consensus: An Introduction." *Review of International Political Economy* 20 (2): 241–255. doi:10.1080/09692290.2013.779374

Booth, W. J. 1994. "On The Idea of The Moral Economy." *The American Political Science Review* 88: 653–667. doi:10.2307/2944801

Brautigam, D. 2011. *The Dragon's Gift: The Real Story of China in Africa*. Oxford: Oxford University Press.

Browne, K. E., and B. L. Milgram, eds. 2008. *Economics and Morality: Anthropological Approaches*. Lanham: Altamira.

Cummings, S. 2012. *Understanding Central Asia*. London: Routledge.

Cummings, S., and R. Hinnebusch, eds. 2011. *Sovereignty after Empire: Comparing the Middle East and Central Asia*. Edinburgh: Edinburgh University Press.

Gleason, G. 2003. *Markets and Politics in Central Asia: Structural Reform and Political Change*. London: Routledge.

Hale, H. 2014. *Patronal Politics: Eurasian Regime Dynamics in Comparative Perspective*. New York: Cambridge University Press.

Harvey, D. 2009. *Social Justice and the City*. Athens, GA: University of Georgia Press.

Hattori, T. 2001. "Reconceptualising Foreign Aid." *Review of International Political Economy* 8 (4): 633–660. doi:10.1080/09692290110077610

Heathershaw, J., and A. Cooley. 2015. "Offshore Central Asia: An Introduction." *Central Asian Survey* 34 (1): 1–10. doi:10.1080/02634937.2015.1008816

Junisbai, B. 2010. "A Tale of Two Kazakhstans: Sources of Political Cleavage and Conflict in the Post-Soviet Period." *Europe-Asia Studies* 62 (2): 235–269. doi:10.1080/09668130903506813

Kandiyoti, D. 1996. "Modernization Without The Market? The Case of The 'Soviet East'." *Economy and Society* 25 (4): 529–542. doi:10.1080/03085149600000027

Khalid, A. 2007. "Introduction: Locating the (post-) Colonial in Soviet History." *Central Asian Survey* 26 (4): 465–473. doi:10.1080/02634930802017895

Martin, T. 2001. *The Affirmative Action Empire*. New York: Cornell University Press.

Özcan, G. B. 2010. *Building States and Markets: Enterprise Development in Central Asia*. Basingstoke: Palgrave MacMillan.

Özcan, G. B., and U. Gündüz. 2016. "Energy Privatisations, Business-Politics Connections and Governance Under Political Islam." *Environment and Planning C: Government and Policy* 3: (forthcoming)

Payne, M. J. 2001. *Stalin's Railroad: Turksib and the Building of Socialism*. Pittsburgh: University of Pittsburgh Press.

Pieterse, J. N. 2010. *Development Theory*. Santa Barbara: University of California.

Pirani, S. 2011. "China's Energy Geopolitics: The Shanghai Cooperation Organization and Central Asia." *Central Asian Survey* 30 (1): 172–175. doi:10.1080/02634937.2011.558699

Sabol, S. 2003. *Russian Colonisation and the Genesis of Kazak National Consciousness*. New York: Palgrave.

Sen, A. 1999. *Development as Freedom*. Oxford: Oxford University Press.

Sinha, R. P. 1974. "Soviet Aid and Trade with the Developing World." *Soviet Studies* 26 (2): 276–282. doi:10.1080/09668137408410950

Tan-Mullins, M., M. Giles, and M. Power. 2010. "Redefining 'Aid' in the China–Africa Context." *Development and Change* 41 (5): 857–881. doi:10.1111/j.1467-7660.2010.01662.x

Woods, N. 2008. "Whose Aid? Whose Influence? China, Emerging Donors and The Silent Revolution in Development Assistance." *International Affairs* 84 (6): 1205–1221. doi:10.1111/j.1468-2346.2008.00765.x

# Ideology in brick and tile: Timurid architecture of the 21st century

Elena Paskaleva

*Leiden Institute for Area Studies, Leiden University, Leiden, The Netherlands*

This study analyses the impact of politics on urban development and, in particular, on Timurid heritage in present-day Uzbekistan. It outlines the problem of landscape manipulation for the advancement of a political ideology. After presenting a brief overview of Tsarist and Soviet restoration practices, the article focuses on the post-Soviet nation-building schemes through public iconography, urban renewal measures and heritage construction. Architectural and epigraphic restorations of Timurid monuments in Samarqand and new constructions in Tashkent provide a valuable illustrative framework. As world heritage sites, the Samarqand monuments are examined both in their historical and current socio-political contexts; the role of UNESCO is also analysed. The study benefits from and contributes to critical heritage studies and urban development as a narrative of power-making and relational space.

## Introduction

After 1991, political and cultural elites of independent Uzbekistan adopted the medieval ruler Amir Timur (1336–1405) as the embodiment of Uzbek national identity. The worldwide acclaimed Timurid architecture is being used to promote nationhood and to signify progressive urban development in post-Soviet Central Asia. Timurid heritage, in turn, has become a visual protagonist of a nationalist rhetoric. As a result, in 1996 the surviving Timurid monuments were methodically restored for the celebrations of Timur's 660th birthday, and later on in 2007 for the 2750th anniversary of Timur's capital Samarqand.

Akbarzadeh (1996), Laruelle (2010) and Cummings (2012) have described the symbolic content of post-Soviet ideologies as the formation of state ethno-nationalism. In this process, the political and ideological field is overwhelmed by the titular ethnic group's symbolism and historicism. In Uzbekistan, the Timurid myth offers 'signs of certainty' (Cummings 2010, 1) familiar to the Uzbek nation. With the alluring persona of Timur used as a symbol, meaning is produced through Timurid artefacts, the majority of which are architectural monuments. In this sense, recent architectural and epigraphic restorations reveal the link between politics and symbolism within the ethno-nationalistic discourse. The various architectural sites are being enshrined in speedy urban development projects across Uzbekistan. These projects are widely promoted by the state within the context of large-scale constructive (*sozidatel'nye*) and urban renewal (*blagoustroitel'nye*) measures meant to raise the level and quality of life of all Uzbeks. In this sense Timurid architecture not only elevates national values and concepts but also celebrates the post-independence prosperity efforts and contributes to the ultimate goal of transforming Uzbekistan to a state with a great future (*O'zbekiston kelajagi buyuk davlat*). Timurid architecture, as part of the country's 'golden heritage' (*oltin meros*), is used to boost the Uzbek population's sense of belonging and pride through the construction of an ethno-national identity. This study treats urban development, and in particular architectural restoration, as a technique of governance and exercise of power used to influence the social acceptance of history.

Since gaining independence in 1991 the Uzbek government has taken the importance of Timurid architecture to heart and key Timurid monuments have been considerably rebuilt. By providing empirical analysis of several Timurid sites in Samarqand, this article aims to contribute to the international discourse on heritage as a non-static phenomenon, and in particular on the notion of authenticity.[1] I analyse Timurid monuments not only as 'cultural heritage' but also through the lens of critical heritage studies. As formulated by Eric Hobsbawm, 'the national phenomenon cannot be adequately investigated without careful attention to the "invention of tradition"' (Hobsbawm and Ranger 1983, 13–14). Hobsbawm puts forward exactly the construction of the notion of nationhood based on a heroic past. Additionally, Smith (2006) shows how the manifestation of contemporary power is validated through the management of heritage sites. The article engages with the discourse on tangible heritage, particularly the role of architecture as a legitimation tool in post-Soviet Central Asia (Alexander, Buchli, and Humphrey 2007; Diener and Hagen 2013). In this aspect, through its direct involvement with restoration projects, the Uzbek elite uses Timurid heritage as a tactic of state legitimation, and the Uzbek authorities are creating their own heritage (Harrison 2009).

Furthermore, the concept of relational space, as defined by Harvey (2009 [1973], 13) in which the space is formed by objects that exist only in relationship to other objects, can be used to define the new pseudo-Timurid developments in Tashkent, which not only quote the architectural vocabulary of their predecessors but also can be only understood and evaluated in relationship to them. What is more, by elevating the concept of collective memory throughout the revival of the Timurid cult, the Uzbek leadership creates a sense of emotional satisfaction and pride among the Uzbek population as a result of their actual/physical interaction with Timurid heritage (Harrison 2013, 88). Tashkent is conceived as the symbolic centre of new Uzbekistan (Alexander, Buchli, and Humphrey 2007).

In this article, I focus on the different approaches to architectural restoration throughout the Soviet and the post-Soviet period. Timurid monuments are studied here as a landscape of layered restorations, each political regime leaving its own mark based on its own ideology.[2] Analysed as imaginary artefacts, the majority of recently restored sites and their epigraphy are not based on direct material evidence (i.e., photographs, films or textual descriptions). Firstly, the article outlines the importance of the Timurid cult and its role in the construction of collective memory from the mid-19th century until present. Secondly, it provides an overview of recent urban development and regeneration practices in Samarqand and the role of UNESCO in stimulating cultural tourism; special emphasis is placed on the selection of monuments to be restored. Thirdly, the regeneration of the Hazrat Imam Complex in Tashkent is discussed. This section offers a comparative approach revealing the interchangeable significance of Timurid (15th century) and Shaybanid[3] (16th–17th centuries) architectural heritage used by the Uzbek elite to unify national traditions in a modern political context.

## Timurid discourse on restoration as a construct of collective memory

In order to understand the profound impact of the Uzbek urban renewal measures and programmes, it is important to evaluate the role of Amir Timur as the pivotal figure of Uzbek collective memory. Timur was a semi-nomadic conqueror whose empire stretched from modern Turkey to India at the beginning of the 15th century. Architectural monuments of the Timurid empire in the modern Uzbek cities of Samarqand and Shahr-i Sabz are known worldwide as masterpieces of Islamic architecture.

The Timurid legacy in 'golden Samarqand' had been claimed for political purposes long before the creation of Uzbekistan as a republic within the USSR in 1924 and the 1929 inclusion of the predominantly Tajik-speaking Samarqand region within the borders of Uzbekistan (Adams 2013, 117). While some of the first European expeditions to Samarqand in 1841 by Nikolai Khanykov and Alexander Lehmann (Helmersen 1852; Gorshenina 2014a, 250) directed the eyes of Western connoisseurs to selected Timurid monuments, their travelogues contained very little information on the local population. In 1841, Lehmann notes: 'Unaffected, the Uzbek walks nowadays past these grandeur monuments, indulging only in the sensual pleasure of the moment; carefree he sees them in dust and debris and no one from the crowd attempts to preserve these venerable walls' (Helmersen 1852, 146).[4] By the mid-19th century most of the original architectural substance, in particular the *kirpich* brickwork, had been reused for the construction of new buildings. The inhabitants of Samarqand were well aware of the spiritual importance of the sites, however in the eyes of *cultured* Western travellers they had neglected their own heritage and 'have not succeeded in preserving these places' (Radlov 1880, 22–23, quoted by Gorshenina 2014a, 252).

The official discourse of preservation started with General Konstantin Petrovich von Kaufman (1818–82) after his capture of Samarqand in May 1868. The 'civilized' treatment of Islamic artefacts as introduced by the Turkestan administration was opposed to the presumed indifference of the local population in the preceding centuries. Kaufman's restoration efforts established the role of the Russian Empire not only as the legitimate heir to Timur's architectural heritage but also as a profoundly caring colonizer which recognized local religious traditions and values. The refurbishment of the monuments was related to urban development; the sites were cleared of rubble and fences were erected. In 1875, Registan Square in Samarqand was levelled and paved, and the monuments were given a special role in the new imperial urbanization efforts. The purpose of these efforts was to instigate respect for the new ruling power among the Samarqand pious religious elite and the masses.

The systematic study of Samarqand's monuments was initiated in 1895 when the Archaeological Commission sent a group of scholars under the supervision of Nikolai Iv. Veselovskii. Among them were the young talented architect Aleksei V. Shchusev and the artist Samuil M. Dudin who were supposed to carry out the first archaeological survey of Samarqand (Iakubovskii 1940, 292). The expedition resulted in the publication of the only volume of the lavishly decorated catalogue *Mecheti Samarkanda* (The Mosques of Samarqand) in 1905 (Veselovskii 1905), solely dedicated to Timur's dynastic mausoleum of Gur-i Amir (early 1400s) and financed by Empress Aleksandra Fedorovna (1872–1918). This prototype of an officially politicized edition on Timurid architecture marked a new trend in the study of Timurid heritage: the monuments were not regarded as potential targets for implementing urban renewal measures but as a source of comprehensive academic studies. Gur-i Amir was depicted as an idealized work of art, stripped of any religious or socio-cultural importance (McChesney 2003, 19).

The dichotomy between the cultured and academic Russian-speaking elite and the ill-informed local tourist guides could be clearly seen at the turn of the 20th century. G. A. Pankrat'ev describes the local guides as 'completely ignorant', unable to read and understand the Arabic inscriptions; they were simply entertaining storytellers who were unaware of the exact construction dates and mistakenly attributed monuments to different patrons. Pankrat'ev stresses the fact that the local population spoke with deep respect about Amir Timur as a builder of *madrasas* (Islamic religious schools) and mausoleums, although the actual surviving inscriptions confirm that some were built before and others were built after his reign (Pankrat'ev 1910, 1).

In October 1918, Vladimir Lenin personally signed a decree on the importance of conservation of cultural artefacts of scientific importance. This decree set the tone for the creation of museums and organizations dealing with the preservation of architectural heritage. In May

1920 the first commission for the preservation of architectural monuments was created under the regional commissariat for education in Samarqand.[5] The commission stressed the importance and urgency of architectural preservation. As a result, on 22 May 1921 the Turkomstaris was established: the acronym stood for the Turkestan Committee for Museums and Preservation of Ancient Monuments, Art and Nature (*Turkestanskii komitet po delam muzeev i okhrane pamiatnikov stariny, iskusstva, i prirody*). Turkomstaris's leader, D. I. Nechkin, pleaded for extra funding for the upkeep of the monuments by pointing out that 'the loss of the architectural monuments will be a real national sorrow' (Gorshenina 2013a, 55). He insisted that the prestige of the Soviet government was at stake as the destruction of the Timurid heritage would be used by Western scholars and museums to accuse the Soviet leadership of negligence. Nechkin suggested that foreign museums would buy some of the portable artefacts (Gorshenina 2013a, 56). Funding for reconstruction work was being sought through the *waqf* (endowment deeds) of several monuments[6] kept in Bukhara and a special commission was established to bring the documentation back to Samarqand and to relocate any potentially available funds.

The Turkomstaris was renamed Sredazkomstaris (Central Asian Committee) after the creation of the new Soviet Central Asian republics (1924–36).[7] Its main office was situated in Samarqand, the then capital of the Uzbek SSR. The two main duties of the Sredazkomstaris were carrying out necessary repair measures and preventing further destruction (Nechkin 1926, 7, quoted by Kruikov 1990, 35). Sredazkomstaris activities involved architectural conservation and restoration in all Central Asian republics: 64 monuments in Uzbekistan, seven in Turkmenistan, seven in Kyrgyzstan and five in Kazakhstan, with Uzbekistan having by far the largest number of monuments within its newly defined administrative borders. The first comprehensive scientific research on Timurid architecture was carried out by the exclusively Russian members of the Sredazkomstaris, namely the architect Boris N. Zasypkin (1891–1955), the historiographer Vasilii V. Bartol'd (1869–1930), the art historian Ivan I. Umniakov (1890–1976), the archaeologist Vasilii L. Viatkin (1869–1932) and the palaeographer Aleksandr A. Semenov (Kruikov 1990, 35). This group of scholars not only drew the first architectural plans of the monuments but also studied primary sources on the history of their construction (Bartol'd), translated the epigraphy of key Timurid sites (Semenov) and carried out excavation and restoration work (Viatkin and Zasypkin). The Sredazkomstaris existed until 1928 when its duties were formally transferred to the Uzkomstaris, established in early 1927 in Samarqand. In 1931, the Uzkomstaris was relocated to the new Uzbek capital of Tashkent and carried out its work until 1946. However, the growing restoration duties and responsibilities were split up among several regional units, dominated by centrally controlled administrators. Within the prevailing ethnocentric discourse, all buildings situated on the territory of the Uzbek SSR were regarded as part of Uzbek national heritage.

In 1937, a specialized restoration school (*masterskaya*) opened in Samarqand teaching traditional building and decoration techniques employed in Timurid architecture. Boris Zasypkin, together with local craftsmen, developed a manual on the construction methods including the building of vaults and the design of complicated geometrical patterns (*girikh*) containing more than 200 drawings and photographs. The practical training took place under the guidance of master (*usto*) Shirin Muradov, who later became an honorary academician at the Uzbek Academy of Science. Attracting local craftsmen and exploiting their knowledge of traditional building techniques that had been passed down from generation to generation could be also seen as a political move to integrate local collaborators, who were no longer treated as backward or ignorant but as the guardians of centuries' old knowledge and traditions. Yet the Russian architects and archaeologists had a leading role in these collaborative projects. Their activities were regarded as a social obligation, as a contribution to the preservation of rich heritage traditions across Central Asia and their popularization among all Soviet citizens (Kruikov 1990, 1991; Demchenko 2011; Shaw 2011; Gorshenina 2013a,b).

In the 1930s, Joseph Stalin 'added a marked Russian nationalist character to the concept of Soviet citizenship' (Keller 2007, 262). In the process of establishing national identities corresponding to the new boundary delimitations, Uzbek cultural achievements were illustriously narrated and heroic figures such as Amir Timur were celebrated. The pioneering scholar of Central Asian national histories was Aleksandr Iu. Iakubovskii (1886–1953), who created the image of Timur as a strong and powerful leader. He emphasized Timur's contribution to the consolidation of Russia as a result of Timur's defeat of the Golden Horde in 1395 (Iakubovskii et al. 1950, 356). In 1941, Stalin himself ordered the opening of the Timurid tomb at Gur-i Amir in Samarqand. McChesney suggests that according to 'Marxist ideology and public discourse, Timur was a reactionary feudal but for Stalin he may have been a role model'; Stalin revered Timur's military victories (McChesney 2003, 24). As outlined by McChesney, the construction of new Uzbek identity might have also involved the creation of typical Uzbek facial features. The renowned Moscow forensic anthropologist Mikhail M. Gerasimov (1907–70) was sent to Samarqand in May 1941 as part of a controversial expedition to 'document the authenticity of Timur's burial' under the leadership of Tashmukhammed N. Kary-Niazov.[8] This clearly atheist expedition violated the Muslim sanctity of the dead and desecrated Timur's burial. It can also be regarded as an assault on Islamic practice in Uzbekistan. Based on the exhumed skulls at Gur-i Amir, Gerasimov reconstructed the faces of Amir Timur, his son Shah Rukh and grandsons Ulugh Beg and Muhammad Sultan. Throughout his article *Portret Tamerlana* Gerasimov refers to Timur as a 'Mongol' and concludes that Timur had 'typical Mongoloid features' (Gerasimov 1947, 18), Shah Rukh belonged to the Europeoid race, while Ulugh Beg and Muhammad Sultan both belonged to the Europeoid race with an admixture of Mongoloid characteristics (Oshanin, quoted by McChesney 2003, 29). In his memoirs Kary-Niazov describes a conversation he had with Oshanin and the celebrated Tajik poet Sadriddin Ayni (1878–1954), while trying to identify the skulls of Timur and Ulugh Beg (Kary-Niazov 1967, 241–242). Ayni comments that the one was illiterate and the other was a scholar. In this way the official Soviet discourse differentiating between the uneducated Timur and his cultured grandson Ulugh Beg is legitimized by a respected poet trusted by the local people and the Islamic community at large.

With the advent of socialist ideology, which aimed at culturing the backward nomads in Central Asia, the image of collective memory was strengthened by the cultural potential of the Timurid legacy (Iakubovskii 1933, 1946). It was thus Timur's grandson, Ulugh Beg (1394–1449), who became the patron of the Soviet state propaganda regarding Central Asian heritage and cultural values (Shaw 2011; Arends 1965). This undoubtedly cultured scholar, astronomer and architectural patron ruled in Samarqand but had, unlike his grandfather, neither extraordinary military achievements nor the ambition for excessive military power (Barthold 1958, 103). The sedentary Ulugh Beg fitted perfectly with the aspirations of the Soviet government to culture and thus modernize the life of Central Asia 'nomads' from within their own cultural environment and legacy. Industrial and cultural development of Central Asia was high on the USSR's political agenda and the importance of local, educated elite and intelligentsia was needed for the promotion of the Soviet model in the 1950s (Stronski 2010; Kalinovsky 2013). Ulugh Beg was thus the ideal knowledgeable predecessor not only to instigate pride in the Uzbek intelligentsia but also to promote its qualities and potential among other Soviet co-patriots. Ulugh Beg was a Timurid heir, but he was not 'burdened' by his grandfather's brutal legacy as Timur died when Ulugh Beg was just 11 years old. Furthermore, Ulugh Beg was portrayed as an atheist and a free-thinker by Soviet propaganda as he was beheaded in a conspiracy plot by the Islamic clergy, presumably murdered for his scientific endeavours (Keller 2007, 274). In this sense the figure of Ulugh Beg was a convenient instrument in what Adeeb Khalid has called 'the displacement of Islam from the public arena' (Khalid 2014, 522). In his haven city, Samarqand, Ulugh Beg created one of the greatest libraries and one of the finest observatories in the Islamic world, which produced impressively accurate astronomical tables. The gem of his architectural legacy was the Ulugh Beg Madrasa on Registan Square (1417–20). This *madrasa* was the first Timurid monument to be completely restored. In accordance with Soviet propaganda that aimed to 'educate' the Central Asian proletariat, the partially restored new epigraphy contained prophetic sayings related to the importance of knowledge. Soviet leaders including Nikita Khrushchev and Leonid Brezhnev had their photographs taken in front of that building during their state visits to Samarqand. All international guests were paraded across Registan Square as it became the landmark of the Soviet protection of cultural memory in Central Asia.

In 1973, the Central Committee of the Communist Party of Uzbekistan took the decision to condemn Amir Timur. As a consequence, the Presidium of the Uzbek Academy of Science issued a ruling stating that all copies of Yazdi's *Zafarnama*, the celebrated Timurid chronicle from the 15th century, were to be confiscated and burned in the courtyard of the Fan publishing house in Tashkent. Ibrahim Muminov's *Role and Place of Amir Timur in the History of Central Asia* (1968) was also condemned, as were all publications that showed any positive side of Timur's deeds (Bababekov 2006). During the Soviet period, Timur was not considered an Uzbek national hero, but a brutal Mongol warlord, an illiterate statesman and a devout Muslim. As a result the philosophy behind the restoration of Timurid monuments did not honour the personality of Timur but celebrated hereditary indigenous craftsmanship within the USSR. The restorations with steel and reinforced concrete after the devastating Tashkent earthquake of 1966 were the climax of socialist technological progress combined with the skills of local craftsmen (Demchenko 2011; Shaw 2011). At home and abroad, Timurid architecture boosted Uzbekistan's image as the cradle of cultured socialism in Central Asia (Stronski 2010).

After independence in 1991, the most populous post-Soviet Muslim state rejected the Marxist–Leninist communist legacy and replaced it with the Timurid cult. Timur, the 'Uzbekified' conqueror of the Turkic steppe, became the national hero. Although not an ethnic Uzbek and born almost two centuries before the Uzbeks settled in Samarqand, Timur has a mass appeal in a predominantly Muslim nation with nomadic roots.

> The name of Amir Temur was blacked out from the pages of our history in an attempt to bury him in oblivion. The goal was to remove the national consciousness from the soul of the people so that it might lose its sense of national pride and reconcile itself to its dependence and subordination. Our people, trapped for so many years in the clutches of the colonial vice, are no longer deprived of the opportunity to honour our great compatriot and render to him his historical due. (Karimov 1996, 344)

The powerful personality of Timur and his grandiose architectural ambitions fostering state legitimation (Woods 1987; Manz 1989, 2002) have made him a popular figure among post-Soviet political elites (Allworth 1990; Adams 2010). They in turn elevated the status of Timur as the father of the Uzbek nation in the post-Soviet period (Karimov 1998, 384). Since Timurid monuments belong to all Uzbeks and their maintenance is solely in the hands of the state as postulated by the Uzbek Constitution (1992),[9] they are not directly related to any political party or platform and can be framed as apolitical. Their proper maintenance and the reverence accorded to them by the Uzbek population are seen in direct relation to religious virtues. As pointed out in the widely manifested work *Ulozhenie Timura* (Azimova 1992), Timur understood well that society cannot live without religion. The fact that although being illiterate, Timur knew the Quran by heart and engaged in theological disputes testifies to his 'elevated spirituality, the purity and firmness of his faith' (Karimov 1998, 412). However, the division between the secular state and religion was also understood by Timur and is clearly manifested throughout the independence discourse. In modern Uzbekistan, Timurid cultural heritage is seen as a representation of Timur's humanistic achievements and intrinsically belonging to Timur. Timurid monuments are no longer described as megalomaniacal buildings erected by a brutal warlord, an approach that was central to Soviet Timurid discourse (Iakubovskii 1933; Muminov 1968). On the contrary, state policy in independent Uzbekistan is propagated through the collective memory of Timur. As pointed out by Islam Karimov at the opening of Timur's monument in Samarqand on 18 October 1996: 'Glorifying Amir Timur – this means strengthening our faith in the great future of our county based on our deep historical roots, our culture and strength' (Karimov 1998, 394).

Michael Herzfeld argues that 'it is not as though the idea of heritage is unimportant to the anti-intellectual forms of populism; on the contrary, it is the linchpin of some of the most egregiously chauvinistic ideologies in the world today' (Herzfeld 2010, S262). Heritage is often used as an image for the production of cultural authority, but it can also be a tactic of legitimation, as in Uzbekistan. Thus, aside from Timur's rehabilitation as a national hero, the value of the Timurid discourse lies in the attempt to evoke pride in the primacy of the Uzbek nation (Matveeva 2009) and also in strong Uzbek leadership modelled after the Timurid statehood example, as shown by March (2002, 2003a, 2003b). The statehood legacy of Amir Timur (*Ulozhenie Timura*) is the flagship of modern Uzbek government. Timurid architecture is a mechanism used by the Uzbek political elite to provide a tangible interaction with this Timurid legacy and to re-enact the country's collective memory. The sanctity of the Timurid shrines, lost during the Soviet period, has been reinstated throughout the years of independence via numerous restoration campaigns and urban development projects. Apart from their material existence, the monuments also form an inseparable part of Uzbek daily life – they are incorporated into television news bulletins; they are portrayed on massive posters and billboards throughout Uzbekistan; they decorate the covers of textbooks and magazines; and they provide the backdrop to lavish ceremonies and opulent jubilees (Adams 2010). The Timurid legacy is vibrant, colourful and palpable.

## Conservation, political and economic significance of Timurid heritage in Samarqand

Heritage as a cultural construct is intrinsically linked to the process of selection. Although the Timurid architectural heritage was recognized as an important source for promoting the cultural potential of Central Asia at home and abroad, the majority of the Timurid monuments were sparingly restored during the Soviet period. The early restoration attempts focused mainly on conservation by stabilizing endangered structures such as collapsing vaults, domes and minarets. The choices of what to restore were made by knowledgeable committee members of the Sredazkomstaris (until 1928) and Uzkomstaris (until 1946). New additions to the morphology of the buildings were executed in bare brick with very sparse decoration. In most cases it was obvious that this new fabric did not belong to the original structure. Non-existing domes were indeed rebuilt in reinforced concrete in order to withstand the frequent earthquakes in the region. Initially in the 1950s hand-crafted tiles were used and applied manually to the reconstructed parts. Later on in the 1970s and 1980s manufactured concrete frames were used and polychrome tiling was mass-produced (Demchenko 2011). Even with these innovations, the whole restoration process was still extremely lengthy, carefully planned by interdisciplinary commissions and executed by teams of archaeologists, architects, engineers and local craftsmen (Kruikov 1990, 1991).

All this changed, however, after 1991 when Timurid architecture was branded as the Renaissance of the East (Askarov 2009) and Timur's legacy was seen as a 'spiritual fundament' of the great future of modern Uzbekistan. The Timurid collective memory started to be propagated both in the public independence discourse and throughout actual architectural restoration and development projects in order to create a sense of pride and belonging among the Uzbek population.

The 1992 Uzbek constitution postulated that all 'cultural monuments should be preserved by the state'. Thus, the state made conscious choices of what to restore and when. State policies also determined the new visual symbolism related to Timur, which involved sumptuous public celebrations of jubilees – the 660th anniversary of Amir Timur's birthday in 1996 and the 2750th anniversary of Timur's capital Samarqand in 2007. Three new statues of Timur were erected in Tashkent (1994), Shahr-i Sabz (1996)[10] and Samarqand (1996), designed by the sculptor Ilhom Dzhabarov (b. 1945).[11] The current officially approved image of Timur is different from Gerasimov's facial reconstruction from 1941. Prior to the 1996 celebrations the Uzbek artist Malik Nabiyev (1916–2008) won a competition for a new portrait of Amir Timur in 1994.[12] This new image with Europaeid features and a royal posture depicting Timur seated on his throne and holding a sword (almost copied in the Samarqand monument) is widely propagated by the state. A copy of the portrait is placed at the Gur-i Amir mausoleum and is relentlessly multiplied on blackboards, posters, book covers, textbooks and souvenirs (Figure 1).

The 660th anniversary of Timur's birth was crowned not only with the new museum of Amir Timur in the centre of Tashkent but also with a series of restoration campaigns that affected the Timurid mausoleum of Gur-i Amir (early 1400) and the Bibi Khanum Mosque (1398–1405) in Samarqand (Paskaleva 2013). These two major Timurid sites had been explored as early as 1895. The study of their epigraphy started in 1898 (Iakubovskii 1940, 298). The plans for their reconstruction had been drawn and partially executed during the Soviet period. However, the new approach after independence included a reconsideration of their epigraphic programme[13] and the subsequent addition of new texts.

Figure 1. Present officially approved image of Timur.

An interesting feature of the epigraphic restorations in Uzbekistan is that sometimes similar texts are repeated on monuments of different ages and with different functions. This is the case with the new epigraphy on the main sanctuary mosque of Bibi Khanum. The Arabic text added in the 1990s reveals Sura 2, verses 127–128, and reads:

> And when Abraham, and Ishmael with him, raised up the foundations of the House: 'Our Lord, receive this from us; Thou art the All-hearing, the All-knowing; and, our Lord, make us submissive to Thee, and of our seed *a nation* [emphasis added] submissive to Thee; and show us our holy rites, and turn towards us; surely Thou turnest, and art All-compassionate.[14]

The figure of Abraham combines a spectrum of religious virtues accepted by the followers of Judaism, Christianity and Islam. It might be possible that this text was chosen not only to denote the importance of one nation, one community (*umma*) sharing a common purpose and sense of belonging, but also to stress its multi-ethnic character, given the ethnical and religious diversity in Uzbekistan, in particular in Samarqand. The official state rhetoric is inclusive of all religions and ethnicities.

The same text was also used on the Kök Gunbad Mosque (1435) in Shahr-i Sabz, built by Ulugh Beg[15] and on the main sanctuary of the Kalan Mosque in Bukhara (*c.*1514). One possible explanation for this repetition might be multiple usage of analogous calligraphic templates, a process that saves labour and time. It is generally accepted that the period of independence has brought a unique revival of the art of epigraphy. New impetus has been given to the education of young calligraphers in Tashkent and new epigraphic restoration has flourished. The difference compared with previous conservation efforts is that at present the Timurid monuments are entirely covered in tiling, including the Soviet bare-brick additions. An illusion of authenticity has been consciously created and carefully crafted, paired with unprecedented beautification efforts of the surrounding areas. For its urban development and regeneration campaigns Samarqand was awarded with the highest Uzbek distinction, the medal of Amir Timur on 18 October 1996 and this date is celebrated annually as the day of Samarqand.

In 2007 Samarqand celebrated its 2750th jubilee. As early as 2004, the city started preparing on a grand scale for the festivities, initiated by UNESCO and supported by a presidential decree. The Timurid necropolis at Shah-i Zinda (with mausoleums dating from the 1370s to the 1430s) underwent a massive restoration campaign throughout which new mausoleums were built. Original Timurid tile work was substituted by modern mass-produced tiling. The remains of the portal to the 11th-century Qarakhanid Madrasa (1066) were demolished (Nemtseva 2015, 95).[16] Several Quranic texts (Sura 3, verses 169 and 170) were added to the main entrance originally built in 1435. A decree by the Cabinet of Ministers from 16 July 2004, signed by President Islam Karimov, postulated that the status of Shah-i Zinda was to be changed to a public fund under the Muslim Board of Uzbekistan (*O'zbekiston Musulmonlari Idorasi*).[17] In 2004 the Ministry of Finance granted 300 million *soums*[18] 'for the organization of the reconstruction, restoration and regeneration of Shah-i Zinda' and promised enough funds for the continuation of the work to be secured by the state budget in 2005. The Muslim Board of Uzbekistan granted 50 million *soums* in 2004 and 100 million *soums* in the following years. Prime Minister Shavkat Mirziyoyev was put in charge of the execution. In 2007 the president paid a pilgrimage to Shah-i Zinda. During his visit he recommended that the text of the *bismilla* be put above the main entrance to the necropolis and a gallery be set up with old photographs of the dilapidated mausoleums prior to independence showing numerous images from the restoration campaigns of 2005–07.[19]

Shah-i Zinda is the only complex in the UNESCO-listed city centre of Samarqand that falls directly under the authority of the Muslim Board of Uzbekistan; the imam of Samarqand is its principal guardian. The conservation of Registan Square is governed by the Ministry of Culture. The rest of the monuments including the Bibi Khanum Mosque and Mausoleum, the

Timurid dynastic mausoleum of Gur-i Amir, the Aq Saray, the Hazrat Imam Mosque, etc. fall under the directorate of the Uzbek State Museum of History of Culture (*O'zbekiston madaniyati tarixi davlat muzeyi*).

Although Islamic practice around the monuments is controlled by the state and police are omnipresent, the guardians appear to be genuinely involved and are fairly knowledgeable about the history of the sites. They are perfectly aware of the new additions and are sincerely concerned with the state of preservation. Each guardian could specify the exact location of original tile work or text. All take pride in their work and are eager to collect additional information on the history of the respective site. Showing and selling photographs of the old state of repair and comparing them with new images is being done not only at each listed building but also at all souvenir stalls. Small souvenir shops, sometimes surprisingly selling rare (Soviet) books and recent Uzbek historical novels and posters, are located within mausoleums and mosques across the city.

During the regeneration of Samarqand in 2005–06 the Bibi Khanum Mausoleum, situated opposite Bibi Khanum Mosque, was decorated with a new dome and a grand portal. The old vodka factory *Zarafshan* in the proximity of Gur-i Amir was demolished. The Ruhabad Mausoleum, previously in its shadow, was restored and the meticulously landscaped Amir Timur park that surrounds the mausoleum was created. The Hotel Afrosiyob Palace was built in 1996 on the territory of the citadel opposite Ruhabad Mausoleum.

The beautification of Samarqand continued throughout 2009 when the main building of the Uzbek State Museum of History of Culture, one of the oldest and largest museums in Central Asia situated in the eastern part of Registan Square, was demolished.[20] After 2010, in accordance with a governmental decision, the museum was moved to Mirza Ulugh Beg Street (until 1991, Karl Marx Street). On 1 September 2014 it was officially reopened in a building used for political education during the Soviet period. The majority of tourists are unfortunately unaware of its vast collection, and due to its relocation outside the city centre the number of visitors has remained very limited. The huge and still empty Registan site, on which the museum stood, was transformed into a park and landscaped with the ubiquitous low fir trees and two golden tigers symbolizing Samarqand.

According to the recent regeneration plan, the central urban arteries were widened up to 11 metres and new four-storey housing projects popped up along Mirza Ulugh Beg Street and Al-Beruni Street – the two main roads leading from Samarqand train station into the city centre. Most of the traditional houses along these roads were demolished as they were described as ineffective trading hubs. The new residential projects are deemed as a testament to the profound social and urban regeneration changes that have taken place after independence (Trevisani 2014, 249–250). Financial support for the project along the Ulugh Beg Street was granted by several companies, including the railway company O'zbekiston temir yo'llari and Uztransgas. In turn, these companies received housing for their young employees. Most likely these urban regeneration projects were meant to impress the flocks of international tourists, who pour into the city on the high-speed Afrosiyob train, which runs daily from Tashkent to Samarqand.

Cultural tourism is an increasingly important branch of the Uzbek economy. It is directly linked to the concept of spiritual memory and to the commercialization of architectural heritage. Tourism has a vast potential to contribute to the economic development of Uzbekistan and to generate much needed foreign currency. Unfortunately, it is still not fully exploited. UNESCO has undoubtedly played a major role in the promotion of Uzbekistan as an attractive tourist destination. At present, Uzbekistan has four sites on the World Heritage List: Khiva, the Itchan Kala (1990), the Historic Centre of Bukhara (1993), the Historic Centre of Shahr-i Sabz (2000)[21] and Samarqand – Crossroad of Cultures (2001).[22] The UNESCO Director General Irina Bokova visited Samarqand in August 2013. Her address underlined the global importance of Samarqand's heritage and the personal involvement of the president:

> We see this power all around us this evening – in the majestic beauty of Registan Square, this 'Pearl of the Orient.' I know these words have special meaning for you, Mr President, as a native of Samarkand.[23] All of this is why Samarkand – Crossroads of Cultures is inscribed on the UNESCO World Heritage List – because it embodies values that are outstanding and universal, because Samarkand is part of the story of all humanity. (Bokova 2013, 2)

UNESCO is the only United Nations agency with a specific mandate in the field of culture. Uzbekistan joined UNESCO in October 1993 and the organization has two main bodies in the country. UNESCO's Tashkent office, established in 1999, has its own building and office staff; the head is appointed by UNESCO headquarters in Paris. UNESCO collaborates closely with the Uzbek Ministry of Culture and with the Principal Board on Protection of Cultural Monuments of Uzbekistan. The other body is the National Commission of the Republic of Uzbekistan for UNESCO, which falls directly under the office of the prime minister. Lola Karimova-Tillyaeva[24] has been the Permanent Delegate to UNESCO since 2008. The collaboration with local and international heritage experts is coordinated by the UNESCO International Institute for Central Asian Studies (IICAS), established in August 1995 in Samarqand, which has a vast network of international scholars and a record of outstanding publications. According to UNESCO, 'the cultural heritage of Uzbekistan constitutes a source of national identity and pride and its preservation and promotion enjoys great attention from the government' (UNESCO 2013, 19).

The legal framework of the collaboration is the Uzbek ratification of UNESCO's Convention on the Protection of the World Cultural and Natural Heritage (1972, para. 4), which entrusts cultural heritage to the state. In 1996 the Uzbek government ratified The Hague Convention (1954) regulating the protection of cultural property.[25] The Hague Convention is important as it acknowledges the connection between cultural heritage and national identity.[26] These conventions have been integrated into the national legislation as well.[27] Only recently with the resolution of the Cabinet of Ministers from 21 July 2014 was a new governmental commission set up for the protection of cultural and archaeological heritage objects.[28] The Deputy Prime Minister Adham I. Ikramov was appointed as its chairman.

UNESCO has actively participated in the development of a management plan for the city of Samarqand, submitted in 2013.[29] The need for this plan was urgent due to the detrimental impact of busy roads and the state of conservation of the urban fabric in the old Timurid city. According to the UNESCO (2011) report, Uzbekistan places considerable emphasis on tourism. This is apparent in a ministerial decree from 7 June 2011 that set the restoration and preservation goals for the city until 2015. The programme envisaged the restoration of 22 historical sites in the Timurid capital. The two major monuments to undergo reconstruction are the Mausoleum Ishrat Khana (1464) with a budget of 1.48 billion *soums* (US$628,260) and the Bibi Khanum complex with a budget of 1 billion *soums* (US$424,500). Here it should be pointed out that these two monuments were deemed to be destroyed beyond repair in an inventory carried out by the Sredazkomstaris members Vasilii Viatkin and Boris Zasypkin. These renovations are anticipated to create new tourist routes (in particular in the south-west of Samarqand) and infrastructure services with a 1.5% growth rate with a revenue of 1.7 billion *soums* (US$721,650) expected in the state budget within five years. In addition, approximately 3000 jobs in research and restoration works would be created, complemented by a geographical information system (GIS) database to monitor the tangible and intangible cultural heritage (UNESCO 2011).

On 16 February 2015, Uzbekistan submitted an updated report[30] on the state of conservation of Samarqand's heritage to the World Heritage Centre, examined by the World Heritage Committee at its 39th session in Bonn, Germany (28 June–8 July 2015). Although the report confirms that the management plan was presented to the *khokim* (mayor) of Samarqand region in 2014 and was to be included in the annual budget of the cabinet of ministers, it does not mention any allocated funds or actual costs incurred during the planned restoration of Bibi Khanum and Ishrat Khana;

the latter is still in a ruined state. In response, the World Heritage Commission noted 'the progress made with the implementation of the Management Plan and efforts of the State Party to strengthen the protection of the property' and reiterated the request that the 'World Heritage Committee shall be notified prior to any major restorations or new constructions which may affect the Outstanding Universal Value (OUV) of the property before making any decisions that would be difficult to reverse' (UNESCO 2015, 133). Subsequently, the World Heritage Centre asked Uzbekistan to submit yet another updated report by 1 December 2016.[31] One wonders what is the added value of such reports that list the frequency of official meetings and provide no usable information on the latest measures and state of preservation?[32] In the majority of cases the actual urban development projects have taken place prior to the report submission deadline.

All these monitoring activities demonstrate that UNESCO would like to be actively involved and informed about the restoration and regeneration efforts in Uzbekistan. However, in practice the organization has an advisory function and one of its major tasks is to create awareness of the cultural heritage and to stimulate collaboration between NGOs. The actual decisions are taken, as explained above, by state authorities and the project commissions are divided among local privately owned companies. International collaboration projects related to architectural heritage have dwindled in recent years. Foreign investment seems to have been relegated, in the majority of cases, to the construction of new roads and is used to a lesser extent for the preservation of architectural heritage.

## Redesigning the holiest site in Tashkent: the Hazrat Imam complex

In Tashkent, modern constructions are planned and executed with a meticulous programme that could be related to the political significance of Timurid heritage. Their architectural epigraphy can be analysed as a tool to attest importance to certain, carefully chosen urban sites and at the same time to relate the monuments to the larger context of Timurid (15th century) and Shaybanid (16th–17th centuries) material heritage.

In January 2007, the International Islamic Educational, Scientific and Cultural Organization (ISESCO)[33] declared Tashkent one of the four capitals of Islamic culture. The oldest and the holiest place in Tashkent was chosen to commemorate the occasion. The Hazrat Imam Complex (locally known as Hast Imam) was turned into the largest and most prestigious construction site in Tashkent. The new building activity transformed the image of the Old City and created a large-scale pilgrimage site on what used to be a remote area off the beaten track amidst narrow streets of traditional Uzbek mud-brick housing – one of the oldest areas in Tashkent. The most important construction within the complex was the new Hazrat Imam Mosque (Figure 2).

With the Hazrat Imam Complex, the Old City acquired a new modern centre. Ever since the Russian colonial period, Tashkent has been divided by the Ankhor canal in the rapidly developing New City to the east and the more traditional Old City to the west. The New City was designed by the Russian settlers as a showpiece of progressive Western civilization (Kosmarski 2011, 40–41). By drastically modernizing the Old City in 2007, especially its most religious and sacred nucleus, a new state-controlled tolerance towards Islam was demonstrated that would have been unthinkable during the early years of Uzbek independence. Furthermore, the building project was characterized by directly quoting Timurid and Shaybanid iconography, epigraphy and urban planning. Through the use of architectural elements pertaining to key monuments of the Timurid and Shaybanid dynasty, the modern Uzbek political elite aspires to the status of powerful leaders, creating artefacts on the same grand scale as their predecessors.

Several important architectural approaches can be observed in the Hazrat Imam Complex. Firstly, the project was executed on the holiest site in Tashkent. Secondly, the created architectural ensemble (a *kosh*)[34] consisting of a congregational mosque opposite a *madrasa* has been used by

Figure 2. Hazrat Imam Mosque, 2013. Photo: author.

powerful dynasties such as the Timurids in Samarqand and Herat, and the Shaybanids in Bukhara. Thirdly, the concept of architectural palimpsest and utilization of Timurid and Shaybanid architectural morphology reinforces the legitimacy of the project. Fourthly, the positioning of the Uthman Quran – one of the earliest written versions of the Quran, kept in a museum in the centre of the complex – gave a flair of Islamic superiority to 'Hast Imam' which reaches beyond Central Asia. These four approaches are discussed below.

The Hazrat Imam Complex had evolved around the *mazar* (holy shrine) of Abu Bakr Muhammad Kaffel Shashi (d. 976), one of the first imams of the Shafii *madhab* (school of jurisprudence) of Sunni Islam. The graveyard that grew around the mausoleum of Kaffel Shashi has always been the most popular pilgrimage site in the Sibzar district of the Old City (Bulatova and Mankovskaya 1983, 106). During the 16th century, Tashkent gained cultural and commercial importance across Mavarannahr under the Shaybanid dynasty. The mausoleum of Suyunidz Khan (d. 1525), the first ruler of the Shaybanid dynasty in Tashkent, was erected in the burial ground to the south of the Kaffel Shashi shrine. The Barak Khan Madrasa was built around the mausoleum[35] of Suyunidz Khan between 1530 and 1550. The *mufti* (the highest religious leader) and chairman of the Spiritual Board of Muslims of Central Asia and Kazakhstan (SADUM) was housed in the Barak Khan Madrasa after 1950. This was the only functioning *mufti* on the territory of Central Asia, which had the support of 75 per cent of all Soviet Muslims (Peyrouse 2007, 42).

Other important buildings within the Hazrat Imam Complex include the 16th-century Muyi Muborak Madrasa, or the 'Sacred Hair' Madrasa, which supposedly houses a rarely seen hair of the Prophet Muhammad. The Library of the Muslim Board of Uzbekistan constitutes an important part of the complex. It possesses approximately 20,000 books and 3000 manuscripts on Islamic history, astronomy and medicine, including the Uthman Quran. With the refurbishment of the site, the Muslim Board of Uzbekistan acquired new administrative buildings within the complex.

The new Hazrat Imam Mosque, designed by the architect A. S. Turmatov, was built in a *kosh* opposite the Barak Khan Madrasa. The *kosh* has two main characteristics: location and scale. On the one hand, the location is of primary importance as it represents the significance of the building defined by its position within the urban fabric. Since most of the *kosh* complexes developed over the course of several centuries, a key factor was to build across an already existing compound erected by a famous ruler or dynasty. The location of the *kosh* legitimized the patron, his power and financial means, as he rivalled with the manifestation of power by a previous, established and celebrated ruler. In Tashkent, the Hazrat Imam Mosque was erected exactly on the main axis of the 16th-century royal Shaybanid *madrasa*. In the case of the Hazrat Imam Complex, not only was a new grander mosque created but also the original Shaybanid monument was redesigned.

The site of the Barak Khan Madrasa was redeveloped in a process best described as an architectural palimpsest. By reusing architectural details such as tiled domes, high drums, minarets and monumental portals, the modern Uzbek political elite seeks fame and recognition similar to the Timurid and Shaybanid dynasties. What is more, by placing the same epigraphy from the front facade of the Barak Khan Madrasa onto the main entrance to the Timurid dynastic mausoleum of Gur-i Amir in 2008–09, the symbolism of the site was intensified.

When I first visited the Barak Khan Madrasa in September 2006, the main facade was characterized by two low domes covered with tin sheets; there was no dome above the main mausoleum.[36] Within the remarkably short period of four months in 2007, the front facade was drastically changed. The *madrasa* was adorned with three turquoise pseudo-Timurid cupolas on high cylindrical drums. Two identical cupolas without any structural function were erected above the vestibule simply to keep the symmetry of the main facade. The third largest dome was erected above the mausoleum of Suyunidz Khan.

The Barak Khan Madrasa has been redesigned according to the greatest surviving Timurid model. The only building in present-day Uzbekistan with three cupolas forming one ensemble is the Bibi Khanum Mosque (1398–1405), which Timur erected in Samarqand as the greatest architectural achievement of his reign. The mosque was conceived as the capstone of Timurid craftsmanship and architectural ingenuity, remaining one of the largest mosques in Central Asia. The compound is based on the open courtyard plan with four majestic portals; it is the first mosque in Islamic architecture to display domes behind the side chambers. The main mosque is situated along the east–west longitudinal axis with the two side mosques forming the north–south axis. The side mosques are covered by turquoise ribbed domes resting on high drums (newly built in the 1980s); the main sanctuary is adorned with a tiled blue dome with the largest span in Central Asia. The Bibi Khanum Mosque also forms a *kosh* with the Bibi Khanum Madrasa, built by Timur's chief wife, who secured him the Mongol title of a 'son-in-law' which legitimized Timur's rule. In my opinion, the addition of the three domes to the Barak Khan Madrasa (Figure 3) makes a very clear architectural reference to the Bibi Khanum Mosque. Furthermore, the two domes above the vestibule also refer iconographically to the Shaybanid Mir-i Arab Madrasa (1535–36) that forms a *kosh* ensemble with the Kalan Mosque in Bukhara. The two domes, characteristic of the Mir-i Arab Madrasa, are repeated on the main facade of the Barak Khan Madrasa and on the main facade of the new Hazrat Imam Mosque.

The Uzbek 'Ideology of Independence' stresses the notion of a unified Muslim community, freed from Soviet-imposed atheism. Islamic cultural heritage and values are constantly celebrated by the state in an attempt 'to define Islam as properly national' (Khalid 2014, 525). At present, Quranic verses evoking the creation of a unified Muslim nation are being inscribed onto Timurid monuments throughout numerous restoration campaigns after the UNESCO listing as a World Heritage site. An important example of recent epigraphic restoration is the portal to the dynastic Timurid Mausoleum Gur-i Amir, which was retiled and adorned with Quranic

Figure 3. Barak Khan Madrasa in Tashkent, 2013, after restoration in 2007. Photo: author.

verses in 2008–09 (Paskaleva 2013). The Arabic text is from Sura 3, verse 104: 'Let there be *one nation* [emphasis added] of you, calling to good, and bidding to honour, and forbidding dishonour; Those are the prosperers.' It is interesting to note that the same text, but in an earlier calligraphic rendition, is used on the main portal of the Barak Khan Madrasa (Rtveladze 2011, 419).[37] I suggest that the choice of the verse on the portal of Gur-i Amir is an attempt to create the image of the nation based on shared values such as piety and religious devotion. The original text on the Barak Khan Madrasa added in the 1950s can be explained by the function of the *madrasa* as the seat of the *mufti* and as the only institution propagating Islamic religious values across Central Asia during the Soviet period. The fact that the text was copied from the Barak Khan Madrasa onto Gur-i Amir might also suggest an attempt to increase the 'proto-Timurid' importance of the new Hazrat Imam Complex in Tashkent, completed by September 2007.

The novelty used in the urban development of the Hazrat Imam Complex is the presentation of the Uthman Quran (also known as the Samarqand codex). This approach may have been adopted in order to attach not only regional but also world importance to the complex. The Quran was compiled in Medina under the third Sunni caliph Uthman (r. 644–56). It was completed in 651, only 19 years after Muhammad's death. Its remarkable story cannot be dealt here at length, however it is important to note that the Uthman Quran was one of Timur's treasures that he acquired after the campaign in Syria and Iraq. The Quran is believed to have been kept in the main sanctuary of the Bibi Khanum Mosque in Samarqand; hence, the name Samarqand codex. In 1869, Konstantin von Kaufman, Governor-General of Turkestan, sent it to the Imperial Library in St Petersburg. It attracted the attention of Tsarist orientalists and eventually a facsimile edition was published in St Petersburg in 1905. After repeated appeals by the people of Turkestan, the Quran was returned to Tashkent in 1923, where it has remained ever since. Prior to 2007, the Uthman Quran was kept in a safe at the Library of the Muslim Board of Uzbekistan,[38] which few tourists visited. Nowadays, the Uthman Quran is the highlight of the Hazrat Imam Complex. It has a special place in a glass case in the new museum of the Muslim Board at the Muyi Muborak Madrasa, situated in the middle of the square between the Barak Khan Madrasa and the Hazrat Imam Mosque.

The Hazrat Imam Complex was the key architectural achievement of modern Uzbek architecture in 2007. The new orthogonal landscape was created with wide lanes and flowerbeds; the low vegetation allows for vast, unobstructed views that have become ubiquitous across Uzbekistan (Kosmarski 2011, 46). The outcome is a mix of Shaybanid and modern pro-Timurid iconography (blue domes, high drums, ochre brickwork with tile decoration) meant to unify old architectural traditions in a modern context. The construction was finished ahead of schedule, 1.5 months before the celebration of Uzbek Independence Day on 1 September 2007. The progress was regularly monitored by the president, who was re-elected on 23 December 2007. The popular Hazrat Imam Mosque is visited both by local people on Friday prayers and by governmental officials during state visits.

## Conclusions

In this article I have discussed recent building activities and urban development measures in Samarqand and Tashkent. The continuous renovation and renewal projects initiated in Uzbekistan are changing the urban fabric of the cities on a large, unprecedented scale. The new constructions range from mosques to secular public buildings; their style is eclectic. The importance of Timurid heritage is evoked by integrating its intrinsic morphology into the development of the new architectural landscape of independent Uzbekistan. Timurid heritage is used as the 'symbolic embodiment of their greatest political ideals and national aspirations' (Abashin 2012, 155).

Sally Cummings summarizes that 'symbolic legitimation is crucial to power maintenance and to imbuing a sense of belonging into citizens of newly independent states' (Cummings 2012, 174). In the case of Uzbekistan, the sense of belonging is created by uplifting the status of the Uzbek people as heirs to Amir Timur and upholders of Timurid values such as 'spiritual might', 'justice' and the 'renaissance of science and culture'. The years of independence are described as a 'return to the sources of spirituality, national roots, historical memory' (Karimov 1998, 380). Symbolic legitimation is thus carefully structured around the elevation of the Timurid monuments not only as commemorative religious sites but also as core icons for the formation of new Uzbek identity based on re-evoked Timurid values.

The presented restorations disclose the fact that conscious choices are being made regarding the promotion of certain sites directly related to Timur. Since the monuments are owned by the state, public funds are used for their restoration. These campaigns involve both conservation and new morphological and epigraphic additions. In particular, the epigraphic restorations constitute a medium used to propagate the national ideology. By selecting texts underlining the importance of a unified Muslim nation (Gur-i Amir, Bibi Khanum) and by acknowledging the spiritual and religious diversity of the nation (Bibi Khanum), the new epigraphy seems to serve as a political tool.

Although all five Central Asian republics have underlined the strict separation between state and religion, Quranic texts in Arabic are being used as a legitimation device in present-day Uzbekistan. However, very few people can read Arabic and the message cannot be strictly targeted at the local population. My assumption is that the new texts reach out to other Muslim nations in an attempt to secure a global recognition of Uzbekistan and to denote its Timurid heritage as belonging to the wider Islamic cultural heritage. As Beatrice Manz points out 'Uzbekistan did not have to fight for its independence, but it does have to struggle for recognition as a power in its own right' (Manz 2002, 22).

These local urban development practices raise the more general question of authenticity of architectural heritage and the role of UNESCO in preserving it. The fact that major restoration projects in Uzbekistan have taken place after the UNESCO listing as World Heritage Sites points to the fact that the role of international organizations is restricted by the imposing power of the political elite. International representatives and most scholars are constantly monitored and accompanied by state officials throughout their visit to Uzbekistan (Adams 2013, 117).

Furthermore, heritage (claimed as such by UNESCO) and its use as a marketable commodity for the sake of tourism leads to the commercialization of the historical past (Herzfeld 1991), which has a detrimental and irreversible impact on the architectural artefacts. Using the 'rhetoric of modernization' and urban development, state authorities make conscious choices between large-scale regeneration projects and speedy restoration campaigns elevating Timurid sites within the 'rhetoric of heritage and high culture' (Herzfeld 2010, S266). Although the number of tourists has been growing in recent years, one wonders what percentage of the rapidly dwindling original tile work and decoration will remain intact in the years to come.

## Methodology

The empirical research presented in this paper was carried out during several visits to Samarqand and Tashkent between 2006 and 2015. The analysis is founded on photographs taken throughout these visits. Further historical insights are based on pre-Soviet and Soviet publications and photographic archival material kept at Cambridge University Library and the Harvard collection of the Aga Khan Program for Islamic Architecture. Another source for empirical data is administrative decrees and legislation, the majority of which are available online.


## Acknowledgments

The author thanks the anonymous reviewers for their valuable comments and comprehensive recommendations.

## Disclosure statement

No potential conflict of interest was reported by the author.

## Funding

The study, conducted at Cambridge in 2013–14, was made possible by a postdoctoral research grant by the Dr Catharine van Tussenbroek Foundation. In the autumn of 2014 the author carried out a detailed photographic survey at the Aga Khan Program archives at Harvard University; partial funding was provided by the Juynboll Foundation and by the research cluster Asian Modernities and Traditions at Leiden University.


## Notes

1. The UNESCO debate on heritage values and their importance was initiated during the Conference of Nara (1994), which questioned the notion of authenticity. The full text of the convention can be accessed at http://whc.unesco.org/archive/nara94.htm/.
2. The socio-political importance of Timurid monuments remains largely unstudied. The last two major Western publications on Timurid architecture – the ground-breaking and still most comprehensive study by Golombek and Wilber (1988) as well as O'Kane (1987) – are from the late 1980s. The recent politicized Uzbek study by Askarov (2009) claims Uzbekistan as the cradle of Renaissance across Eurasia. The most relevant publication for this research has been McChesney (2003). Tsarist and Soviet restoration policies towards Timurid architecture have been discussed by Shaw (2011), Demchenko (2011) and Gorshenina (2013a, 2013b, 2014a), but they do not cover the post-Soviet period and,

in particular, the newly created epigraphy. Gorshenina's ground-breaking works (Gorshenina 2012, 2014b) have been removed from the library of the Institute of Archaeology in Samarqand and are not currently accessible to scholars in Uzbekistan.

3. The Shaybanids were a powerful dynasty throughout the 16th–17th centuries. Monuments of the Shaybanid dynasty in Uzbekistan are situated in Bukhara and Samarqand.
4. Author's translation from German.
5. The commission examined 19 monuments in and around Samarqand. One of the first projects was the strengthening of the north-eastern minaret of the Ulugh Beg Madrasa; the commission was led by Viatkin (1869–1932) and the engineers Kastal'skii (1868–1943) and Mauer (1866–1932). The minaret was finally restored in its vertical position in 1932.
6. Endowments of the Ulugh Beg Madrasa and the Abdu Darun complex. I have not been able to find any information on the endowments of the Bibi Khanum Mosque or the Gur-i Amir Mausoleum. The keepers of the monuments in Samarqand also could not provide any details. Robert McChesney quotes Emel'yanov and explains that the Russians surveyed the endowments in Turkestan and 'identified 297 waqfs in Samarqand' (McChesney 2003, 19).
7. The most comprehensive study on the Turkomstaris, Sredazkomstaris, Uzkomstaris was carried out by Gorshenina (2013a). Her article was also published in English (Gorshenina (2013b).
8. Kary-Niazov was the ideal representative of the indigenization (*korenizatsiia*) in which educated titular nationals were encouraged to take leadership positions or participate actively in the social cultural transformations. In 1940 he became a member of the central committee of the Communist Party of Uzbekistan. The other members of the expedition were the anthropologist Professor Lev V. Oshanin, the palaeographer Aleksandr A. Semenov, the architect Boris N. Zasypkin, the archaeologist Vasilii A. Shishkin, and V. N. Koronov from the Hermitage Museum. The widely celebrated Tajik poet Ayni, who lived in Samarqand close to Gur-i Amir, was also involved.
9. Chapter 11, para. 49.
10. The statue in Shahr-i Sabz in front of Aq Saray palace was replaced in 2003 as the crown of Timur was considered to be associated with a Russian tsar and thus deemed inappropriate.
11. Also spelled Ilhom Jabborov. More information on his oeuvre can be found on the website of the Uzbek Art Academy.
12. The original portrait is kept by the family. Several copies were created by Malik Nabiyev'son Husan Nabiyev. In August 2013 one of them was up for sale at the art gallery of the Zarqaynar shopping mall in Tashkent.
13. All exterior and interior texts are conceived as an inseparable part of the decoration in Islamic architecture.
14. All Quranic translations are by Arthur J. Arberry, Oxford (Koran 2008).
15. The calligraphy was designed by Habbibula Solih and the band was added during the restoration campaign in 1992–95 (Olim et al. 2012).
16. Nina B. Nemtseva points out that this entrance to the *madrasa* had survived all conquests of Samarqand and all political regimes, but it did not survive the recent building campaign in 2004. Nemtseva surveyed the whole necropolis as early as 1959; she has created the most comprehensive study on Shah-i Zinda. Her latest book on Shah-i Zinda was published in 2015. Due to lack of funding, only 30 copies were printed.
17. The Muslim Board of Uzbekistan was established in 1993. The organization succeeded the Spiritual Board of Muslims of Central Asia and Kazakhstan (SADUM) that existed between 1943 and 1991. SADUM was the official governing body for Islamic activities in the five Central Asian republics within the Soviet Union, whereby each republic had a *qaziyat* (Muslim directorate). The chairman of SADUM held office in Tashkent and was appointed as a supreme *mufti*.
18. I am unable to provide the respective amount in US dollars in 2004; the present official exchange rate is US$1 = 2560 *soums*.
19. The museum contains a copy of the decree from 2004 and a model of the whole complex.
20. Established in 1896, a new purpose built museum building was designed in 1978 by the famous architect and scholar of Central Asian architecture Mithat S. Bulatov (1907–2004). At present the museum houses around 200,000 artefacts, including the archaeological collections of Vasilii Viatkin.
21. At present (May 2015) Shahr-i Sabz is undergoing a massive regeneration ahead of Timur's 680th birthday celebration in 2016.
22. The historical centres of Khiva, Bukhara and Samarqand were proclaimed by the Uzbek government as state architectural reserves (UNESCO 2004, 25).
23. Islam Karimov was born in Samarqand in 1938.

24. Lola Tillyaeva is the youngest daughter of the Uzbek president Islam Karimov.
25. For the full text of the Hague Convention, see http://portal.unesco.org/en/ev.php-URL_ID=13637&URL_DO=DO_TOPIC&URL_SECTION=201.html/.
26. The other two conventions ratified by Uzbekistan are the Convention on the Means of Prohibiting and Preventing the Illicit Import, Export and Transfer of Ownership of Cultural Property (1970); and the Convention on Safeguarding of the Intangible Cultural Heritage (2003).
27. Law on the Preservation and Utilization of Cultural Heritage Properties (No. 269-II 20 August 2001) and Law on the Preservation and Utilisation of Archaeological Heritage Properties (No. 42 16 June 2009). In 2014, the government of Uzbekistan adopted two more Decrees of the Cabinet of Ministers in addition to the existing legislative acts: No. 53 from 6 March 2014 On Additional Measures for the Further Improvement of Protection and Use of Tangible Cultural and Archaeological Objects; and No. 200 from 21 July 2014 On Additional Measures for the Further Improvement of Protection and Use of Tangible Cultural and Archaeological Objects.
28. Postanovlenie Kabineta Ministrov Respubliki Uzbkeistan, 21 July 2014, No. 200. Accessed August 20, 2015. http://www.norma.uz/novoe_v_zakonodatelstve/ohrana_obektov_kultury/.
29. In September 2014, a meeting was held to discuss the management plans for the three other World Heritage-listed sites in the territory of Uzbekistan.
30. The report is available on the UNESCO website *Samarkand – Crossroad of Cultures*. Accessed August 24, 2015. http://whc.unesco.org/en/list/603/documents/.
31. Decisions adopted by the World Heritage Committee at its 39th session, in Bonn, 2015 (UNESCO 2015, 133).
32. In August 2013, the UNESCO's director general was shown around the Bibi Khanum Mosque, but did not visit the Ishrat Khana.
33. The Islamic Educational, Scientific and Cultural Organization (ISESCO) was established by the Organization of the Islamic Cooperation (OIC) in May 1979. ISESCO is one of the largest international Islamic organizations and specializes in the fields of education, science and culture. Its headquarters are in Rabat, Morocco.
34. The *kosh* is an architectural ensemble of two or three buildings oriented towards each other with their main facades along the same axis. The *kosh* is formed by the buildings and the square between them. Examples of *kosh* ensembles are the Bibi Khanum Mosque and Mausoleum in Samarqand and the Kalan Mosque and Mir-i Arab Madrasa in Bukhara. The Mir-i Arab was the only functioning *madrasa* during the Soviet period; it was reopened in 1945 and is still operating today.
35. An earlier second mausoleum of the Unknown was incorporated into the south-western corner of the *madrasa*.
36. The original dome was destroyed during an earthquake in 1868 (Bulatova and Mankovskaya 1983, 114). A picture of the dome published by Ratiia and Voronin (1936, 69) reveals a *muqarnas* frieze and an epigraphic band above the high drum covered in tile mosaic. It is probable that the decoration on the 2007 domes was inspired by the original tile patterns.
37. The Barak Khan Madrasa was studied for the first time by the Uzkomstaris in 1935 (Ratiia and Voronin 1936, 68). The explorations were led by the key scholars of Uzbek architectural heritage: Masson, Zhukov, Ratiia and Voronin. The text was most likely added during the Soviet restoration campaign in 1956 based on the new design by A. N. Vinogradov. In 1979, a new restoration campaign was initiated but it was not fully executed.
38. The building of the library dating back to the 1880s was demolished in late 2006–early 2007. The location was integrated into Hazrat Imam square.

## References

Abashin, S. 2012. "Nation-construction in Post-Soviet Central Asian." In *Soviet and Post-Soviet Identities*, edited by M. Bassin and C. Kelly, 150–168. Cambridge: Cambridge University Press.

Adams, L. 2010. *The Spectacular State: Culture and National Identity in Uzbekistan*. Durham: Duke University Press.

Adams, L. 2013. "Ethnicity and the Politics of Heritage in Uzbekistan." *Central Asian Survey* 32 (2): 115–133. doi:10.1080/02634937.2013.807580

Akbarzadeh, S. 1996. "Nation-building in Uzbekistan." *Central Asian Survey* 15 (1): 23–32. doi:10.1080/02634939608400931

Alexander, C., V. Buchli, and C. Humphrey, eds. 2007. *Urban Life in Post-Soviet Asia*. London: UCL Press.

Allworth, E. A. 1990. *The Modern Uzbeks. From the Fourteenth Century to the Present. A Cultural History.* Stanford: Hoover Institution Press.

Arends, A. K. ed. 1965. *Iz istorii epokhi Ulugbeka.* Tashkent: Izd. Nauka UzSSR.

Askarov, Sh. 2009. *Arkhitektura Temuridov.* Tashkent: San'at.

Azimova, R. 1992. *Ulozhenie Timura.* Tashkent: Chulpon.

Bababekov, Kh. H. 2006. *Chudesa sud'by istorii Temura.* Accessed 13 September 2014. http://www.centrasia.ru/newsA.php?st=1149494640.

Barthold, V. V. 1958. *Four Studies on the History of Central Asia.* Translated from the Russian by V. and T. Minorsky. Volume 2 Ulugh-Beg. Leiden: Brill.

Bokova, I. 2013. Address on the Occasion of the Official Opening Ceremony of IX International Music Festival '*Sharq Taronalari*' ('Melodies of the Orient'). Samarkand: 25 August 2013.

Bulatova, V., and L. Mankovskaya. 1983. *Pamiatniki zodchetsva Tashkenta XIV-XIX veka.* Tashkent: Literatura i iskusstvo.

Cummings, S. 2010. "Inscapes, Landscapes and Greyscapes: The Politics of Signification in Central Asia." In *Symbolism and Power in Central Asia*, edited by S. N. Cummings, 1–11. London and New York: Routledge.

Cummings, S. 2012. *Understanding Central Asia.* London: Routledge.

Demchenko, I. 2011. "Decentralized Past: Heritage Politics in Post-Stalin Central Asia." *Future Anterior: Journal of Historic Preservation, History, Theory, and Criticism* 8 (1): 65–80.

Diener, A. C., and Hagen, J. 2013. "From Socialist to Post-socialist Cities: Narrating the Nation Through Urban Space." *Nationalities Papers: The Journal of Nationalism and Ethnicity* 41 (4): 487–514. doi:10.1080/00905992.2013.768217

Gerasimov, M. M. 1947. "Portret Tamerlana. Opyt skul'pturnogo vosproizvedeniia na kraniologicheskoi osnove." *Kratkie soobshcheniia Instituta istorii material'noi kul'tury* 17: 14–21.

Golombek, L., and D. Wilber. 1988. *The Timurid Architecture of Iran and Turan.* Princeton: Princeton University Press.

Gorshenina, S. 2012. *Asie centrale. L'invention des frontières et l'héritage russo-soviétique.* Paris: CNRS.

Gorshenina, S. 2013a. "Turkomstaris-Sredazkomstaris-Uzkomstaris: Formirovanie institutsii i etno-tsentricheskii razdel kul'turnogo nasledia srednei azii." *Etnograficheskoe obozrenie* 1: 52–68.

Gorshenina, S. 2013b. "Turkomstaris-Sredazkomstaris-Uzkomstaris." *Anthropology and Archeology of Eurasia*, 52 (2): 51–72. doi:10.2753/AAE1061-1959520204

Gorshenina, S. 2014a. "Samarkand and its Cultural Heritage: Perceptions and Persistence of the Russian Colonial Construction of Monuments." *Central Asian Survey* 33 (2): 246–269. doi:10.1080/02634937.2014.916071

Gorshenina, S. 2014b. *L'invention de l'Asie centrale. Histoire du concept de la Tartarie à l'Eurasie.* Paris: Librairie Droz.

Harrison, R. 2009. *Understanding the Politics of Heritage.* Manchester: Manchester University Press.

Harrison, R. 2013. *Heritage. Critical Approaches.* London and New York: Routledge.

Harvey, D. ([1973] 2009). *Social Justice and the City.* Athens, GA: The University of Georgia Press.

Helmersen, G. 1852. *Alexander Lehmann's Reise nach Buchara und Samarkand in den Jahren 1841 und 1842.* Osnabrueck: Biblio Verlag.

Herzfeld, M. 1991. *A Place in History: Monumental and Social Time in a Cretan Town.* Princeton, NJ: Princeton University Press.

Herzfeld, M. 2010. "Engagement, Gentrification, and the Neoliberal Hijacking of History." *Current Anthropology* 51 (S2): S259–S267. doi:10.1086/653420

Hobsbawm, E., and T. Ranger. 1983. *The Invention of Tradition.* Cambridge: Cambridge University Press.

Iakubovskii, A. Iu. 1933. *Samarkand pri Timure i Timuridakh.* Leningrad: Izd. Gos. Ermitazha.

Iakubovskii, A. Iu. 1940. "Iz istorii arkheologicheskogo izucheniia Samarkanda." *Trudy otdela Vostoka* 2: 286–337.

Iakubovskii, A. Iu. 1946. "Stat'i. Timur (Opyt kratkoi kharakteristiki)." *Voprosy istorii* 8–9: 42–74.

Iakubovskii, A. Iu., et al. 1950. *Istoriia narodov Uzbekistana.* Tashkent: AN UzSSR.

Kalinovsky, A. M. 2013. "Not some British Colony in Africa: The Politics of Decolonization and Modernization in Soviet Central Asia, 1955–1964." *Ab Imperio* 2: 191–222. doi:10.1353/imp.2013.0044

Karimov, I. A. 1996. *Uzbekistan: natsional'naya nezavisimost', ekonomika, politika, ideologiya.* Tashkent: Uzbekiston.

Karimov, I. A. 1998. *Na puti dukhovnogo vozrozhdeniya.* Tashkent: Uzbekiston.

Kary-Niazov, T. N. 1967. *Razmyshleniia o proidennom puti.* Tashkent: Fan.

Keller, Sh. 2007. "Story, Time, and Dependent Nationhood in the Uzbek History Curriculum." *Slavic Review* 66 (2): 257–277. doi:10.2307/20060220

Khalid, A. 2014. "Ulama and the State in Uzbekistan." *Asian Journal of Social Science* 42: 517–535. doi:10.1163/15685314-04205003

The Koran. 2008. Translated with an Introduction by Arthur J. Arberry. Oxford: Oxford University Press.

Kosmarski, A. 2011. "Grandeur and Decay of the "Soviet Byzantium": Spaces, Peoples and Memories of Tashkent, Uzbekistan." In *Urban Spaces after Socialism. Ethnographies of Public Places in Eurasian Cities*, edited by T. Darieva, W. Kaschuba, and M. Krebs, 33–56. Frankfurt/Main: Campus Verlag GmbH.

Kruikov, K. S. 1990. "Organizatsionnye formy okhrany i restavratsii pamiatnikov arkhitektury Uzbekistana (1920–1990)." *Arkhitektura i stroutel'stvo Uzbekistana* 8: 34–37.

Kruikov, K. S. 1991. "Organizatsionnye formy okhrany i restavratsii pamiatnikov arkhitektury Uzbekistana (1920–1990)." *Arkhitektura i stroutel'stvo Uzbekistana* 2: 9–13.

Laruelle, M. 2010. "National Narrative, Ethnology, and Academia in Post-Soviet Uzbekistan." *Journal of Eurasian Studies* 1: 102–110. doi:10.1016/j.euras.2010.04.007

Manz, B. F. 1989. *The Rise and Rule of Tamerlane*. Cambridge: Cambridge University Press.

Manz, B. F. 2002. "Tamerlane's Career and Its Uses." *Journal of World History* 13 (1): 1–25. doi:10.1353/jwh.2002.0017

March, A. 2002. "The Use and Abuse of History: 'National Ideology' as Transcendental Object in Islam Karimov's 'Ideology of National Independence." *Central Asian Survey* 21 (4): 371–384. doi:10.1080/0263493032000053190

March, A. 2003a. "From Leninism to Karimovism: Hegemony, Ideology and Authoritarian Legitimation." *Post-Soviet Affairs* 19 (4): 307–336. doi:10.2747/1060-586X.19.4.307

March, A. 2003b. "State Ideology and the Legitimation of Authoritarianism: The Case of Post-Soviet Uzbekistan." *Journal of Political Ideologies* 8 (2): 209–232. doi:10.1080/13569310306088

Matveeva, A. 2009. "Legitimising Central Asian Authoritarianism: Political Manipulation and Symbolic Power." *Europe-Asia Studies* 61 (7): 1095–1121. doi:10.1080/09668130903068624

McChesney, R. 2003. *Timur's Tomb: Politics and Commemoration*. The Central Eurasian Studies Lectures. Indiana University: Department of Central Eurasian Studies.

Muminov, I. M. 1968. *Rol' i mesto Amira Timura v istorii Srednei Azii v svete dannykh pis'mennykh istochnikov*. Tashkent: Fan UzSSR.

Nechkin, D. 1929. *Zadachi i blizhaishie tseli Komiteta po delam muzeev i okhrany pamiatnikov stariny, iskusstva i prirody v Srednei Azii*. Tashkent: Izd-vo Sredazkomstarisa.

Nemtseva, N. B. 2015. *Shahi-Zinda. Istoria, arkheologia, arkhitektura*. Tashkent: Author.

O'Kane, B. 1987. *Timurid Architecture in Khurasan*. California: Mazdâ Publishers.

Olim, S., et al., eds. 2012. *Epigraphical Monuments of Uzbekistan. Qashqadaryo. Palace and Memorial Ensembles*. Toshkent: Extremum Press.

Pankrat'ev, G. A. 1910. *Istoricheskie pamiatniki g. Samarkanda*. Samarkand.

Paskaleva, E. 2013. "Samarqand Refashioned: A Traveller's Impressions, August 2013" (with a preface by Daniel C. Waugh). *Silk Road Journal* 11: 139–153.

Peyrouse, S. 2007. "The Rise of Political Islam in Soviet Central Asia." *Current Trends in Islamist Ideology* 5: 40–54.

Ratiia, Sh., and Voronin, L. 1936. "Pamiatnik arkhitektury narodov SSSR. Mavzolei Barak-khan." *Arkhitektura SSSR* 11: 67–73.

Radlov, V. 1880. "Sredniaia Zerafshanskaia dolina." Zapiski Imperatorskogo russkogo geograficheskogo obshchestva po otdeleniju etnografii. Vol.6: Sredniaia Zerafshanskaia dolina, pod redaktsiei N. I. Veselovskogo et P. I. Lerkha. St Petersburg: Tip. V. Bezobrazova & c: 1–92.

Rtveladze, E., et al. 2011. *Masterpieces of Uzbekistan's Architectural Epigraphy*. Tashkent: Fund Forum.

Shaw, C. 2011. "The Gur-i Amir Mausoleum and the Soviet Politics of Preservation." *Future Anterior: Journal of Historic Preservation, History, Theory, and Criticism* 8 (1): 43–63.

Smith, L. 2006. *Uses of Heritage*. London and New York: Routledge.

Stronski, P. 2010. *Tashkent: Forging a Soviet City, 1930–1966*. Pittsburgh, PA: University of Pittsburgh Press.

Trevisani, T. 2014. "The Reshaping of Cities and Citizens in Uzbekistan: The Case of Namangan's "New Uzbeks." In *Ethnographies of the State in Central Asia, Performing Politics*, edited by M. Reeves, J. Rasanayagam, and J. Beyer, 243–260. Bloomington and Indianapolis: Indiana University Press.

UNESCO. 2004. *Central Asian Earth 2002–2012*. Tashkent Office. National Commission of the Republic of Uzbekistan for UNESCO.

UNESCO. 2011. *Decisions adopted by the World Heritage Committee at its 35th session (Paris, 2011)*. WHC-11/35.COM/20. Samarkand decision: 35COM 7B.80.
UNESCO. 2013. *Country Programming Document (UCPD) for the Republic of Uzbekistan* (2014 – 2017).
UNESCO. 2015. *Decisions adopted by the World Heritage Committee at its 39th session (Bonn, 2015)*. WHC-15/39.COM/19. Samarkand decision: 39 COM 7B.73.
Uzbek Constitution. 1992. Tashkent: Uzbekiston.
Veselovskii, N. 1905. *Mecheti Samarkanda*. Vypusk 1. Gur- Emir. St. Petersburg.
Woods, J. E. 1987. "The Rise of Tīmūrid Historiography." *Journal of Near Eastern Studies* 46 (2): 81–108. doi:10.1086/373225

# The ideology of development and legitimation: beyond 'Kazakhstan 2030'

Diana T. Kudaibergenova

*Department of Sociology, University of Cambridge, Cambridge, UK*

The paper analyses the multifaceted discourse of development and nation-building in post-Soviet Kazakhstan. It addresses the regional clan–central elite relations and Nursultan Nazarbayev regime's legitimating agenda through the Kazakhstan 2030 Strategy for development. The economic developmental component in Nazarbayev's ideological discourses is primarily an exercise of control over regional economic and political elites and that helped building further legitimacy for the regime in various socio-ethnic constituencies on both the regional and central levels. Kazakhstan 2030 was deployed by the regime to substitute the Soviet version of ideology, legitimize the regime among various ethno-lingual audiences, and discipline the behaviour of regional elites. The paper shows how the study of elites' interests can best explain the nature of national ideology and development projects.

## Introduction

The modernizing and developmental goals in economic, social and political spheres are the focal points of the Nursultan Nazarbayev regime's state-building in Kazakhstan. These goals form politico-economic discourses of the state strategic programmes, in the visions of Kazakhstan 2030 and other programmes such as Kazakhstan 2010, Kazakhstan 2020 and, finally, Kazakhstan 2050. The Kazakhstan 2030 developmental programme is one of the first cornerstones of the modernizing nationalism in Kazakhstan defined by Alima Bissenova (Bissenova 2012, 10, 11) as 'a phenomenon of collective aspiration' for collective improvement and as something promising by the government, namely, future enhancement and development of citizens' lives. Modernizing nationalism does not always appear as an ethnically divided discourse; on the contrary, it is an overarching agenda for all citizens of Kazakhstan, regardless of their ethnic, religious or social identity, who should strive to live better and continue building important conditions (stability and interethnic harmony) for the further progress and prosperity of Kazakhstan. Such nation-building continues to be semi-ideological, both mimicking the ideological framework of goal-oriented and commonly shared set of values for all, but also distancing the regime from an open declaration of one dominant ideology.[1] It provides the space for the commonly shared a-cultural and non-ethnic developmental values and ideals, but leaves space for the unsettled 'national idea' in the socio-political and socio-ethnic spheres.

The programmes similar to Kazakhstan 2030, products of modernizing nationalism, are called upon to serve multiple goals of the regime as they: (1) substitute old (Soviet) versions of 'concrete ideologies', with flexible economic objectives; (2) simultaneously legitimize the regime in the eyes of the two distinct socio-linguistic and socio-ethnic groups (Kazakh ethno-nationalists and Russian speakers[2]), which were traditionally (from the Soviet period) presented as differentiated political audiences; and (3) exercise control over regional economic and political elites (Table 1) by creating blueprints for their political identity and behaviour codes.

Intra-elite relations have occupied a prominent role in Central Asian studies. Issues of regionalism and centre–periphery relations (Cummings 2000, 2002, 2005, 2006; Schatz 2000, 2006; Jones Luong 2002), intra-elite relations and clans (Junisbai and Junisbai 2005; Collins 2006; Schatz 2004, 2005, 2006; Junisbai 2010), and elite-led ideological processes in state- and nation-building and legitimation (March 2003; Cummings 2006, 2010; Adams 2010; Isaacs 2010, 2011; Koch 2010; Bissenova 2012; Ó Beacháin and Kevlihan 2013) were extensively analysed. These works highlighted the importance of elites in processes of power-formation consolidation, nation- and state-building, and future development of these states. Building on this literature and addressing the regional clan–central elite relations and the Nazarbayev regime's legitimating agenda via the Kazakhstan 2030 Strategy, the paper expands on the existing dichotomy between the regional and central elites in Kazakhstan. I identify central and top elites as the main decision-making body defined formally (positional) and informally (power bargaining) and geographically separated as the centre currently moved to the capital Astana (see Koch 2013 for the debate on centre location and distribution of power from Astana). The central elite is primarily represented by President Nursultan Nazarbayev (thereafter the president) himself and his closest power-elite field: Prime Minister Karim Masimov, several influential ministers, such as Asset Issekeshev and Vladimir Shkolnik, and others. (Table 1 has a representation of current regional heads and the economic importance of each region in terms of (regional) gross domestic product (GDP).) However, various top elites are simultaneously situated in the centre and represent the regional elite divisions or so-called regional *clans* (Schatz 2004, 2005; Collins 2006; Azadi 2010; Isaacs 2011).

The clan networks in Kazakhstan are no longer identified just by the kinship lines or a sole regional identity, but are more strictly established by the financial interests of the network and its geographical location. It is also important to highlight that clans may be comprised of both formal positions in regional administrations (regional, local and village *akims* may belong to the clan structure in a specific region) as well as more informal players who are placed outside the politico-administrative hierarchy (such as leaders and members of local communities, large and small business groups). Regional elites who comprise clans are also connected to the clan-specific central elites who may occupy higher political and power positions.[3] It is also important to note that not all central and regional elites may belong to a specific clan and there is no reason to focus one's attention entirely on clan politics. Regional clans exist and influence the political processes but are not the main influence in the complex processes of state- and nation-building in Kazakhstan at this point in time. Following Rico Isaacs' timely criticism of the 'informal politics' approach (Isaacs 2011, 2013), I highlight the importance of the formal structures of regional and central political administration. These are defined by the centrist control mechanism where even local governors (*akims*) are selected and appointed by the president himself (Cummings 2000 analyses centre–periphery relations in Kazakhstan). Informal structures of regional clans may intervene in this process of formal and informal administration simultaneously with the 'virtual politics', the existence of certain formal institutions on the surface (Wilson 2005; Heathershaw 2014).

The paper addresses the important role played by the modernizing mission of the Kazakhstan 2030 Strategy in the regional–central elites' relationships and in disciplining of the regional elites by central powers. It does so from a sociology-of-development point of view, which tracks socio-political processes and changes in the centre–regional politics. While development policies were created to frame national and nationalist discourses and to legitimize the Nazarbayev regime while providing a goal-oriented vision of development, these policies also played an important mutual bargaining role in the regime's relations with the regional elites and clans.

Although it is hard to disagree with scholars who dismissed the Kazakhstan 2030 Strategy as a post-Soviet 'counterpart' of five-year plans and similar projects 'about the bright future of communism' (Schatz 2000, 88; see also Cummings 2005, 2006; Bissenova 2012; Pomfret 2013), it is important to study the strategy because it is one of the first solid attempts of the regime to propose a discursive and structural framework for the implementation of its goals and its legitimacy building (Pomfret 2013). The fate of the Kazakhstan 2030 Strategy may eventually be forgotten and even ridiculed, but so far its role in legitimization and state-building has been remarkably effective. First, the framework provided blueprints for the participation of regional and centrist elites in state-building. Second, it disciplined the administrative corps within a specific domain, which was envisioned in the document as the 'professional state'. Finally, the strategy had conceptualized the initiation of the modernizing nationalism framework of the regime and a new balance between Russian-speaking and Kazakh identities by providing the common ground of economic prosperity for all and the vision of the development and progress that could be collectively achieved via such a programme (Figure 1 shows the language-based divisions of the two political communities).

## Kazakhstan 2030: development and nation-building discourses

The Kazakhstan 2030 Strategy programme was the first visionary programme in the post-independence and post-transition period, and was entirely a future- and goal-oriented project. It focused on a managerial assessment of the situation in 1997 with a complete SWOT analysis (strengths, weaknesses, opportunities and threats) and the projection of the future developmental possibilities. Structurally, the strategy consisted of seven long-term priority areas: (1) national security; (2) domestic political stability and consolidation of the society; (3) economic growth based on an open market economy with high foreign investment and internal savings; (4) the health, education and well-being of Kazakhstani citizens; (5) energy resources; (6) infrastructure, especially transport and communication; and (7) professional state.[4]

The text of the strategy offered a visionary and developmental approach mainly in the economic sphere without touching upon the specifics of economic jargon or any real concrete projects, but providing the blueprint for their future operations. However, the main goals of the strategy and, thus, the regime were well focused and formed the backbone of Nazarbayev regime's semi-ideological system of presidential annual addresses which specify the developmental plans for the upcoming year and summarize already achieved development of the passing year (this is why the annual presidential addresses usually occur either at the end or at the very

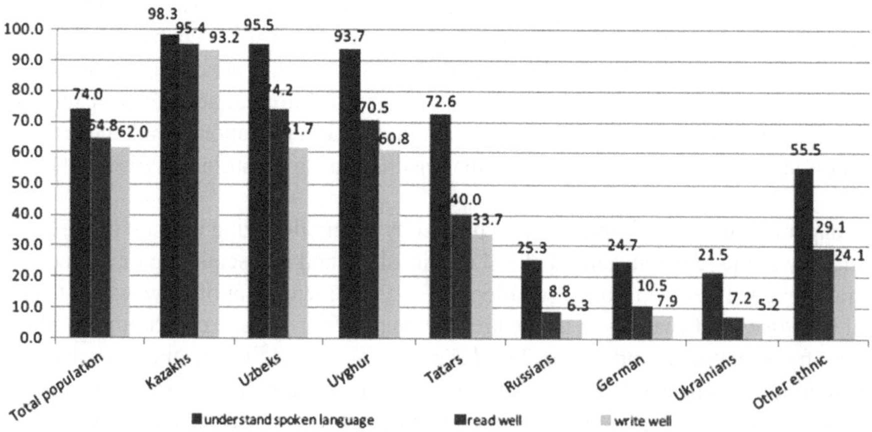


Figure 1. Socio-linguistic composition of population in Kazakhstan, 2009: extent of Kazakh language skills. Source: Agenstvo Respubliki Kazakhstan po statistike, 2010.

beginning of the year – December or January). Although the Kazakhstan 2030 Strategy and further similar programmes on Kazakhstan 2020 and 2050 were able to provide the sense of 'where we are going', which is usually ascribed to an ideology, the criticism about the absence of a 'concrete' vision about the country's and the nation's future development continues to be the most heated and popular topic in media.[5] The main trouble with the absence of ideology for numerous local commentators is the lack of a coherent and usually nationally oriented doctrine about the country's development not only in economic terms but also in social and political spheres. Thus, Kazakhstan 2030 for many local commentators provides the economic and developmental basis of what could be identified as a partial, semi-ideology. These economic and development discourses in Kazakhstan 2030 were based on economic growth and integration, restrictions of state interventions to economic processes, but also state involvement when it is needed, restrictions and disciplining of political cadres and especially regional elites and, most importantly, the attraction of foreign investment.

The main goals of Kazakhstan 2030 were based on the seven priorities and were fairly simple. The major goal of the strategy from the regime's perspective was the creation of a stable socio-political and economic foundation for international investments so that the county would not face economic problems and shortages. During the transition period of 1993–97, 'industry operated under tight financial constraints due to the shortage of working capital' and was unable 'to complete the entire production cycle resulting from the shortfall in deliveries of raw materials and components' (Jandosov 1998, 1). In this context it was not surprising that the rhetoric focused around the importance of foreign investments. For these reasons the regime had facilitated the semi-ideological paradigm of 'stability' following the discursive field of 'stable Kazakhstan = stable development'. The initial text of the Kazakhstan 2030 Strategy and its step-by-step programmes have emphasized the importance of foreign investment that could only be guaranteed by the stable socio-political situation in the country, and vice versa relational development.

The importance of foreign investments during the transition was crucial for the regime's as well as for regional elites' interests (Jandosov 1998). Following the introduction of Kazakhstan 2030, a special state committee for investments[6] was created. The 'pursuit for [*sic*] foreign investment' envisioned as a 'long and never-ending' process became the leitmotif of the regime's domestic and foreign policy (Kazakhstan 2030, 111). Annual events such as the Astana Economic Forum became important tokens of this objective.

The whole discourse of 'stability' was important for the legitimation of the regime's projects in regional domination. For example, the text of Kazakhstan 2030 specifically indicates that 'the central and regional power should stop intervening in economic processes', but 'the state has to intervene where market system is still underdeveloped' specifying the situational approach to the state (and central elites') intervention but circumscribing the regional elites' interference (Kazakhstan 2030, Professional State section).

The Kazakhstan 2030 Strategy has laid out a strong basis for many policies and state-led programmes, including the modernizing nationalism that has originated on the basis of the developmentalist perspectives and strategies offered by the Nazarbayev regime in this strategic programme. In this section I offer a discursive reading[7] of the programme on two important domains: the separation of powers (definitional level) and state-building level (modernizing nationalism level).

The discursive core of the strategy and its efforts for modernizing nationalism can be divided along the following categories: state, government, neighbouring countries and integrative processes and citizens of the Republic of Kazakhstan. It is important to discuss the discursive categories offered despite the intentional or accidental blurriness of the text. These categories help to identify (1) the agents of political power and bargaining within the regime and (2) the regime's dominant narratives and goals in nation-building laid out by the strategy.

The 'State' category was defined as above and beyond the government, regional administration and society. Through the text of the strategy one can read the ambiguous developments of the state category as a state of Kazakhstan with its emergence and re-emergence following 'epochs in which various empires: Ottoman, Austro-Hungarian and Soviet' intervened in the state-building (Nazarbayev 1998/2005, 74). The 'State of Kazakhstan' and 'our country' discourses constitute the territorial domain as well as the first priority of the strategy – national security (see also Koch 2013 on the similar argument of geographical and power-related discourses of state and capital in Kazakhstan). Here 'state' also is described in the strategy as a nation. 'State-nation' (rather than a nation-state) was defined as a unity of all citizens living in Kazakhstan who have and should have equal opportunities for their development. The national domain was described in priority number 2 – domestic stability and social consolidation. The discourse of stability became the central emphasis of the regime's discursive and ideological projects even prior to the formal 1991 independence[8] as it guaranteed stable investment and, thus, economic and social development. So, the 'priority of stability' became central to the strategy and regime's ideological field as a precondition for economic development. One can conclude that stability and economic development have become two interdependent variables in the official state-building discourses. Further, the state sometimes was personified with the figure of Nazarbayev himself (in the text and within the discourse of political development).[9] The main priority of the state and the head of the state (Nazarbayev) was to maintain peace and stability and lead economic development built on these stable bases.

The 'government' was also presented as a personified agent but represented both in a multiplicity of individual agents (although not defined clearly, these are ministers and high political elite members in power) and their volatility. The strategy indicated that the government was supposed to change by default:

> As the Head of State I [President Nazarbayev] must say the following. The time that we could spare for our officials [*chinovniki*] to adapt to the new situation is up. We no longer can afford being kind-hearted at the expense of other people, endangering the development destiny of the country. We have to most seriously undermine this potential for reproduction of pernicious habits and step up capital reforms among the government staff and that of civil servants. (Nazarbayev 1998/2005)

Because each member of the government and society was projected as responsible for the success of the development project envisioned by the regime, the framework of this development strategy is expected to influence their behaviour and discipline them. The text of Kazakhstan 2030 reminded each member of society that there were important sacrifices to be made and that economic change would not happen immediately, but steadily. This has created the discourse of the future-oriented and future-anticipated strategy of development. It also facilitated the regime's use of other future-oriented and developmental discourses, for example, the Kazakhstan 2050 Strategy. For example, the anticipation of change or fulfilment of the final project became a short-term prospectus for nation-building where national identity had to be found in the future rather than immediately:

> Not everyone is able to answer the question of 'Who are we the Kazakhstanis?' To settle [this] self-identification process will take some time and it requires a historical period of development.
>
> It took communist regime more than seventy years to create Soviet people – a project that failed. Many postcolonial and multinational states still did not finalise these processes after so many years [of independence]. We will be able to form and mature this feeling only after some decades would pass.[10]

Although this ambiguous temporal anticipation did not lead to some specific and 'concrete' ethno-nationalistic projects and policies that the majority of Kazakh speaking population expected from the regime, it nevertheless paved the way to the regime's other legitimating projects in a cautious manner. This approach has allowed the regime to invest into and build an alternative, modernizing nationalism, and situational projects for nation-building which I term elsewhere as 'substitution for the absence of ideology' (Kudaibergenova 2015; Ó Beacháin and Kevlihan 2013; Karin and Chebortarev 2002).

Modernizing nationalism was another important goal set out by the Kazakhstan 2030 Strategy. The success of the Kazakhstan 2030 Strategy, as in other similar projects, was dependent on the 'support of Kazakhstani citizens'[11] who had to be united and supportive of state programmes, calling for the collective aspiration and action in the fulfilment of the country's development. As already noted above, the Kazakhstan 2030 Strategy rarely mentioned the 'nation' but rather focused on the dimension of the state: a prosperous, successful and strongly developed state became the core templates envisioned by the creators of Kazakhstan 2030. Furthermore, ethnic, religious and class distinctions were seen as threats to the successful development of this state-nation of Kazakhstan 2030:

> If various ideological, religious, ethnic or class oriented groups remain in the state of confrontation it will lead to a dangerous situation where society/people [*narod*] will be distracted from the main goal – the achievement of common welfare and realisation of our national interests.[12]

In its mission to build a new state and a new system that had never existed in the history of Kazakhstan, the producers of the strategy proposed the notion of *civicness* rather than nationness prioritizing a *jus soli* approach over *jus sanguinis* as had happened in Latvia and Estonia, for example. It was vital for the development and bright successful future that the Kazakhstan 2030 Strategy argued to 'guarantee the development of our uniform civicness [*grazhdanstvennost'*] based on the equality of opportunities for all citizens of our country' and create conditions under each so that 'all ethnic groups would have equal rights' (Nazarbayev 1998/2005, 99–100).[13] The grand idea of the modernizing nationalism was 'to build a successful and rich Kazakhstan which will ensure political stability and societal consolidation in the long-term perspective' (Nazarbayev 1998/2005, 100). Although the strategy was available in both Kazakh and Russian languages (the text was identical in both translations), Kazakhstan 2030 has never focused on the national character identified beyond the 'state' or 'citizenship' civic categories. In other words, the regime was not engaged solely in ethno-national nation-building or just the civic modernizing one, but rather in both. However, the main domain of all strategies, including the following Kazakhstan 2050, was the strength of the state and success of its administrative apparatus in achieving the economic goals set by the regime. This approach clarified the state-nation rather than nation-state paradigm of national development. This, however, does not mean that other discourses did not adopt more ethno-nationalist approaches. On the contrary, the development of a Kazakh nationalist field represented by the key individuals or small marginal parties still continues to be a vocal representation of differing views. But the regime opted for the non-primordialist and not specifically ethnicity-driven approach which provided the space for the civic discussions in nation-building in Kazakhstan, but only to the extent in developmental discourses rather than discussions on Kazakh language empowerment and Kazakhification of public offices (e.g., Cummings 2006).

According to the vision of the Kazakhstan 2030 Strategy, the strong state was primarily important and vital for the economic and financial development of Kazakhstan and its further modernization. This approach of rapid economic modernization[14] proved to be the most successful of the regime's ideational (but not ideological) projects. In a study of the property (real estate) boom and consumption culture in Kazakhstan, Bissenova (2012), for example, successfully argued that the 'discourse of material progress' was driving the legitimacy of the regime in post-Soviet Kazakhstan.

> I maintain that this ideology is shared by the vast majority of the consumer-citizens in Kazakhstan regardless of their ethnic, religious, and even political affiliations. These consumer-citizens might disagree on

> many so-called identity issues: whether to refer to themselves as Kazakhs or Kazakhstanis, what language to speak in public or private settings, how to address questions of ethnicity and religion in the public sphere, whether to follow the democratic path of the West or follow the 'Eastern tigers' model. Nevertheless, the consumer-citizens tend to agree with the premise that the primary purpose of the state is to ensure order and material well-being for all or at least for the majority of the population. (26)

These findings are also backed up by the results of the recent sociological studies on social attitudes and political support in Kazakhstan. According to the 2011 KISI sociological study on identification in Kazakhstan, almost 60% of respondents supported the idea that the state should regulate the economy, focusing on the interests of social equality of all citizens (Sultanov et al. 2011). Among these respondents, 45.8% identified themselves as loyal supporters (*predanniy storonnik*) of President Nazarbayev, and more than 83% as citizens of Kazakhstan as their first priority of identification (Sultanov et al. 2011, 19–20). Moreover, around 34% of respondents agreed with the establishment of 'iron discipline' (*zhelezniy poryadok*) in case of instability and threat of a bloody conflict for the country, and 25.6% agreed to this only for the period of crisis, but with a condition that 'everything needs to be balanced and without further bending [radicalization]' (Sultanov et al. 2011, 42). In these conditions support for the regime's economic policy and vision, which was first established in Kazakhstan 2030 based on support for President Nazarbayev's politics, is distributed proportionally among Kazakh speakers (around 50%) and non-Kazakh population (37–39%) (Sultanov et al. 2011, 22). These results partially demonstrate the success of developmentalist strategies similar to Kazakhstan 2030 in forging popular ideas of the strong state, strong leadership, stability and an attractive basis for 'consumer-citizens' in Kazakhstan, as Bissenova (2012) coins them. Other successes of Kazakhstan 2030 also include a particular discourse of elite discipline, which is discussed in the following section.

## Kazakhstan 2030 and regional elites

Apart from the legitimating role of the Kazakhstan 2030 Strategy in the regime's modernizing nationalism, it was also envisioned to bring coherence to regional governmentality and to provide the administrative grid and hierarchy of control to the non-democratic regime and regional elites. Kazakhstan with its regional complexities of geographical dispersion and competition of regional elites (Table 1), thus, becomes a space for the study of important technologies of governing elites and their interests at different levels of power. The introduction of Kazakhstan 2030 was in many ways a timely ideological tool in which to provide legitimacy for the regime, discipline regional elites and a bargain with the interests of top financial/political elites by vesting the strategy's goals in their interests in various economic development sectors, e.g., oil and gas and industry.

The Republic of Kazakhstan is comprised of 14 provinces (*oblast*) and two cities with provincial status, Astana and Almaty (Table 1). Each province is represented by the administrative unit – the regional *akim* (governor) appointed by the president himself. Apart from the extensive state apparatus in each region, which is comprised of the network of lower-level provincial administration in each unit and by the self-governing bodies, *maslikhats*, each region is also represented by an array of bigger industrial financial groups and smaller businesses. The level of investment and production potential of each region thus forms and regulates these formal and informal financial networks. The rapid development of the Western Kazakhstan region (Aktobe, Western Kazakhstan, Mangystau; Table 1) also indicated, for example, the growth and empowerment of these regional elites.

The vast wave of privatization initiated in 1994 has resulted in the growth of the ratio of GDP generated in the private sector, amounting to 55% in Kazakhstan in 1997 (Kaser 1998). This has

Table 1. Regional Kazakhstan: Governors, investment and regional GDP as of 2013.

| Province | Head of the province (*akim*), since (year) | External investment, 2013 (%) | Capital of the province (city) | Regional gross domestic product (GDP) in 2012 (tenge, billions) |
|---|---|---|---|---|
| Akmola | Sergey Kulagin, 2014 | 1.2 | Kokshetau | 803.9 |
| Aktobe | Archimed Mukhambetov, 2011 | 15.7 | Aktobe | 1674.7 |
| Almaty | Amandyk Battalov, 2014 | 2.2 | Taldyqorgan | 1454.3 |
| Atyrau | Baktykhozha Izmukhambetov, 2012 | 23.1 | Atyrau | 3292.5 |
| West Kazakhstan | Nurlan Nogaye v, 2012 | 7.3 | Uralsk | 1711.4 |
| Zhambyl | Karim Kokrekbayev, 2013 | 2.5 | Taraz | 763.7 |
| Karaganda | Nurmukhambet Adbibekov, 2014 | 7.3 | Karaganda | 2459 |
| Kostanai | Nuraly Saduakasov, 2012 | 2.7 | Kostanai | 1156.2 |
| Kyzylorda | Krymbek Kushurbekov, 2013 | 7.6 | Kyzylorda | 1176.6 |
| Mangystau | Alik Aydarbayev, 2013 | 8.9 | Aktau | 2170.8 |
| South Kazakhstan | Askar Myrzakhmetov, 2009 | 4.3 | Shymkent | 1870.6 |
| Pavlodar | Kanat Bozumbayev, 2013 | 2.6 | Pavlodar | 1528.4 |
| North Kazakhstan | Samat Yeskendirov, 2013 | 0.3 | Petropavlovsk | 683 |
| East Kazakhstan | Berdybek Saparbayev, 2009 | 5.5 | Ust-Kamenogorsk | 1819.5 |
| Astana | Imangali Tasmagambetov, 2008 Adilbek Dzhaksybekov, 22 October 2014 | 1.9 | – | 2582.9 |
| Almaty | Akhmetzhan Esimov, 2008 | 7.1 | – | 5730 |

Sources: Agentstvo Respubliki Kazakhstan po statistike; Sbornik Regioni Kazakhstana 2012; Taldau 2014 (Agentstvo Respubliki Kazakhstan po statistike), official website of Akmola, Aktobe, Almaty, Atyrau, West Kazakhstan, Zhambyl, Karaganda, Kostanai, Kyzylorda, Mangystau, South Kazakhstan, Pavlodar, North Kazakhstan and East Kazakhstan provinces.

also resulted in the growth of regionally powerful financial groups. Local political and economic commentators usually include the following groups: Eurasian Financial Group, Bulat Utemuratov's Group, *Kazakmys* (Vladimir Ni), and Timur Kulibayev's group. Alongside these financial groups a middle tier of regional administration operates under provincial *akims*.

The informal networks and interrelations between the financial groups and local administration are hard to trace methodologically, and if even partially successful such analysis would be speculative. Therefore, I would separate the concepts of regional administrative corps from the regional financial clans. The clan networks and the structure of big regional financial groups are surrounded by a cloud of secrecy and speculation. So it is important first to focus primarily on the formal structures of governance (Isaacs 2011).

However, this does not save Kazakhstani politics from personalization of the regime and cabinets. The core of the power elite, for example, Umirzak Shukeev, Imangali Tasmagambetov, Timur Kulibayev, Bulat Utemuratov, Nurlan Balgymbayev,[15] Akhmetzhan Esimov and Karim Masimov have not only remained in power since the introduction of the strategy discussed here, but also came to identify the regime clearly with their personalities and speculations about their power share. These key elites have remained in the most powerful field within the Kazakh informal and formal political hierarchy, occupying both formal positions in the government (Nurlan Balgimbayev served as prime minister during the turbulent moments of 1997–99 right after Akezhan Kazhegeldin's oppositional insurgence[16]; Karim Masimov as the prime minister; Umirzak Shukeev as a talented apparatchik and former deputy prime minister), and in the most important regional administrative positions (Imangali Tasmagambetov as former *akim* of Almaty and Astana; and Akhmetzhan Esimov as former *akim* of Almaty) or within important governmental financial structures, for example, the Samruk Kazyna Development Fund (chaired by Timur Kulibaycv in 2011 and by Umirzak Shukeev since December 2011).

These power-positioned elites were able to survive intra-elite competition that has pushed many other prominent political and economic actors, for example, Akezhan Kazhegeldin, Oraz Jandosov, Galymzhan Zhakiyanov and Bulat Abilov, to leave the political scene or go into exile. The intra-elite competition for financial resources was the trigger for the formation of such viable opposition movements as Kazakhstan's Democratic Movement (DVK) in 2001. It was formed from the political and economic elites who were pushed out of the political field, apart from Kazhegeldin who left his political career before this date (Junisbai and Junisbai 2005). The remaining power elites were also more successful in building their networks of support regionally and centrally and in lobbying for their interests within the regime.

The introduction of the Kazakhstan 2030 Strategy has impacted all these groups extensively by providing the semi-ideological framework of work conduct and code of practice through formal institutions and directing the goals of big regional business groups within this developmental perspective. Thus, the development project in Kazakhstan was largely invested in the promotion and bargaining around the interests of various power and regional elites within the framework of the strategy.

### *Disciplining elites*

In the final introductory paragraphs of Kazakhstan 2030, President Nazarbayev has justified the strategic side of the plan by highlighting that it 'allows [one] to focus and discipline the attention of the state on short-term priorities', and that it 'disciplines the government to work on these programs and strategies on a daily basis' (Nazarbayev 1998/2005, 76). The disciplining nature and task of the Kazakhstan 2030 Strategy was highlighted further in the programme, where

> it is highly important to create a system in which each ministry and each bureaucratic unit will organise its work in such a way that each day, each month and each year we would come closer to the realisation of our goals. (76)

State officials were called upon to strategize their work in the matter of the Kazakhstan 2030 goal orientation rather than 'being distracted by less important daily routine' (76). In this affirmatory but also demanding fashion, the strategy had set up a special disciplining discourse or the charter, work convention for the public officers and all those governing bodies to work within the strategy's framework and have a 'focused and coordinated work' (85–86).[17] This has provided a long-lasting effect on the strategic planning and project-oriented implementation in the regional politics. Following the 'virtual politics' approach of surface creation in the form of numerous programmes, plans and small-scale developments at the local level, many of these documents and projects cited and mirrored Kazakhstan 2030.

The disciplining nature of the strategy envisioned the creation of a cadre of loyal and 'progressive-looking state-officials' who would become 'the key carriers of this ideology' (Cummings 2006, 182). The strategy had largely followed the managerial and corporate-like plan of development where key implementers of the strategic project were also viewed as political managers. The regime viewed them as capable of managing the project at regional and lower levels, but also aimed to manage them from above in a top-down management style within a business corporation: 'Our task is to create in Kazakhstan an efficient modern state service and management structure best suited for market economy; form the Government capable of realising priorities; build a state protecting national interests.'[18] The strategy's seventh priority 'Professional

State', for example, envisaged that central and regional governments had to follow seven strategic principles. These were general recommendations for self-efficient and less bureaucratic administration and a decentralization of power from the ministries to the regions.[19]

The proposed managerial approach to the 'strategic development' of the state organs' work was in reality a tightening of the authoritarian regime at the top as well as at regional levels (Cummings 2000; Jones Luong 2002). Thus, Kazakhstan 2030 had initiated a new form of regime control over the central and regional bureaucracy where a state strategy was not only replicated and propagated in each region and regional village but also became a political handbook for every bureaucrat.[20] Beyond that, each region's economic development was evaluated according to whichever strategy (Kazakhstan 2030 or 2050) was in vogue in Astana at that moment. In other words, the regional elites at all levels not only propagated the key principles of the regime's strategic management of its cadres but also unofficially (without turning the strategy into a specific law) and rhetorically influenced the economic development priorities. These priorities were reflected in the state's statistical language (Table 1) and translated back to the presidential speeches and addresses to the nation where modernizing nationalism flourished.

The regime has technically succeeded in creating a viable semi-ideological umbrella for its various discursive frames, for example, Kazakh revival and people's friendship of internationalism. This was largely tied up with the personification of this state-nation ideology and the figure of President Nazarbayev as the main developer and builder of the country. Isaacs (2010) argues that the processes of charismatic legitimation were not truly legitimate and mostly elite-facilitated. However, the growing glorification of Nazarbayev's rule, who was seen as the main guarantor of inter-ethnic stability and economic prosperity, which are the two main paradigms of the modernizing nationalism, structurally eliminated any alternative ideas and projects. The lack of pluralism in contemporary Kazakhstani social and political sphere is seen as the main threat to the desired stability as it does not generate alternative scenarios to Nazarbayev's regime after it might break up or transform (Satpayev et al. 2013). Moreover, because the ruling political and economic elites just like the foreign investors (Schatz 2000) are all interested in contributing to this authoritarian-type legitimacy (Matveeva 2009), which allows 'stable and peaceful development' only under President Nazabayev's rule, there were not many successful attempts to break this cycle.

Ruling elites are interested in facilitating the modernizing nationalism discourse in conjuncture with further personalization of the regime with the name of Nursultan Nazarbayev for their own interest. Recent projects facilitated by the presidential administration such as the Law on the Leader of the Nation, *elbasy*[21] (the Father of the Nation) project and the new project of the *Mangilik El*[22] (Eternal Nation) personify the state and the nation with the figure of Nazarbayev.

### *Guiding development*

Since the introduction of the Kazakhstan 2030 Strategy, the politico-economic public sphere has seen vast state support in the development of industrial and natural resources' production in which specific regional elites or clans have vested their interests. From the oil-rich Western Kazakhstan's developmental projects to the privatization schemes in the late 1990s, these projects were led by the vanguard of such powerful elites as former prime ministers Balgymbayev and Kazhegeldin. In the late 2000s, identical blueprints of technological and innovative development projects are similarly led by the new powerful elites, such as Asset Issekeshev (since 2009 Minister of Industry and New Technologies and Deputy Prime Minister) and Karim Masimov (since 2007–12 and currently, and since April 2014, Prime Minister). The modernizing nationalism paradigm continues to serve the internal interests of the powerful financial–political groups via the larger investments in Western Kazakhstan, for example, and in the growing development of Southern Kazakhstan (Table 1).

The Kazakhstan 2030 Strategy has developed many other similar projects, for example, development strategies on regional and urban growth, in numerous 'Roadmaps' of development (so-called *Dorozhnaya Karta*). Roadmap-project developments emerged as a similar discourse in the mid-2000s[23] for region- or sector-specific development projects. It had served as a blueprint for developmentalist strategies and projects, but most importantly for the development of sectors and specific elite groups at the regional level. While the vast privatization of diverse industrial plants in central, northern and western Kazakhstan has created first Kazakh oligarchs, it also divided regional economic production along the lines of those who controlled these assets (Esirkepov 1999; Peck 2002; Suleimenov and Ashimbayev 2003; Ashimbayev and Khlupin 2008; Junisbai 2010).

Finally, the paradigm of the 'professional state' and its importance for efficient development may also restructure the whole formal institution and thus elite positioning. In August 2014, President Nazarbayev restructured the government by merging two or three important ministries into one by creating more 'compact' and strategic offices. The number of ministries was downsized from 17 to 12.

## Conclusions

This investigation focuses on the developmental approach of the regime in Kazakhstan in order to analyse the processes of state-building, elite interrelations and elite discipline. The developmental approach of the Kazakhstan 2030 Strategy has played a crucial role in nation-building, legitimation of the regime, and in structuring and disciplining the elitist field.

The results of Kazakhstan 2030 were specifically important for disciplining the regional elites by providing them with the blueprint of a semi-ideological agenda, but also re-creating the code of the regime for a loyal public administration apparatus. Secondly, the strategy offered the perspective of building the 'the strong State' and a society of equal opportunities for all ethnic groups who would nourish this inter-ethnic and socio-political stability for a brighter future. This constituted the developing state- and nation-building agenda, which the regime is still pursuing in the absence of a viable political ideology for national consolidation. The new project of *Mangilik El*, the Eternal Nation of Kazakhs, which was introduced in 2014, develops slowly. As Cummings (2006) argued, none of the categories used in the official vocabulary in the ideological field was clearly defined. The strategic ambiguity of concepts used and blurring the boundaries between various different categories was the regime's favourite but also possibly only approach to situate itself in the pressing contexts of intra-elite competition, legitimacy building and foreign investors' anxieties.

Even if the regime were not yet able to create a new national ideology that could compete with the former Soviet instruments of domination, channelling information and dismissing disloyal cadres, but also turning some of them into the true believers, it nevertheless succeeded in creating a semi-ideological system that performed the same functions. The firm placement of Nazarbayev's figure at the centre of the modernizing nationalism as a guarantor of stable and prosperous development has also facilitated the discourse of charismatic leadership.

## Methodology

This paper benefited from a multilayered methodological approach used in my doctoral dissertation on comparative sociology of two nationalizing regimes in post-Soviet Eurasia (Kazakhstan and Latvia). The 18 months of fieldwork mainly involved elite interviews and discourse analysis of ideological texts, content analysis of archival documents and newspapers spanning from 1989 to 2013 in Kazakhstan, Latvia and, most recently, Ukraine. Most of the data used in this article were based on the use of the expert and elite interviews in Kazakhstan from 2011 to September 2014. These informant interviews constituted the backdrop of the analysis. The main method in this work was based on the deconstruction and discourse analysis of ideological texts, contextualization and interpretation of these texts, and the author's reliance on insider confidential information about intra-elite relations. The informal nature of the clans creates a difficulty in studying these informal links and the factuality of the data. This creates further ethical and legal issues concerning the revealing of identities, the confidentiality of interview sources and possible libel charges.

However, the popular approach to clan-based relations that, as I argue in this article, is not a monopolizing structure in its entirety, has caused some further conceptual and ethical issues. Part of my criticism is the speculative nature of the clan research and if a certain researcher is able to get into some clan structure (in my case I had a brief study encounter with the Western Kazakhstan clan), it is neither entirely evident nor safe for the researcher to use these informal and, thus, very sensitive and untraceable data. It would be extremely hard to pinpoint specific financial links and ownership of one clan or of one elite group to a specific property and may result in lawsuits on libel (of which I was constantly reminded during my research) or worse consequences. Therefore, the analysis of informal structures requires further methodological innovations to ensure in-depth reliable and valid data collection and analysis, and safety for the researcher.

## Acknowledgments

The author thanks Dr Gül Berna Özcan for the fantastic work undertaken behind this edited issue, and for her many valuable comments and longstanding support and interest in my work. Her detailed comments and suggestions were invaluable and my experience working with her during the workshop on Social and Economic Development in London was a great inspiration in writing this paper. I also thank two anonymous reviewers for their valuable comments that helped to shape my argument, and Professor Deniz Kandiyoti for attentive reading of the paper which helped me to shape the argument. I am also indebted to my supervisor, Dr David Lane, and numerous colleagues at the University of Cambridge and beyond who have helped me to conceptualize this paper.

## Disclosure statement

No potential conflict of interest was reported by the author.

## Notes

1. The archival analysis (Fund 5-H, presidential archives) of the early post-Soviet discussions in the so-called ideological committee in the Presidential Administration (Administratsiya Prezidenta, AP) revealed this double-faceted dilemma of the regime. On the one hand, majority of the ruling elites (many of whom still remain in power up to the present) emphasized the importance of the commonly shared value system that until the late 1990s still was called 'ideology', but distinguished from the one-party Communist ideology of the Soviet period. On the other hand, President Nazarbayev himself was openly against setting one dominant ideology, but rather allowing the multiplicity of views which would not overspill or radicalize the situation in the ethnic–linguistic divide. These discussions are followed even after the publication of *Ideinaia konsolidatsiya kazakhstanskogo obshestva kak uslovie progressa Kazakhstana* (The Societal Ideational Consolidation as a Condition for Kazakhstan's Progress, 1993), the regime's ideological programme.
2. The disparity of the state language acquisition and use (Figure 1) in both communities where many ethnic Kazakhs are not fluent in their native language creates further tensions in the identity politics in contemporary Kazakhstan.
3. In an interview with *Central Asian Monitor*, a political newspaper in Kazakhstan, the famous political analyst and writer Daniyar Ashimbayev stated that the development of the so-called 'clan' system in contemporary Kazakh politics went through the stages of kinship selection of the 'political

office' team but moved towards the personality centred financial groups. According to this analysis, in such a system it is more or less easy to identify the leader of the group. Ashimbayev stated: 'There is [Timur] Kulibayev's group which is very strong. There is Kelimbetov.' But where one group's interests end and another group's starts 'is a very difficult question', he concluded. Most powerful figures are usually associated with the stronger power position in the centre (Khen n.d.; also Maksudov 2013).

4. For the Kazakhstan 2030 Strategic Program in English, see www.akorda.kz/, for example. Here I use a direct quotation from the English text of the strategy; further in the text I use my own translations.
5. One of the enquiries into the issue by Madi Alimov's (2013) piece entitled 'Un-ideational country: Kazakhstan's state ideology is still under construction' (*Bezideinaia strana. Gosudarstvennaya ideologiia v Kazakhstane vse eshe strukturiruetsya*) in *Central Asian Monitor*, a newspaper that has raised numerous and continuous debates on the absence of state ideology in Kazakhstan, asserted that 'such popular searches for national idea which is supposed to consolidate the society were ineffectual'.
6. The investments committee is currently based under the Ministry of Industry and New Technologies that has been headed for a very long time by young and powerful Asset Issekeshev. The Strategy for the Development in Kazakhstan has advanced through years; in the 2000s one of the main discourses of development was directed towards the technological and innovative development led by the Ministry of Industry and New Technologies. Current paradigms of the regime's development strategy are directed towards the green economy, and the forthcoming Expo-2017 is solely dedicated to this discourse.
7. Stavrakakis (1997, 263) defined 'discursive/symptomal reading' as a process of 'demonstrating how a given ideological field is the result of a montage of heterogeneous "floating signifiers", of their totalisation through the intervention of certain "nodal points"'.
8. Prior to the 16 December 1991 independence, the Republic of Kazakhstan declared its sovereignty on 25 October 1990. My analysis of the official press, such as Kazakhstanskaya Pravda, as well as the Kazakh press, for example, Ana Tili, Qazaq Adebieti, demonstrates the formation of two distinct discourses of sovereign Kazakhstan within the Soviet Union and the future Confederation of the Independent States (as it was envisioned by Nursultan Nazarbayev) and the independent Kazakhstan post-1991. Many of the processes and discourses of state-building started forming during the 'sovereign' period of late 1990 and throughout 1991 and then transformed during the independence era. Both periods saw very little differentiation in the top ruling elites of the country.
9. The strategy text suggests that the perspective and development plan originates as a blueprint for all of the parts of the state (government, society, centre and regions as these are loosely identified in the text itself) but also by the Head of the State (Nazarbayev). The text reads as a powerful proposal from the first person, the Head of the State (as it is mentioned in some parts, e.g., on page 85), Nazarbayev himself.
10. Nazarbayev (1998/2005, 100) from the Priority # 2: Domestic Political Stability and Consolidation of the Society.
11. Nazarbayev (1998/2005, 90), 'Kazakhstan's Mission'
12. Nazarbayev (1998/2005, 99), from the Priority # 2: Domestic Political Stability and Consolidation of the Society.
13. See also in Greenfield (1993) for a similar argument.
14. For example, see President Nazarbayev's 2005 address to the nation.
15. Nurlan Balgymbayev died on 14 October 2015.
16. In 1998, the ex-prime minister and main manager behind the privatization policy in Kazakhstan, Akezhan Kazhegeldin, also formed one of the first strong oppositional campaigns against the Nazarbayev regime forming the Republican People's Party and opening the first oppositional press, such as the newspapers of '451° by Fahrenheit' and 'XXI Century' (see Kondyzgakova 2001 for a discussion). Although Junisbai and Junisbai state that 'despite his considerable success in garnering support in the West', Kazhegeldin's parties and oppositional work did not have 'much impact on Kazakhstan's political development' (Junisbai and Junisbai 2005, 378). Kazhegeldin continues publishing his texts even presently on the pages of *Novaya Gazeta Kazakhstan*, which is very prominent among urban intelligentsia and the so-called Kazakh creative class.
17. The Law on Public Administration of Kazakhstan (1999) did not directly quote the Kazakhstan 2030 text, but it reflects on its core values of the 'Professional State' of disciplined and responsible work of the public servants.
18. The Kazakhstan 2030 Strategic Program in English (Kazakhstan 2030 Strategy 1997/2013; and see note 4), text quoted from the Priority 7 Professional State, 37.
19. Nazarbayev (1998/2005, 125), Professional State section.

20. The strategy and every presidential address to the nation, which followed similar developmental and managerial structure, had to be replicated in the official regional media, especially in print. Special meetings and public discussions were organized on the matter and the Kazakhstan 2030 (which was published as a brochure) was widely disseminated regionally.
21. *Elbasy* in Kazakh means the Leader, Father of the Nation. The 2010 Law on the Leader of the Nation in Kazakhstan stated the special role of President Nazarbayev and expanded his representative powers.
22. *Mangilik Eli* in Kazakh means Eternal Nation. *Mangilik El* or Eternal Nation was presented as a new national idea for Kazakhstan which combined the main values of Kazakhstan's independence – tolerance, unity, stability and rights of all – and was announced by President Nazarbayev during his annual address to the nation in January 2014.
23. Initial projects were designed by the prominent Kazakhstani sociologist Sabit Zhussupov; for his collection of articles, see Zhussupov (2008).

## References


Adams, L. 2010. *The Spectacular State: Culture and National Identity in Uzbekistan*. Durham, NC: Duke University Press.

Alimov, M. 2013. "Un-Ideational Country: Kazakhstan's State Ideology is Still Under Construction [*Bezideinaia Strana. Gosudarstvennaya Ideologiia V Kazakhstane Vse Eshe Strukturiruetsya*]." *Central Asian Monitor*, April 2013. Accessed June 25, 2015. http://www.centrasia.ru/newsA.php?st=1366324200.

Ashimbayev, Daniyar, and Vitalii Klupin. 2008. *Kazakhstan: Istoriya vlasti. Opyt rekonstruktsii*. Almaty: Credo.

Azadi, A. 2010. "V etoi voine klanov samoe glavnoe – vizhyt, ili, po krainei mere ne ne byt' ubitymi." *DAT*, October. http://www.taszhargan.info/в-этой-войне-кланов-главное-—-выжить-и/.

Bissenova, A. 2012. "Post-Socialist Dreamworlds: Housing Boom And Urban Development In Kazakhstan." PhD dissertation, Cornell University.

Collins, K. 2006. *Clan Politics and Regime Transition in Central Asia*. Cambridge: Cambridge University Press.

Cummings, S. 2000. *Kazakhstan. Centre-Periphery Relations*. London: Royal Institute of International Affairs.

Cummings, S. 2002. "Understanding Politics in Kazakhstan." (DEMSTAR Research Report No. 10). edited by Ole Norgaard, and Lars Johannsen.

Cummings, S. 2005. *Kazakhstan: Power and the Elite*. London: I.B. Tauris.

Cummings, S. 2006. "Legitimation and Identification in Kazakhstan." *Nationalism and Ethnic Politics* 12 (2): 177–204. doi:10.1080/13537110600734547

Cummings, S., ed. 2010. *Symbolism and Power in Central Asia: Politics of the Spectacular*. London: Routledge.

Esirkepov, T. 1999. *Privatizatsya Gosudarstvennoi Sobstvennosti V Respublike Kazakhstan V Usloviyah Perepoda K Rynky*. Almaty: Universitet "Turan" [Privatisation of State Property in the Republic of Kazakhstan under transition conditions].

Greenfield, L. 1993. *Nationalism: Five Roads to Modernity*. Cambridge, MA: Harvard University Press.

Heathershaw, J. 2014. "The Global Performance State: A Reconsideration of the Central Asian 'Weak State'." In *Ethnographies of the State in Central Asia*, edited by Madeleine Reeves, Johan Rasanayagam, and Judith Beyer, 29–54. Bloomington and Indianapolis: Indiana University Press.

Isaacs, R. 2010. "'Papa' – Nursultan Nazarbayev and the Discourse of Charismatic Leadership and Nation-Building in Post-Soviet Kazakhstan." *Studies in Ethnicity and Nationalism* 10 (3): 435–452. doi:10.1111/j.1754-9469.2011.01089.x

Isaacs, R. 2011. *Party System Formation in Kazakhstan. Between Formal and Informal Politics*. London: Routledge.

Isaacs, R. 2013. "*Nur Otan*, Informal Networks and the Countering of Elite Instability in Kazakhstan: Bringing the 'Formal' Back in." *Europe-Asia Studies* 65 (6): 1055–1079. doi:10.1080/09668136.2013.802547

Jandosov, O. 1998. "Development, Prospects and Challenges of Financial System in Kazakhstan." In Prospects and Challenges of Financial Systems in Transition Economies, IMF report. https://www.imf.org/external/np/eu2/kyrgyz/pdf/jandosov.pdf.

Jones Luong, P. 2002. *Institutional Change and Political Continuity in Post-Soviet Central Asia. Power, Perceptions and Pacts*. Cambridge: Cambridge University Press.

Junisbai, B. 2010. "A Tale of Two Kazakhstans: Sources of Political Cleavage and Conflict in the Post-Soviet Period." *Europe-Asia Studies* 62 (2): 235–269. doi:10.1080/09668130903506813

Junisbai, Barbara, and Azamat Junisbai. 2005. "The Democratic Choice of Kazakhstan: A Case Study in Economic Liberalization, Intraelite Cleavage, and Political Opposition." *Demokratizatsiya: The Journal of Post-Soviet Democratization* 13 (3): 373–392. doi:10.3200/DEMO.13.3.373-392

Karin, Erlan, and Andrey Chebortarev. 2002. "The Policy of Kazakhization in State and Government institutions in Kazakhstan." In *The Nationalities Question in Post-Soviet Kazakhstan*, edited by N. Masanov, et al., 69–108. Chiba: Institute of Developing Economies.

Kaser, M. 1998. "Stabilization and Reform: Experience of Five Central Asian States." IMF Report "Challenges to Economies in Transition Stabilization, Growth, and Governance". https://www.imf.org/external/np/eu2/kyrgyz/.

Kazakhstan 2030 Strategy. 1997/2013. *Kazakhstan 2030. Prosperity, Security, and Ever Growing Welfare for All the Kazakhstanis. English version*. www.akorda.kz.

Khen, I. n.d. *Na Vlastnom Olimpe* [At the Power Olympia]. Accessed June 22, 2015. http://www.kazbio.info/?S=101.

Koch, N. 2010. "The Monumental and the Miniature: Imagining 'Modernity' in Astana." *Social and Cultural Geography* 11 (8): 769–787. doi:10.1080/14649365.2010.521854

Koch, N. 2013. "The 'Heart' of Eurasia? Kazakhstan's Centrally Located Capital City." *Central Asian Survey* 32 (2): 134–147. doi:10.1080/02634937.2013.802487

Kondyzgakova, M. 2001. "Issledovanie po gazete '451° by Fahrenheit.'" MA dissertation, Kazakhstan National University, Department of Journalism.

Kudaibergenova, D. 2015. "Elites and the Making of Post-Soviet Nations: Nationalising Regimes in Kazakhstan and Latvia." PhD dissertation, University of Cambridge, Cambridge, UK.

Maksudov. 2013. Accessed June 23, 2015. https://zonakz.net/articles/74545 and http://tengrinews.kz/kazakhstan_news/vse-luchshie-doljnosti-v-kazahstane-zanimayut-yujnyie-klanyi-213961/.

March, A. 2003. "State Ideology and the Legitimation of Authoritarianism: The Case of Post-Soviet Uzbekistan." *Journal of Political Ideologies* 8 (2): 209–232. doi:10.1080/13569310306088

Matveeva, A. 2009. "Legitimising Central Asian Authoritarianism: Political Manipulation and Symbolic Power." *Europe-Asia Studies* 61 (7): 1095–1121. doi:10.1080/09668130903068624

Nazarbayev, N. 1998/2005. *Kazakhstan 2030 Strategy*. Almaty: Zheti Zhargy.

Ó Beacháin, Donnacha, and Rob Kevlihan. 2013. "Threading the Needle: Kazakhstan between Civic an Ethno-Nationalist State-Building." *Nations and Nationalism* 19 (2): 337–356. doi:10.1111/nana.12022

Peck, A. 2002. "Industrial Privatization in Kazakhstan: the Results of Government Sales of the Principal Enterprises to Foreign Investors." *Russian and East European Finance and Trade* 38 (1): 31–58.

Pomfret, R. 2013. "Kazakhstan's 2030 Strategy: Goals, Instruments and Performance." Paper presented at the American Economic Association annual conference in Philadelphia on 4 January 2014.

Satpaev, Dosym, Tolganai Umbetaliyeva, Andrey Chebortarev, Rasul Zhumaly, Aidos Sarym, Aiman Zhusupova, Zamir Karazhanov, and Rustem Kadyrzhanov. 2013. *Sumrechnaya zona ili 'lovushki' perehodnogo perioda* [The Twilight Zone: Traps of Political Succession in Kazakhstan]. Almaty: Gruppa otsenki riskov.

Schatz, E. 2000. "Framing Strategies and Neo-Conflict in Multi-Ethnic Kazakhstan." *Nationalism and Ethnic Politics* 6 (2): 71–94. doi:10.1080/13537110008428596

Schatz, E. 2004. *Modern Clan Politics. The Power of "Blood" in Kazakhstan and Beyond*. Seattle and London: University of Washington Press.

Schatz, E. 2005. "Reconceptualizing Clans: Kinship Networks and Statehood in Kazakhstan." *Nationalities Papers: The Journal of Nationalism and Ethnicity* 33 (2): 231–254. doi:10.1080/00905990500088594

Schatz, E. 2006. "Access by Accident: Legitimacy Claims and Democracy Promotion in Authoritarian Central Asia." *International Political Science Review* 27: 263–284.

Stavrakakis, Y. 1997. "Green Ideology: A discursive Reading." *Journal of Political Ideologies* 2 (3): 259–279. doi:10.1080/13569319708420763

Suleimenov, Nurlan, Daniyar Ashimbayev, and Viktor Andreev. 2003. *Kazakhstan 90-h. Pravitel'stvo Kazhegeldina: privatizatsiya, korruptsiya i bor'ba za vlast'* [Kazakhstan in 1990. Kazhegeldin's Government: Privatisation, Corruption And Struggle For Power]. Almaty: Credo.

Sultanov, B. et al. 2011. *KISI Report Sotsial'no-politicheskaya stratifikaciya kazakhstnskogo obshestva (po rezultatam sotsiologicheskogo issledovaniya KISI i nauchno-issledovatel'skogo proekta IFiP).* Almaty: KISI, p. 40.

Therborn, G. 1980. *The Ideology of Power and Power of Ideology.* London and New York: Verso.

Wilson, A. 2005. *Virtual Politics: Faking Democracy in the Post-Soviet World.* London: Yale University Press.

# Social, environmental and economic sustainability of Kazakhstan: a long-term perspective

Marzhan Thomas

*Department of Geography, Environment and Development Studies, Birkbeck, University of London, London, UK*

This paper explores the evolution of Kazakhstan's development through an analysis of population trends, infant mortality, air emissions, water management, oil production, income, cost of living and average salary. The longitudinal data analysis demonstrates that the development of Kazakhstan during the Soviet period was far from sustainable in terms of uncontrolled environmental pollution. Time-series analysis illustrates that the 1990s transition to the market economy temporarily eased environmental degradation but also brought about initial socio-economic disarray and decline in living standards. Further support for rural areas and economic diversification is needed to move away from Kazakhstan's heavy reliance on mineral resource extraction to a more sustainable path of development.

## Introduction

Sustainable development (SD) has grown in importance for both public bodies and the business community since the 1970s. One of the most important early attempts at modelling future potential future was the book *Limits to Growth* (1972), which used 12 probable scenarios of resource use, population growth and economic development from 1972 to 2100 (Meadows et al. 1972). The major conclusion was that growth in the human footprint (associated with growing pollution and resource use) can exceed the planetary limits, unless emissions and resource use rates are reduced (Randers 2010). However, *Limits to Growth* did not account for some parameters, such as change of technology and use of renewable energy. If resource consumption is slowed down and energy efficiency, recycling and effective use of raw materials are increased, then a sustainable future looks more realistic.

SD is a contested and vague concept, meaning different things to different people (Robinson 2004).[1] There is no common philosophy of sustainable development-ism, in contrast to the schools of neo-liberalism or socialism (Pearce, Markandya, and Barbier 1989; Giddings, Hopwood, and O'Brien 2002). Diverse interest groups approach SD according to their objectives. The confusion over SD can also be observed in transitional countries. In the 1990s the concept of SD was widely supported in Russia; however, two decades later, environmentalists were struggling to promote its case (Henry 2009). The major drawback was that the Russian administration often used the phrases 'economic development' and 'sustainable development' interchangeably, which slowed down understanding of sustainability principles and pursuing its goals.

Another major drawback of SD is that it does not encompass ethical, cultural and philosophical issues. In Kazakhstan, despite many historical changes, the nomadic lifestyle of ancient

Kazakhs had exerted a strong influence on sustainable living and surviving as a nation (Kaldybay et al. 2013). Based on seasonal climatic conditions, the Kazakh *auls* (mobile villages) rotated to different areas – *kokteu*, *zhailau*, *kuzdeu* and *kystau* – i.e., spring, summer, autumn and winter pastures. The environmentally sustainable husbandry and pastoralism protected the existence of several generations of Kazakh tribes. Therefore, local understanding of sustainability plays an important role in implementing SD approaches of various nations, shifting away from the top-down one-size-fits-all approach.

Studies have been conducted for developing and transitional countries in the areas of energy pricing, corporate social responsibility, sustainable energy development, quantitative policy analysis in water-stressed regions, and sustainable rural development (Dahl and Kuralbayeva 2001; Verbitskaya, Nosova, and Rodina 2002; Kojima 2005; Sarkeyeva 2007; Streimikiene, Simanaviciene, and Kovaliov 2009; Pasakarnis and Maliene 2010). However, there is limited research on SD issues in Kazakhstan and Russia to date. These analyses focused either on a certain type of indicator (e.g., energy or higher education; Verbitskaya, Nosova, and Rodina 2002; Sarkeyeva 2007; Streimikiene, Simanaviciene, and Kovaliov 2009) or on a separate geographical area of development (e.g., rural areas in Central and Eastern Europe (CEE); Pasakarnis and Maliene 2010). An interesting investigation of sustainability with a focus on financial support for SD was carried out for Ukraine (Vahovitch 2008). Although the list of indicators was quite comprehensive, the SD analysis for Ukrainian regions was limited from the intergenerational equity viewpoint because it was done primarily for the periods of 1990–2000 and 2000–05. Another relevant study on SD perspectives was done for 12 countries of South-East Europe (SEE) (Ivanovic et al. 2009). The results showed the mutual sensitivity of economic and ecological indicators. Using energy indicators in the Baltic States, Streimikiene, Simanaviciene, and Kovaliov (2009) offered recommendations for developing a sustainable energy policy for the accession of Baltic States to the European Union.

These two studies on the Ukraine and the SEE covered different areas of development. The investigation of SD in the SEE countries (Ivanovic et al. 2009) considered national aggregate data without a deeper analysis of the various regions within a country (Vahovitch 2008). The study on SD indicators in the SEE was also partial as it analysed the status of sustainability rather than the course of development.

Based on this analysis, this paper argues that it is important to look at both the bigger picture on an extended time scale and the local context of regional development for a comprehensive analysis of intergenerational sustainability. It develops an analysis of Kazakhstan's SD path through a multi-measure investigation that takes inter-generational and intra-regional contexts into account.

Kazakhstan (which is the world's ninth biggest country and the largest landlocked country) has a vast territory, huge natural resources and a multi-ethnic population. In addition, its location between Europe and Asia makes it a historically multicultural region with both eastern and western characteristics (Bendas 2003). Due to substantial energy resources (especially oil and gas), Kazakhstan is an important player in socio-economic, geopolitical and environmental development in Central Asia.[2] These specific features served as a primary call for the application of SD theory to this country. Kazakhstan's progress (or lack of it) towards sustainable socio-economic welfare improvements and environmental protection can be a role model for other neighbouring countries and influences the development of the whole region of Eurasia.

## Sustainable development indicators

Many attempts to define sustainability and characterize SD have been made at local, national and global levels by governmental bodies, academics and various institutions. The definition of sustainability and SD, as argued above, is not straightforward. Many researchers have agreed that it is not possible to define a single indicator for SD, or to capture the whole range of significant aspects of SD (Bossel 2001). Thus, the selection of SD indicators is a complex and context-driven process.

The human development index (HDI), which consists of life expectancy, education and income indices, is a useful tool, first launched and promoted by the United Nations Development Programme (UNDP) in 1990, and based on Amartya Sen and Mahbub ul Haq's works (UNDP 1990; Stanton 2007). It did not, however, account for crime, environmental pollution and unemployment, which often accompany development. Using these indicators may be problematic, as income may incorporate costs of pollution control measures (Redclift 1987).

Another contribution to SD indicators was made at the World's Economic Forum where an environmental sustainability index (ESI) for 148 countries based on 68 indicators was developed. To some extent, this scheme was similar to the wellbeing index (WI), which was developed by the World Conservation Union in 2001 as a set of 88 indicators for 180 countries (Prescott-Allen 2001).[3]

Population has been used as an indicator in many studies by various institutions. From a sustainability point of view, the size of the population is important as it allows appraisal of resources needed to provide food, access to water, sanitation and housing to satisfy basic human needs. Another useful social sustainability indicator is infant mortality rate (IMR),[4] used by the Organisation for Economic Co-operation and Development (OECD 2008). IMR is an important indicator of public health because it reflects the health of women and the overall health situation (curative and preventive).

Air emissions analysis is another measure for human health and wildlife. Air emissions from stationary sources were chosen for this analysis both because they are often the main contributors to air emissions and as they are fixed they are easier to tackle. All the major pollutants were considered, including sulphur dioxide ($SO_2$), nitrogen oxides ($NO_x$), carbon monoxide (CO), volatile organic compounds (VOCs) and heavy metals.

Freshwater quality and quantity affects human health, especially the health of children and women of reproductive age. Freshwater withdrawal was included in the OECD (2008), World Bank (WB) (2012) and United Nations (UN) indicators (UN 2007); and domestic water consumption was included in the UK SD indicators (DEFRA 2011). Due to data limitations, water abstraction from natural sources was used in this study. Water abstraction is a broader withdrawal of water, whereas freshwater consumption reflects on withdrawals from freshwater sources only.

Although oil production could be considered as an economic indicator, oil is a finite natural resource demonstrating depletion of fossil fuels. In addition, oil extraction, transportation and processing cause pressure on wildlife, release of air pollution and oil spills. Crude oil production, as an indicator, was used by the OECD (2008).

As for economic sustainability indicators, salaries are important for SD as they stimulate work efficiency and increase human satisfaction, leading to a mutually beneficial situation for both society and the economy. A similar indicator, price and wages, was used by the European Bank for Reconstruction and Development (EBRD) (2013).

Gross national income (GNI) per capita and income per household were included as indicators in the studies by the OECD (2008), Ukraine (Vahovitch 2008), WB (2012) and UN (2007). This paper uses income per capita that comes from formal and informal employment, property, sales and social transfers (pensions, social benefits, scholarships and loans).

Income growth is closely linked to inflation (which is based on consumer price index – CPI); and high inflation negatively influences people on low incomes. Nominal income is presented in current prices and does not account for inflation. Real income is calculated as nominal income divided by CPI, thus real income is a better indicator as it reflects goods and services that can be purchased. To understand income distribution, Gini coefficient data were used. The Gini coefficient is expressed between 0 and 1 (the higher the number – the more unequal is income distribution).

## Research methods

The selected SD indicators (population, infant mortality, air emissions, water abstraction, oil production, average salary and income per capita) were examined using time-series analysis. The main data sources for the pre-transitional period come from annual reports of the Union of the Soviet Socialist Republics (USSR) national economy (1956–91) and annual reports of the Kazakh Soviet Socialist Republic (1958–1990), stored in the Russian State Library, Moscow. The main sources for the post-transitional period were the annual statistical reports of the Republic of Kazakhstan (RoK) (1992–2012), accessible through the state libraries and official website of the RoK statistical agency.[5] It was difficult to verify the state statistics. The cross-checking allowed verification of the state statistics to avoid human error arising from the manual transcription of the data from the Soviet reports into Excel spreadsheets.

There are several advantages of using state statistics. First, governmental statistics provided an extensive dataset on various social, economic, industrial and agricultural systems. Second, it would not have been possible to obtain such general data on Kazakhstan for the pre-transitional period without the Soviet reporting style. Although there were gaps in the datasets, official statistical sources provided feasible and sufficient ground for understanding and exploring the trends.

There are, however, limitations of the Soviet statistical reports. First, the Soviet statistics were politically motivated and data were often adjusted to fit into official propaganda, for example, classified population census in 1937 (Davies 1994). The second limitation of Soviet data was that many data tables were provided in percentages rather than in absolute units. Third, the Soviet statistics selectively omitted some data in their calculations, for example, salaries did not include military industry, and estimates of deaths did not cover victims of repression (Bergson 1947; Ellman 2002). During Mikhail Gorbachev's '*perestroika*', reliability and quality of the state statistics slightly improved (Treml 1988).

The regular data collection in Kazakhstan started with the first population census of the Russian Empire in 1897. During the Soviet period, Kazakhstan had to report (like many other FSU republics) to the Central Statistical Board in Moscow. After gaining independence in 1991, Kazakhstan began developing its own monitoring system. Following an audit in 2008, the RoK Statistical Agency was granted a certificate of compliance with ISO 9001:2008 requirements, which validates the document management system, including timely update for legitimate research.

As of January 2015, there were 16 administrative units in Kazakhstan: 14 '*oblasts*' (regions) and two state-cities: Almaty and Astana. The latest available regional data were plotted on maps to help a reader visualize the various regions of Kazakhstan.

## Analysis of social sustainability indicators

### *Population*

Allegedly tribes living on the territory of modern Kazakhstan had a traditionally nomadic lifestyle since the first millennium BCE, grazing their livestock on the common pastoral lands (Olcott 1995). Before the inception of the USSR, rich owners of livestock (*bais*) granted some part of their livestock to the poorer herdsmen, who grazed and looked after the animals in exchange for their milk and wool (Pianciola 2004).

Although the Russian presence in Kazakhstan began in the 16th century, large-scale Russian resettlements took place in the 19th century with the construction of forts and the use of fertile land in northern and eastern areas of the Kazakh steppe (Figure 1). With the establishment of Soviet power in the 1920s, especially after the introduction of the collectivization campaign in 1929 30, the Kazakhs were forced to settle to make them easier to administer. This broke down sensible ecological adaptations in the process. The state-enforced top-down collectivization and confiscation of livestock from *bais* posed a massive risk to the whole subsistence of Kazakh *auls* (Pianciola 2001).

Many Kazakhs were forced to emigrate to neighbouring countries, including China and Mongolia, or chose to kill their livestock rather than hand them over to the Soviet authorities. As a result, there was a loss of 12 million (80%) of sheep and cattle and more than 1.8 million human deaths due to famine and starvation (Alekseyenko 2000). Among other Soviet republics, Kazakhstan was the worst affected state with population losses of 38% of the Kazakh ethnic group, the highest among other national groups (Pianciola 2001).

Another large-scale loss of human life occurred during the 1941–45 Great Patriotic War between the USSR and Nazi Germany, when an estimated 27 million Soviet people (mostly civilians) died (Overy 2011). Besides the direct human losses, the war also adversely affected marriage and fertility (Brainerd 2007). Nearly 3.3 million people were deported from Russia to Siberia and to the Central Asian republics between 1941 and 1949, but around 43% of the resettled population died of disease and malnutrition (Shubnaya 2011). Deportations of entire nationalities (including Soviet Koreans, Germans, Crimean Tatars, Chechens, Kurds and Greeks), resettlements of 'anti-Soviet' people, and large-scale labour force transfers took place during and after the war (Kim 2009).

Between 1954 and 1962, about 2 million people, mainly Russians, moved voluntarily to Kazakhstan during Nikita Khrushchev's publicly advertised campaign to develop *tselina* or 'Virgin Land', which made the number of ethnic Russians in Kazakhstan to increase rapidly,

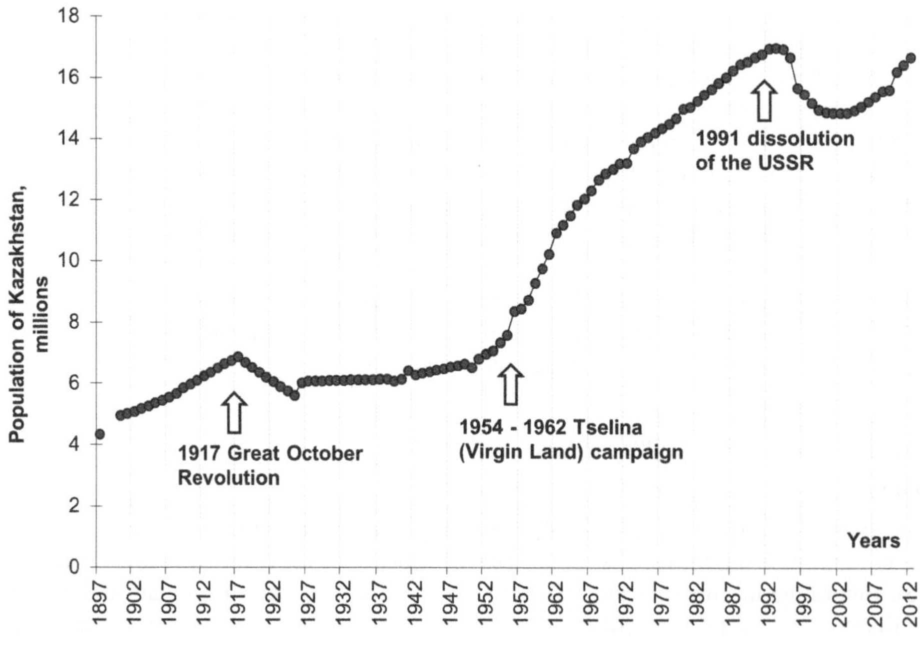


Figure 1. Population.

reaching 43% by 1959 (Minorities at Risk 2006). Ethnic Kazakhs became a minority comprising only 30% of the total population, and Kazakh ethnic identity was largely distorted through strong assimilation to Russian culture and language, especially among urban Kazakhs (Ramazanova 2011).

Figure 1 demonstrates that there were two peaks in the population of Kazakhstan: in 1917 and 1993. Although Kazakhstan's population was adversely affected by collectivization in the 1930s, the famine and the Great Patriotic War in the 1940s, the total population size is seen as not hugely altered, probably due to ethnic relocations and labour transfers from other Soviet republics and most likely due to exaggeration of the population figures for political reasons during the Soviet period.

The last demographic shock in Kazakhstan was experienced in the 1990s (Figure 1). Following market liberalization after the dissolution of the USSR in 1991, inflation and income inequality increased and the number of people living below the poverty line grew. The population of Kazakhstan began to decline, mainly due to falling life expectancy and a decline in fertility rates (Thomas 2015) (Figure 1). The relocation of people took place again, with Germans, Russians, Greeks and Ukrainians emigrating from Kazakhstan. However, between 1991 and 2005, over 1.1 million *oralmans* (returnees) arrived in Kazakhstan from China, Mongolia and other countries.

The introduction of state policies for protection of women's health positively contributed to population recovery since the 2000s (Figure 1). In addition, in line with the state development strategy for Kazakhstan until 2030, programmes to combat unemployment and poverty reduction were also adopted. These helped low-income families to access benefits, which improved living standards. The Russian population declined to 30% due to migration to the Russian Federation, while the growth in proportion of ethnic Kazakhs continued (Shustov 2010).

During the Soviet period, most of the towns were small and medium size (fewer than 100,000 people) and only one city, Almaty, had a population of more than 1 million. New towns were founded (and expanded rapidly) next to industrial centres, coal mining and metal manufacturing areas (e.g., Karaganda and Temirtau).

Generally, the rural population dominates in the south-east and north of Kazakhstan (Figure 2). This distribution has been driven mostly by the mild climate in the south and the heritage of the Soviet *tselina* campaign in the north. The highest urban population is in the coal-mining Karaganda *oblast*, which had the highest number of towns (11) due to mining and metallurgy centres (Figure 2).

The highest population density was in Almaty city (Figure 3), while the population density of Astana city has grown rapidly since it became a capital city in 1998. Apart from the two state cities, South Kazakhstan *oblast* is the highest populated area (Figure 3).

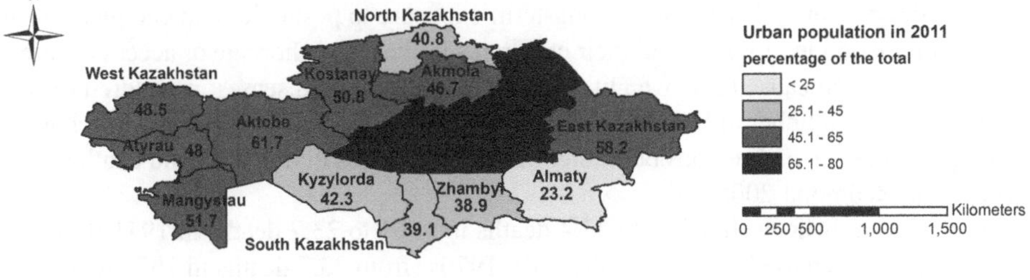


Figure 2. Percentage of the urban population.

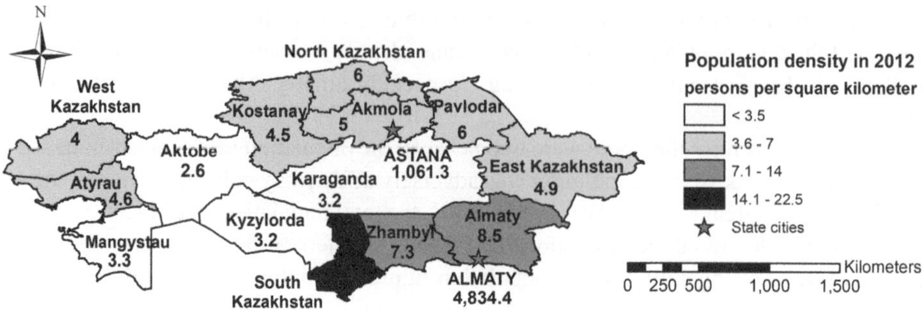


Figure 3. Population density.

In south and south-east of Kazakhstan, warmer winters and longer summers created favourable conditions for living and farming. Additionally, these areas had mountain-fed water resources and were located along the Great Silk Road route, which over time promoted development of market towns. Almaty city, as the capital of Kazakhstan for 68 years (1929–97), has been a major cultural, political and socio-economic centre, attracting people in search of employment. Since the move of the capital in 1998, there has been a similar effect in Astana, and its population has been constantly rising. This allowed a certain regional balance between south and north of the country.

### *Infant mortality rate (IMR)*

In pre-Soviet Kazakhstan, some medical practices, especially those applied during childbirth, were traditionally performed by *shamans* (i.e., tribal healers) (Jones and Grupp 1983; Michaels 2000). Significant improvements in infant mortality happened between 1917 and 1925 with the establishment of the Maternity and Child Welfare Department in the USSR. Soon after the Great Patriotic War, infant mortality in the USSR declined as new medicines introduced during the war (including penicillin) were applied (Jones and Grupp 1983). Additionally, since the majority of people with weak health or chronic diseases were no longer alive, a more robust generation emerged. As a result, IMRs in the USSR declined steadily (Dutton 1979).

In the 1970s, however, IMR in the USSR went up again as a result of the deteriorating healthcare infrastructure caused by stagnation and militarization, and improved recording in the Central Asian republics (Jones and Grupp 1983). In addition, the IMR growth in the 1970s was linked to the increase in death rates from diarrhoea and respiratory and infectious diseases (Velkoff and Miller 1995). This was especially true for the rural areas in Central Asian republics where homebirths were widely practised (Anderson and Silver 1986).

IMRs in Central Asia remained high during the transition, particularly in rural areas (Buckley 1998). This high IMR in the region was associated with unsustainable agricultural practices (such as Aral Sea desiccation in Kazakhstan), long-term exposure to pesticides and chemicals resulting in their accumulation in mothers' and their children's bodies, and shortage of access to safe water and sanitation, which caused low weight, anaemia and digestive diseases in children (Franz and FitzRoy 2006). In a number of Soviet republics infant mortality was misreported, which was not a result of governmental instructions but rather due to differences in live birth and death definitions (Aleshina and Redmond 2005).

In Kazakhstan, IMR declined from 37.4 deaths in 1961 to 23.7 deaths in 1971 (Figure 4). A particularly sharp increase happened in the early 1970s (from 23.7 deaths in 1971 to 39.5 deaths in 1976, i.e., 67% growth) due to poor environmental conditions, anaemia in mothers and their

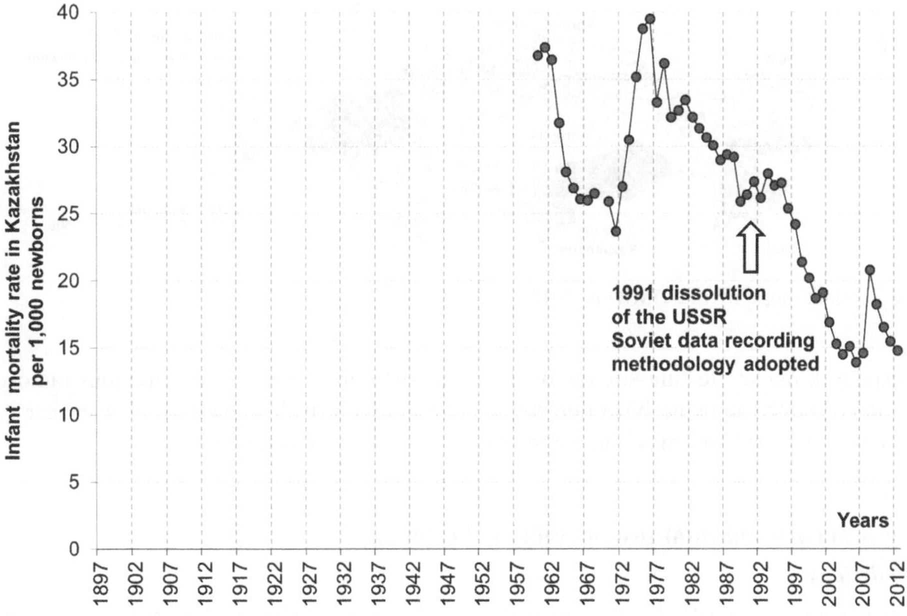


Figure 4. Infant mortality rate (IMR).

newborn children, and deteriorating healthcare infrastructure (due to militarization). Since the 1980s, IMR in Kazakhstan has declined (due to stimulation of childbirth by the state, improved perinatal healthcare and reduced maternal mortality), until the early 1990s when it was negatively affected by intensive migration and socio-economic instability (Figure 4).

Different methods of reporting IMR (World Health Organization (WHO) versus the previously used Soviet method) could change the numbers considerably. If IMRs in Kazakhstan were calculated using the WHO methodology, the rates might have been considerably higher (Anthopolos and Becker 2010).

Among the five Central Asian republics, Kazakhstan had the lowest IMR (Buckley 1998). Overall, the higher rates were at the beginning of the transition during the early 1990s due to economic recession, lack of medical supplies, decline in living standards and increased poverty. Since the late 1990s, IMRs in regions of Kazakhstan have fluctuated, but, overall, were in decline. A low IMR tended to be in *oblast*s with lower content of urban population, for example, Almaty *oblast*, so a higher IMR was often linked to urbanization (Figures 2 and 5) with the exception of Kyzylorda *oblast*, which is explained below.

Figure 5 illustrates that Kyzylorda *oblast* had the highest IMR. Around one-third of infants' deaths in Aral Sea area in Kyzylorda *oblast* were caused by perinatal complications: respiratory diseases, diarrhoea and nutrition deficiency (Kiessling 1998). Desiccation of the Aral Sea uncovered huge salt deposits contaminated with industrial and agricultural chemical residues, which were applied against boll weevils (i.e., severe agricultural pest) during the Soviet period (Spoor 2002). Continuous exposure to the insecticide DDT (dichlorodiphenyltricholroethane) contributed to the higher infant mortality in Kyzylorda *oblast*.

Other regions with high IMRs were East Kazakhstan and Mangystau *oblast*s (Figure 5). Mangystau *oblast* also had the highest maternal mortality of 115.1 deaths per 100,000 live births. Numerous uranium mines caused a high level of oncology diseases in Mangystau *oblast* that contributed to higher IMRs (Grid-Arendal 2012). East Kazakhstan *oblast* has remains of the

Figure 5. Infant mortality rate (IMR) in 2011.

Semipalatinsk nuclear testing site (active between 1949 and 1989), where previous radioactive explosions resulted in acute birth defects, genetic illnesses, leukaemia and other cancer types, mutations and severe chromosomal abnormalities in several generations.

## Analysis of environmental sustainability indicators

### *Air emissions*

To satisfy growing industrial and municipal needs during the 1920s, an 'electrification' plan that prioritized construction of large-scale thermal power stations/units and hydropower stations in a very short time period was developed in the USSR. Emissions from power stations were notorious for excessive sulphur dioxide, nitrates and acid sulphates pollution (Jedrychowski 1999). During the Great Patriotic War many plants were evacuated to Siberia and Kazakhstan and new factories with no pollution control were built rapidly (Josephson 2007). The nuclear testing site in Semipalatinsk also contributed radioactive pollutants causing cancer and leukaemia.

From the 1960s, the Soviet economy experienced long-term industrial decline (Easterly and Fischer 1995). Further economic recession and falling industrial production in the 1990s helped to improve the environmental situation in Kazakhstan and was positive from a sustainability perspective. Whilst this industrial decline would be welcomed by proponents of the de-growth concept, it was not intentional (Martinez-Alier et al. 2010).

Air emission volumes in Kazakhstan went down following the transition to a market economy (Figure 6). Among stationary sources, the biggest polluter was the energy sector (especially coal-based heat and power production) – 50% of all the emissions were from stationary sources in 1990 and 40% in 1995. The high air emissions were associated with energy production in the 1980s and fell sharply after the USSR collapsed (EBRD 2011) (Figure 6).

There might, however, be other reasons behind the decline in air pollution in the 1990s (Figure 6). Reporting of air pollution changed during the transition, making primarily big enterprises accountable, thus underestimating pollution levels (Oldfield 1999). Moreover, to cut costs during the transition, some enterprises simply switched off their pollution control equipment and cut the number of air-monitoring stations.

Various international treaties may have contributed to this decline as well. Kazakhstan joined the Montreal Protocol on ozone layer-destroying substances in 1997, ratified the Kyoto Protocol in 2009 and developed national programmes to reduce greenhouse gas emissions.

Figure 7 demonstrates that the main polluters of air emissions were Pavlodar and Karaganda *oblasts*. About 96% of all coal production in Kazakhstan came from just three cities: Ekibastuz (Pavlodar *oblast*), Karaganda and Temirtau (both in Karaganda *oblast*) (Dahl and Kuralbayeva 2001). Kazakhstan coal has a high ash content (39% in Karaganda coal and 55% in Pavlodar coal).[6]

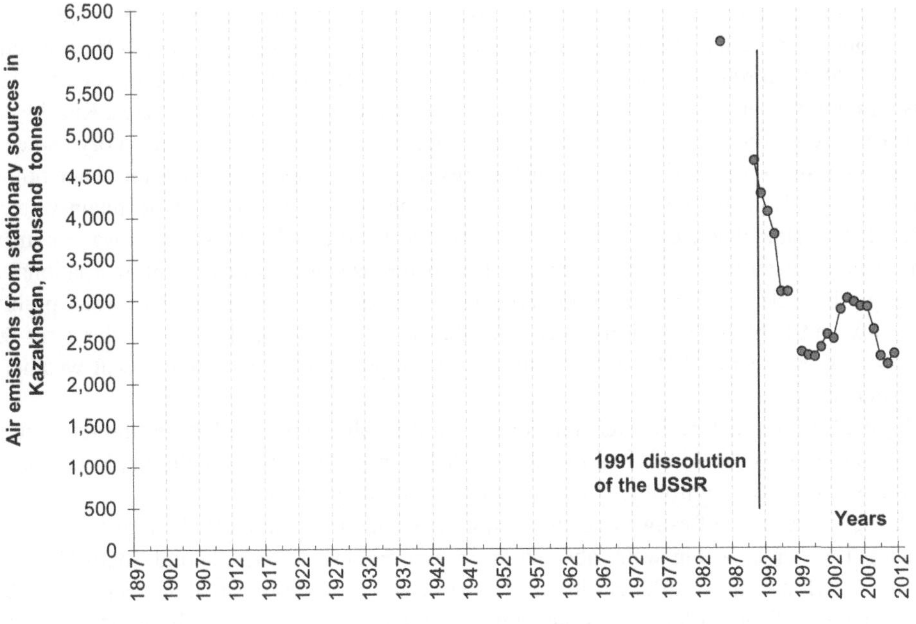


Figure 6. Air emissions.

Figure 7. Air emissions in 2011.

Karaganda and Pavlodar *oblasts* were the most urbanized and had a high output of coal, power, ferrous and non-ferrous metals (Figure 2) (Dahl and Kuralbayeva 2001). Pavlodar aluminium plant had high air emissions of manganese and vanadium metals, while steel and metallurgy complexes in Temirtau (Karaganda *oblast*) emitted phenols, dust, ammonia, carbon monoxide and nitric oxides (Simonenkov et al. 2010).

### *Water management*

Water in the USSR was considered a free resource. Water consumption was not restricted, which caused its wasteful usage due to lack of maintenance, recycling and treatment facilities. The biggest disaster with water management in Kazakhstan began in the 1960s, when the Soviet government decided to turn Central Asia into the world's greatest cotton region. This significantly limited inflow of water from the Syr-Darya and Amu-Darya rivers that feed the Aral Sea (Czarra 2003). As a result, the Aral Sea lost 75% of its volume, causing severe damage to the local fishing economy, environment and human health (*New Scientist* 1989).

Water in Kazakhstan is mostly consumed by the agricultural sector. From 1992 to 2001, water consumption for regular irrigation and industrial needs has fallen by 65% and 40% respectively (UNDP 2004). Moreover, previously shared water resources were spread among the FSU states, causing political bargaining and conflict over water. Among Central Asian states, Kazakhstan is the least water-sufficient republic, as it has no major rivers originating on its territory and experiences water stress due to limitations of the freshwater supplies and upstream water pollution (Zhylkybayev, Bondarenko, and Tsun-sin 2012). Therefore, different tools to retain water and promote its sustainable use were introduced after the 1990s, including efficient water consumption, fines for water pollution and excessive freshwater use, and ratification of international treaties (e.g., the Helsinki Convention on prevention and control of transboundary water pollution) (Kirsanov and Kim 2007). Efforts to recover the Aral Sea were undertaken in the early 2000s by Kazakhstan and the WB, which brought some improvements in fishing, local weather and ecosystems.

Figure 8 shows that freshwater consumption in Kazakhstan was in decline, and fell especially sharply during the early 1990s mainly due to reduced industrial and agricultural production. This illustrates short-term environmental benefits caused by de-growth.

A slight increase in freshwater consumption happened in the mid-2000s (Figure 8). This was associated with increase in water abstraction in two regions: Kyzylorda and South Kazakhstan *oblasts*, which are more sufficient in water than central and western regions (Figure 9). At the same time, significant volumes of water (up to 65%) are often lost through inefficient irrigation and old infrastructure. Kazakhstan might face an acute water deficit by 2030 if water wastage is not resolved (Pavlovskaya 2013). The problem might become even more severe in view of the expected growth in droughts, 20% decline of the major water basins and 20% fall in grain yield in Kazakhstan (Severskiy 2004).

Figure 9 shows that the southern Kazakhstan regions had higher water abstraction than their northern counterparts. The highest water abstraction in Kyzylorda *oblast* is disproportionate to its

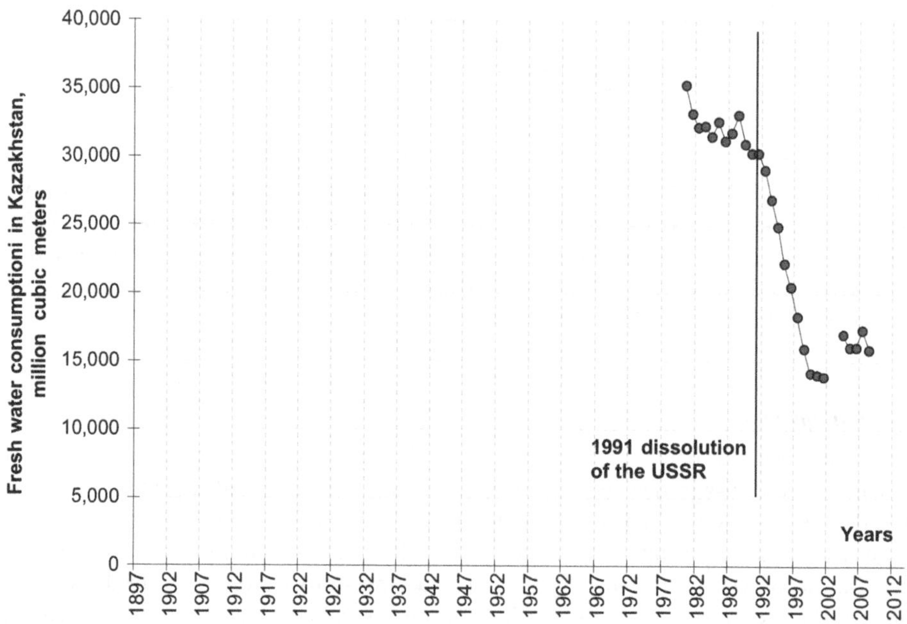


Figure 8. Fresh water consumption in Kazakhstan.

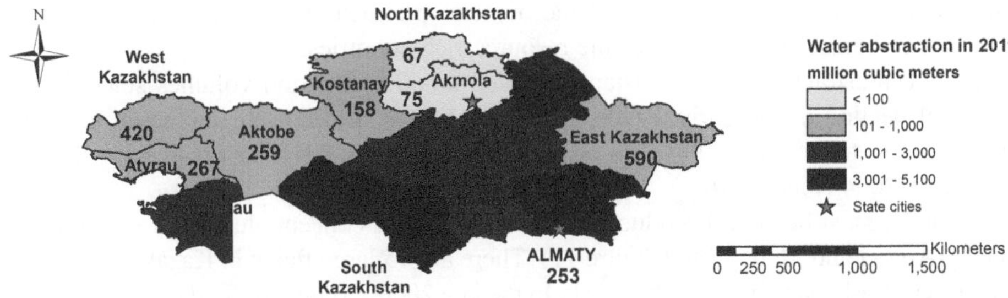


Figure 9. Water abstraction in 2011.

low population density, and is related instead to agriculture (Figure 3). Water in Kyzylorda *oblast* was used for water-intensive irrigation of rice fields, as precipitation in the arid southern regions is very low and the region supplies more than 80% of all rice production in the country (Beurs and Henebry 2004).

Almaty *oblast* is the most water-sufficient area due to its location in the Zhety-su (seven rivers) region. However, one of the main freshwater rivers in Almaty *oblast*, Ili River, originates in China and carries considerable wastewater pollutants (Greenberg 2007). The Ili River flow into Kazakhstan is likely to decline and salinity of Balkhash Lake to rise as the Chinese government plans to relocate about 40 million people from its central regions to the north-west.

### *Oil production*

Oil production in Kazakhstan began in 1899; however, rapid growth started in the 1960s with the discovery of several oilfields in the western part of the country. In order to attract more workers into the oil industry, the USSR set up extra privileges, including longer vacation, the highest salaries and an earlier pension for prolonged service (*za vyslugu let*). However, the oil industry generated high volumes of air and water pollution and posed threats to biodiversity and ecosystems.

Environmental pollution from the oil industry continued after Kazakhstan gained independence and had a destructive impact on the health of oil workers and the population (Granovsky 2003). As oil production and air pollution increased, so did the number of people with respiratory diseases, diseases of digestive organs and infections.

Between 1992 and 2010 Kazakhstan exported on average 73% of its oil production, 70% of its gas and 31% of its coal output, making it very dependent on energy exports (Oskenbayev, Yilmaz, and Abdulla 2013). Tengiz and Kashagan oilfields were discovered in the 1990s and attracted considerable foreign investments from both Western (United States and Europe) and Eastern (China) countries (Ipek 2007), so joint ventures (JVs) with foreign oil companies were created. Subsequently, Kazakhstan built two oil pipelines to China; in addition, oil is also transported through the Caspian Sea by tankers to Baku (Azerbaijan) and distributed through railways or pipelines.

Recent years have seen increased unrest amongst those working in the oilfields. For example, in Zhanaozen (Mangystau *oblast*) local oil workers demanded better pay for harsh working conditions in 2011, but their protests were deemed 'illegitimate' by the government. The deeper reasons for the conflict seemed to rest in their frustration over poverty, as western regions remain among the poorest in the country despite being rich in oil reserves (Pomfret 2006).

Additionally, enormous oil and gas resource development resulted in low economic diversification, and a strong autocratic political system (Franke et al. 2009; Özcan 2010). This paradox is not a new phenomenon and similar cases of 'resource curse' could be found around the globe, including Nigeria, Angola and Venezuela (Sachs and Warner 1995; Neumayer 2004). Jones

Luong and Weinthal (2010) believe that the ownership structure and weak institutions are the 'curse' as they hinder development of the resource-rich countries.

Figure 10 illustrates that Kazakhstan increased its oil production volumes since the 1960s. After initial decline in the early 1990s, oil production in Kazakhstan increased enormously: from 26 million tonnes in 1998 to its peak of 80 million in 2011, or on average 15% every year in 1999–2004 (Figure 10).

Regionally, most of the oil production in Kazakhstan is concentrated in its western *oblasts*, especially Atyrau and Mangystau (Figure 11). There are 15 large fields in Kazakhstan, including Tengiz, Uzen, Kashagan and Karachaganak. In the late 2000s, Tengiz oilfield (Atyrau *oblast*) was expanded with a new method of sour gas injection and a new refinery plant. This increased oil production from 310,000 barrels a day to 540,000 barrels a day, i.e., 1.7 times (Kazmunaygas 2010).

High oil production levels in Atyrau and Mangystau *oblasts* cause a negative impact on the unique marine environment of the Caspian Sea through the introduction of invasive species by oil tankers, pollution from oil extraction, processing and transportation of oil, and sulphur dioxide and hydrogen sulphide emissions from the oil refineries (Kalb et al. 2004; Kaiser and Pulsipher 2007).

Being an isolated water body, the Caspian Sea has a large number of endemic species, for example, the Caspian seal and the Caspian sturgeon. Offshore oil and gas projects disrupt seal habitats, while pipeline construction disturbs sturgeon habitats (Raloff 2006). The Caspian seal is now listed by the International Union for the Conservation of Nature (IUCN) as endangered, as its population has declined by 90% in the last 100 years (and from 500,000 in the 1960s to 111,000 in 2005) due to loss of habitats, by-catch in fisheries (i.e. unintentional catching of fish and/or sea mammals), over-hunting and construction of artificial islands (IUCN 2013).

At the same time, rapid extraction of the oil and gas industry contributed to social conflicts, such as the 2011 Zhanaozen uprising, which left at least 14 people dead. While the average salary

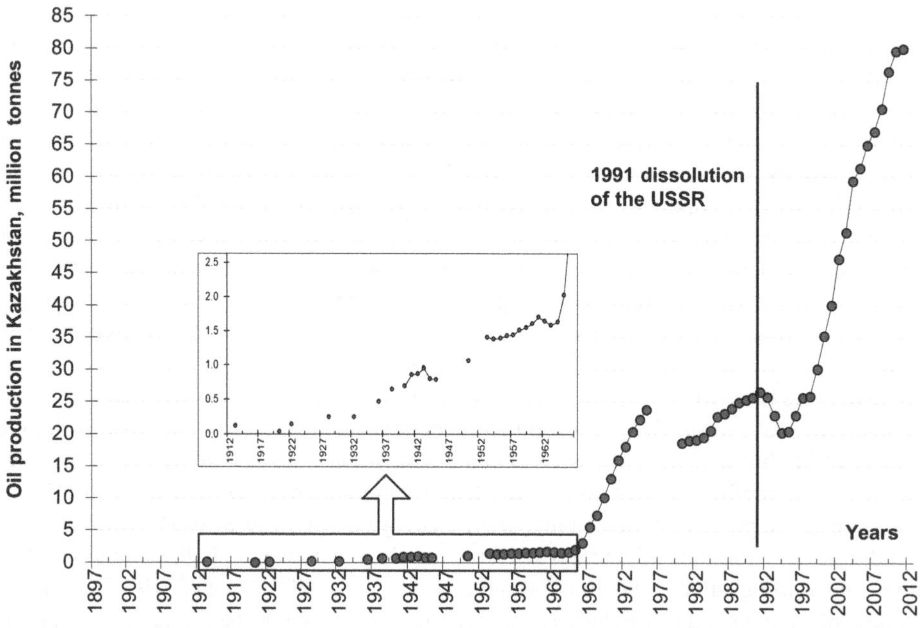


Figure 10. Oil production in Kazakhstan.

Figure 11. Oil production in 2011.

in western Kazakhstan was higher than in other regions, the cost of living was also high (Figures 13 and 18). The western regions also have high infant mortality, especially in Mangystau *oblast* (Figure 5).

## Analysis of economic sustainability indicators

### *Average salary*

Vladimir Lenin believed that the goal of the national economy in socialism was a complete satisfaction of increased material and spiritual needs of the society. However, Stalin's focus on industrial production fuelled by the Cold War led to a shortage of consumer goods, despite adequate salaries. To reduce the amount of money in circulation, money reform took place regularly, for example, in 1961, making salaries smaller.

Statistics concerning salaries were concealed, hiding the differential between and within sectors and occupations, and social inequality (Nove 1966). Since the first wage scale in 1918, membership of the Communist Party and its associated unions had a considerable impact on salaries. For example, a civil servant had a salary of 350 roubles per month whereas a *commissar* (an officer allocated to military troops to teach Communist Party policies and principles) had 800 roubles per month (Bergson 1984).

From the late 1940s, fraud (*pripiski*) in relation to official five-year planning targets was common (Harrison 2011). Although official salaries were low, a single bribe could easily exceed it, making bureaucracy and corruption flourish (Black and Tarassova 2003). Labour efficiency, work remuneration and motivation were very low, with huge gaps between salaries of workers and *nomenklatura*. To survive on such a low salary and to fill the gap in payments, workers also cheated the salary system by stealing products from workplaces.

At the turn of 1990, salaries of the general public remained low, but enough to survive till the next month's payment. In the 1990s, following trade liberalization, many state-owned enterprises were privatized. Numerous cooperatives were offering goods and services, mostly by buying goods at the state price and reselling them at a market price (Nuti 1989). Subsequently, some of the cooperatives became big enterprises, trading on minerals, metals and raw materials, and the wealth accumulated in the hands of their directors, who became the new oligarchs.

Following independence, Kazakhstan introduced its own currency in 1993, the tenge, replacing the FSU rouble at a rate of 1 tenge to 500 roubles. However, in the mid-1990s hyperinflation made the tenge unstable and salaries weak. Rising energy prices and exports brought economic recovery and in the early 2000s Kazakhstan, along with Russia, had the highest average monthly salary (about US$200 in local equivalent) among other FSU states (Pravda 2004).

Figure 12 illustrates that in the first year of tenge introduction, salaries increased from 128 tenge in 1993 to 1726 tenge in 1994, and by 1999 there was a 93 times increase (since 1993) due to hyperinflation. From 1997 to 2012, however, the growth in average salary gradually slowed and was on average 18% per year.

Some professions, like teachers and physicians, have historically been paid lower salaries. The highest salaries were observed in the extractive industries, financial services and insurance industry, whereas the lowest salaries were in fisheries, rural and timber industries (Kazakhstan Today 2010). In addition, Kazakhstan has also been experiencing rapid emergence of the middle class and, subsequently, decline in people living below the poverty level (Maulenova 2009). Entrepreneurs were the biggest group in the new middle class of Kazakhstan actively looking for market opportunities (Özcan 2010).

Figure 13 shows that the regional salaries' distribution was unequal. Despite superficially high salaries, Mangystau *oblast* had the highest cost of living and the highest unemployment in Kazakhstan for several years (Figures 13 and 18) (Nasimova 2011).

Overall, regions with a predominantly urban population got significantly higher average salaries than *oblasts* with rural populations (Figures 2 and 13). In addition, the salary within an *oblast* could differ. For example, in West Kazakhstan *oblast* the salary of farm workers in 2004 was almost four times lower than an average salary in the *oblast*. There was a big variation within enterprises, where the gap in salaries among workers, non-manual specialists and management could differ by a scale of 20 times (Bisekov 2013).

### *Income per capita, Gini coefficient, inflation and cost of living*

Historical information on Soviet income and cost of living were difficult to find. In the USSR, the concept of minimum living costs per se was not established; however, minimum salary and minimum pension were set up instead. In 1967, the minimum salary was set at 60 roubles and kept increasing, making 70 roubles (or 37% of the average salary of 190 roubles) in 1985 (Karpukhin 1978; Nizhegorodskaya 2011). After the transition, however, the minimum salary

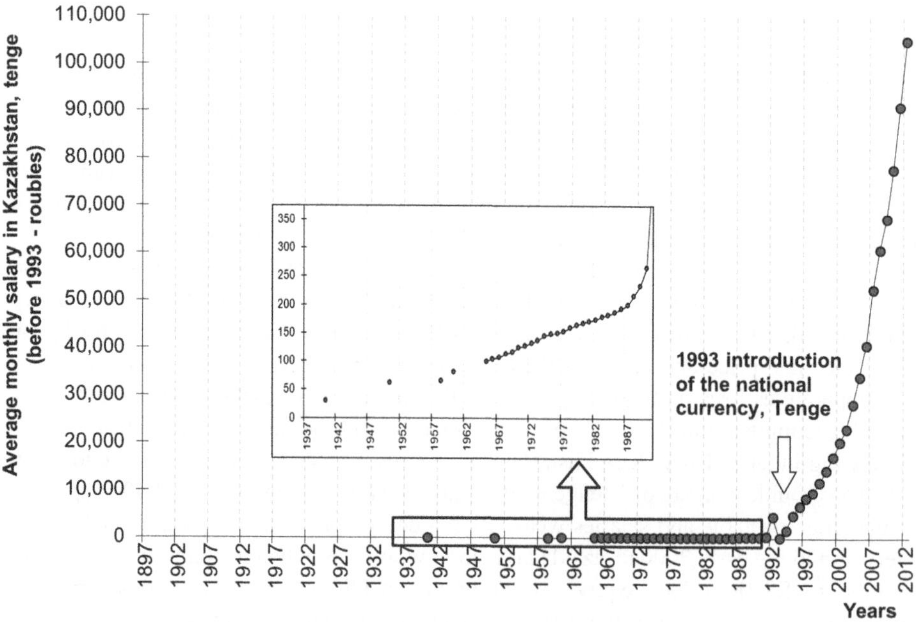


Figure 12. Average monthly salary in Kazakhstan.

Figure 13. Average monthly salary in 2011.

declined to about 10% of the average salary increasing the number of people living in poverty. A minimum cost of living in independent Kazakhstan was set up based on a consumer goods basket and consumer prices; 70% of the minimum cost of living comprised food items (Biekenov 2006).

The income inequality gap increased and income levels in various regions varied greatly (Guriev and Rachinskiy 2006). This rise was believed to be necessary for developing essential institutional transformation, a democratic political system and to promote economic efficiency. New laws, such as one on income legalization introduced in 2001, allowed the population to legalize the 'shadow' income without paying tax on it. This revealed that about US$480 million in total was kept by the population (Sheretov 2003).

Transfer of state-owned assets to private ownership was launched in 1991. However, there was a lack of transparency during privatization and the income distribution gap increased (Mitrofanskaya 1999). Average income fell by 59% and incomes of the majority fell below the minimum cost of living (Darimbetov and Spanov 2001). A recent study reported that half the respondents in Kazakhstan believed that incomes were more equally distributed during Soviet times, although 40% of them stated that their welfare had improved in comparison with the Soviet times (Eshpanova, Narbekova, and Biekenova 2012).

Inflation data were not available in the state reports, but the WB data (WB 2014) were used instead (Figure 14). Inflation peaked dramatically in the early 1990s: 1472% in 1992, 1243% in 1993 and 1547% in 1994. This explains the rapid growth in salaries in Kazakhstan (Figure 13).

The hyperinflation that occurred between 1991 and 1995 declined to 39% in 1996 and then to 16% in 2011 (Figure 14). Income inequality can be traced using the Gini coefficient (Figure 15); when closer to 0 it shows more equality; closer to 1 indicates higher inequality. Here, Gini coefficient of Kazakhstan is plotted together with that of Russia for a better understanding of Kazakhstan's position in comparison with another FSU country that is also rich in natural resources and has a multi-ethnic population living on its vast territory.

Figure 15 illustrates that in 1989 Kazakhstan had slightly higher inequality in income distribution (0.28) than Russia (0.27). During the transition in the 1990s, income distribution inequality increased in both countries – in Russia to 0.41 in 1993 and in Kazakhstan to 0.32 in 1996 – due to privatization and redistribution of the previously state-owned assets. According to Pomfret (2006), inequality in Kazakhstan in the 1990s and 2000s remained at the same level, while Howie and Atakhanova (2014) concluded that income inequality declined between 1996 and 2009. Figure 15 also shows that the Gini coefficient fell: from 0.34 in 1997 to 0.29 in 2007, while in Russia it was slowly growing. The lower Gini coefficient illustrates that Kazakhstan is doing better than Russia in providing more equal income distribution among its citizens.

In terms of real incomes, Figure 16 shows that the highest real incomes in 1998–99 and 2001–03 were in Astana and Almaty cities. Overall, rural areas of Kazakhstan had lower real income per capita than urban ones. Despite a high monthly salary and nominal income in Mangystau *oblast*

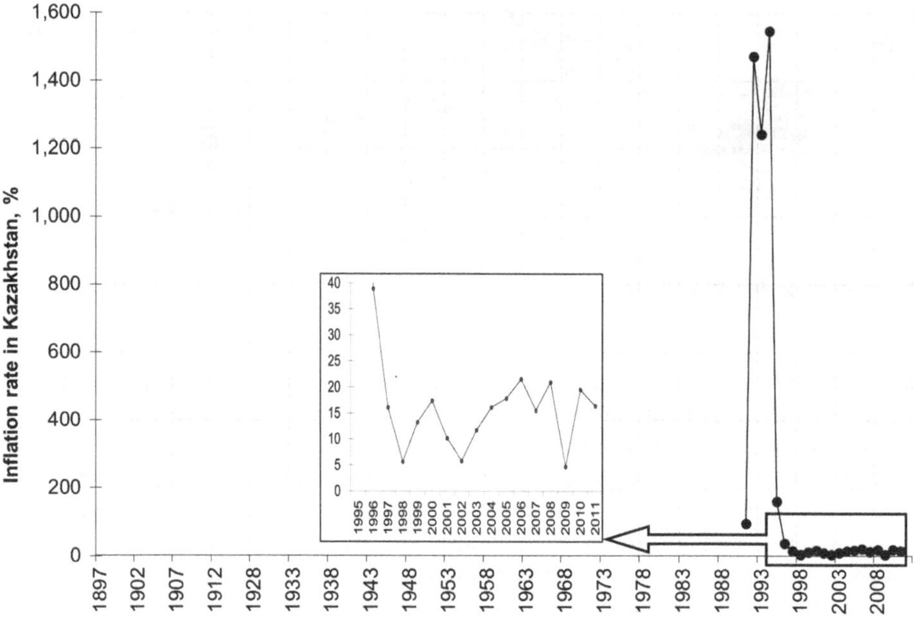


Figure 14. Inflation.

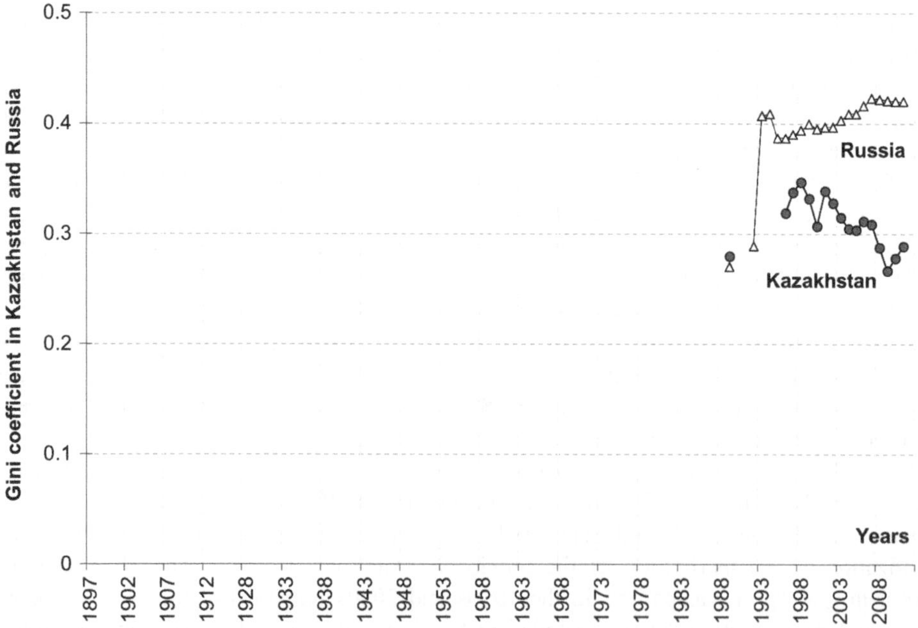


Figure 15. Gini coefficient of Kazakhstan and Russia.

(Figures 13 and 17), its real income in 2003 was one of the lowest in Kazakhstan, and comparable with that of Zhambyl *oblast* (Figure 16). The discrepancies between high nominal income/salary and low real income were most likely caused by high inflation and high living costs in western regions.

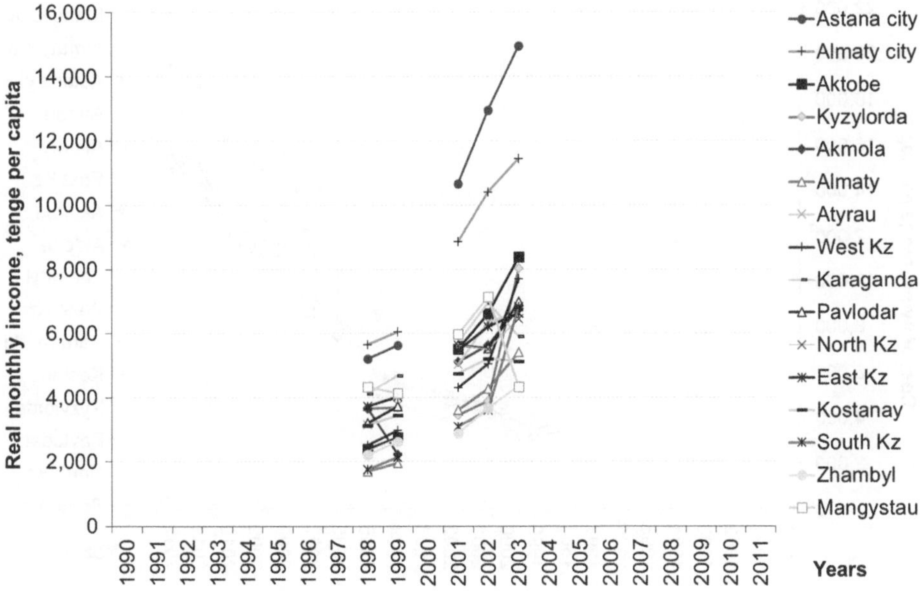


Figure 16. Real income.

Nominal income (i.e., not accounting for inflation) increased in all regions during the period 2001-2011 (Figure 17). However, the gap between income levels in the four regions (Atyrau, Mangystau, Astana and Almaty city) and the rest of Kazakhstan (especially its southern areas) increased greatly (Figure 17).

Figure 18 illustrates that the cost of living grew in all regions with especially high levels in Mangystau *oblast*. As 70% cost of living consisted of food items, it can be assumed that this

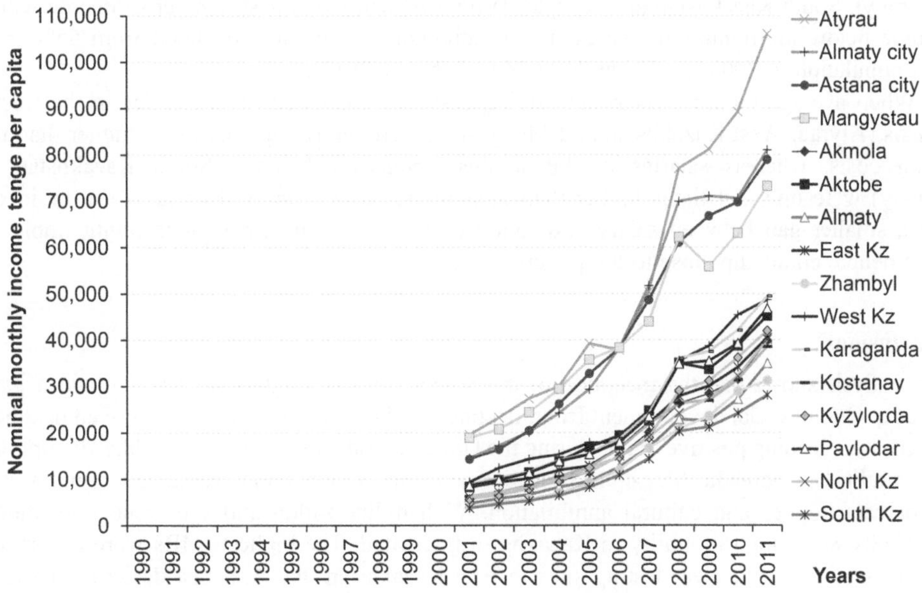


Figure 17. Nominal income.

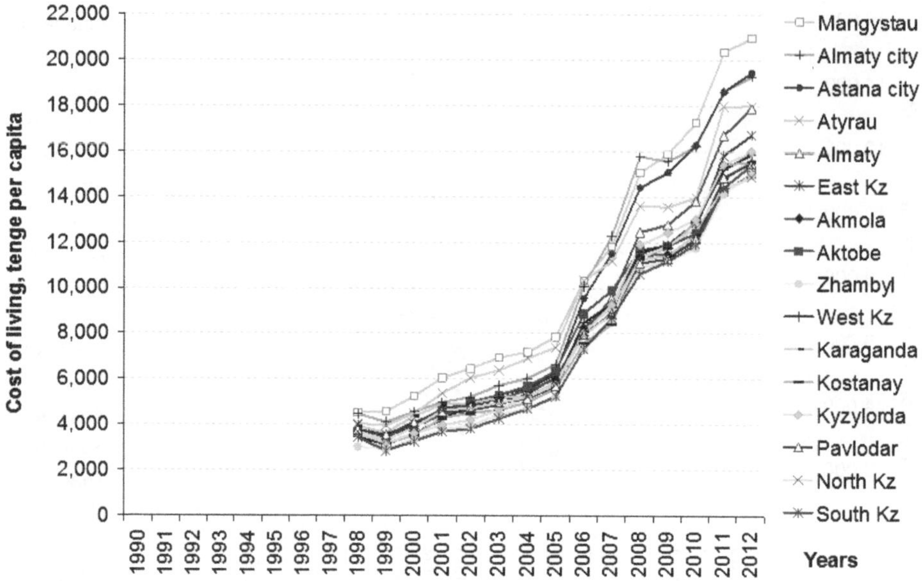


Figure 18. Cost of living.

region had more expensive food with a lack of agricultural produce due to the lowest precipitation in south-west Kazakhstan (fewer than 100 millimetres per year). In Mangystau *oblast* intensive exploitation of uranium, oil and gas resources on the barren Ustyurt plateau since the 1960s contaminated the land heavily. In the case of Astana and Almaty cities, higher population densities have caused a higher demand for essential goods, like food and accommodation.

The low cost of living in the southern regions (Zhambyl, South Kazakhstan and Almaty *oblasts*) is associated with the fact that their population was predominantly rural and could grow their own food (Figure 3) (Kazpravda 2005). Nevertheless, three southern regions (Zhambyl, South Kazakhstan and Kyzylorda *oblasts*) had the largest number of people with an income below the minimum cost of living, although their number declined from 55% in the total population in 2003 to 12% in 2009 (Zhankubayev 2012).

When average monthly salary and living costs are compared, then salaries in the western *oblasts* (Atyrau, West Kazakhstan and Mangystau) were on average 6.5 times higher than their living costs, whereas salaries in the southern *oblasts* (Zhambyl, South Kazakhstan and Almaty) were only 3.4 times higher than their living costs (Figures 13 and 18). Low income and a smaller gap between salary and living costs in the southern regions might imply that more people could slip close to the poverty line.

## Conclusions

The analysis shows that the inception of the Soviet Union brought both positive and negative impacts. On the social development front, decline in infant mortality and an improved healthcare system were leading positive trends during the USSR period. However, for Kazakhs, disruption of their traditional nomadic life, collectivization and the 'Virgin Land' campaign brought about major catastrophes and cultural annihilation. With militarization and economic stagnation in the 1960s–80s, infant mortality in Kazakhstan fluctuated. The highest IMRs were observed in the areas of former nuclear testing sites in East Kazakhstan, the Aral Sea desiccation zone in Kyzylorda and uranium mining areas in Mangystau *oblast*.

Rapid industrialization and relocation of industrial plants during the Great Patriotic War contributed to widespread pollution and environmental damage. While pollution levels in Kazakhstan went down in the 1990s, the decline was not intentional. The largest volumes of air emissions from stationary sources were in the urbanized Karaganda and Pavlodar *oblasts*, which used locally mined coal with a high ash content for generating heat and power.

During the Soviet period, water management in Central Asia was regulated centrally. Since the 1960s excessive water use for cotton irrigation led to the desiccation of the Aral Sea. The idea of diverting Siberian rivers into Central Asia has recently been revisited by regional leaders. Since independence, Kazakhstan had the lowest water availability among the CIS countries and the issues of transboundary rivers management and pollution (especially those originating in China) became crucial. Water preservation and efficient water management are necessary to prevent water deficit in Kazakhstan in future.

Kazakhstan has historically been very dependent on energy exports, especially oil and gas. However, high oil production in Atyrau and Mangystau *oblasts* pose significant risks to the unique Caspian Sea environment and biodiversity.

Despite improvements since the 1990s, Kazakhstan shows stark inter- and intra-regional inequality. Salaries in Kazakhstan were devalued due to hyperinflation in the 1990s. Among regions, as well as among various professions, salaries and incomes are distributed unequally. Despite high salaries, the western regions (especially Mangystau *oblast*) had the highest living costs, low real income and remain among the poorest in the country. This leads to occasional social unrests as seen in Zhanaozen in 2011. Although nominal incomes and salaries have risen massively in post-transition, the regional income gap also increased. However, since the late 1990s, wealth inequality dropped, demonstrating more equal income distribution, especially in comparison with Russia.

In 2006 Kazakhstan accepted the strategy for its transition to SD for 2007–24. Although the population and life expectancy increased according to the strategy, the SD strategy, along with environmental security strategy, was made void in 2011. This might be associated with a lack of funding or lack of long-term commitment and management over the implementation of the SD strategy's actions.

The findings suggest that change in ownership and management of environmental and economic assets was associated with initial social and economic turmoil, environmental pollution decline, hyperinflation and wealth inequality. Later, however, the development of Kazakhstan became more sustainable as its demographic situation improved and citizens were provided with new opportunities. In order to move to a more sustainable course of development, Kazakhstan should apply policies aimed at improving quality of life, encouraging equal wealth distribution among social groups as well as regions, developing renewable energy sources and ensuring decoupling of socio-economic development from wasteful use of natural resources.

Kazakhstan can choose different scenarios of development, and whether or not the country achieves its 'limits to growth' mainly depends on its current and future paths of development and policy choices. The Kazakhstan 2030 Development Strategy focused on socio-economic affairs and raising living standards. It also provided a basis for a national consolidation and nation-building. With recent falling oil prices there are concerns over economic growth, but at the same time this can be an opportunity for institutional reforms and the promotion of economic diversification.

While Russia's annexation of Crimea in 2014 might look threatening to the territorial sovereignty of Kazakhstan (especially to its northern regions), separatism is highly unlikely. First, there is a lack of a political movement in Kazakhstan. Second, Kazakhstan legitimized the Russian language as the language of inter-ethnic communication, whilst making Kazakh the state language. In addition, the 1998 move of the capital city from Almaty in the south (with a predominantly Kazakh population) to Astana in the north (with a predominantly Russian population) caused a positive long-term effect in attracting more ethnic Kazakhs to the northern regions. Finally, Kazakhstan's balanced foreign policy and equal representation of Russian people in political, social and economic life have been a key factor in retaining political stability.

Providing that political stability is maintained, more renewable energies sources are used and the finite natural resource extraction (and associated pollution) is slowed down, Kazakhstan stands a better chance of achieving the SD targets of meeting the needs and aspirations for several generations. Historically, traditions and the mentality of Kazakh people were coherent with SD principles, as they were based on empirical observations, self-sufficiency and environmental protection. There should be a renewed effort to bring these values alive again through public education, raising environmental awareness and standard setting by the government, scholars and businesses in modern Kazakhstan.

**Acknowledgements**

The work for this article was done as a a part of the author's PhD, which was supported by International Students Research Studentship from Birkbeck, University of London.

**Disclosure statement**

No potential conflict of interest was reported by the author.

## Notes

1. There are more than 80 various definitions of SD (Williams and Millington 2004). The most commonly used definition was introduced by Gro Harlem Brundtland, former prime minister of Norway. This states that SD 'seeks to meet the needs and aspirations of the present without compromising the ability to meet those of the future' (WCED 1987, 43).
2. Central Asian republics of the FSU (and later the Commonwealth of the Independent States – CIS) include the republics of Kazakhstan, Kyrgyzstan, Tadzhikistan, Turkmenistan and Uzbekistan.
3. Their predecessor was an international professional team established in 1996 and called the Consultative Group on Sustainable Development Indicators (CGSDI), which published a 'Dashboard of Sustainability'.
4. IMR is defined as death in the period between when a baby is born and when (s)he reaches the age of one year.
5. The data presented here were collected over the course of three years (2010–13) as part of the author's doctoral research.
6. A total of 70% of power plants in Kazakhstan use coal, 15% use hydroelectric power and 15% use natural gas (Atakhanova and Howie 2007). More than half of domestic energy needs are satisfied with coal; however, the energy efficiency of a typical coal power plant is very poor at 27%, and that of a combined heat and power (CHP) coal plant is even lower at 18–21% (Sarbassov et al. 2013).

**Data sources**

***Pre-transitional period***

The main source of data for the pre-transitional period was found in annual reports of the USSR National Economy, stored in the Russian State Library (RSL) in Moscow. The earliest country-wide report I found in the RSL archive was dated 1956. In addition, each Soviet republic used to issue separate reports on their socio-economic development, and these reports were available for the Kazakh socialist republic. The reports included numerous detailed tables with statistical data necessary for the five-year planning scheme ("*pyatiletka*").

A typical report of the USSR National Economy in 1956 consisted of useful and detailed information on development in various areas, including: population growth, industry, transport, trade, science, finance, construction, agriculture, education, and employment. It also contained comparative tables with data for the years 1939 and 1955. Some of the data were compared with 1913, i.e. prior to the First World War. The annual reports were large (up to 520 pages) and often contained comparable tables with other socialist and capitalist countries, demonstrating overall progress of the Soviet socio-economic system. The data were available in hard copy and had to be transcribed manually into spreadsheets during my visits to the Russian State Library in Moscow and Kazakhstan National Academic Library in Astana (2010–13).

Data collection for this research occurred over a period of three years, in stages as follows:

- April–May 2010: trip to Kazakhstan, collection of data from the statistical agency;
- November 2010: data collection for Kazakhstan regions through remote access;
- April–May 2011: trip to Russia, collection of statistical data from the RSL;
- February–March 2013: trip to Kazakhstan, data collection from the National Library.

*Sources of SD indicators data for the pre-transitional period*

*Narodnoye khozyaistvo SSSR v 1956 godu (1957, 1958, etc. ... 1990, 1991). Statisticheskiy ezhegodnik. Gosudarstvennyi komitet SSSR po statistike. Moskva. Financy i statistika* (in Russian). National economy of the USSR in 1956 (1957, 1958, etc. ... 1990, 1991). Statistical yearbook. State statistical committee of the Union of the Soviet Socialist Republics [USSR]. Moscow (36 reports).

*SSSR v tsifrakh (1981, 1982 ... 1987). Kratkiy statisticheskiy sbornik. Tsentral'noye statisticheskoye upravleniye. Moskva. Finansy i statistika* (in Russian). USSR in numbers (1981, 1982 ... 1986, 1987). Brief statistical report. Moscow (seven reports).

*Narodnoye khozyaistvo SSSR 1922–1972. Yubileynyi statisticheskiy sbornik. Moskva, 1972* (in Russian). National economy of the USSR in 1922–1972. Anniversary statistical report. Moscow, 1972.

*Dostizheniya Sovetskoy vlasti za 40 let v tsifrakh. Gosudarstvennoye statisticheskoye izdatel'stvo. Moskva* (in Russian) Achievements of the Soviet government during 40 years. Statistical report. Moscow, 1957.

*Narodnoye khozyaistvo Kazakhskoi SSR v 1958 (1959 ... etc. ... 1989, 1990). Statisticheskiy sbornik. Statisticheskoye upravleniye Kazakhskoy SSR. Alma-Ata* (in Russian). National economy of the Kazakh Soviet Socialist Republic [KazSSR] in 1958 (1959, 1960, etc. ... 1989, 1990). Statistical yearbook. Statistical administration of the Kazakh SSR (33 reports).

*Narodnoye khozyaistvo Kazakhstana za 70 let. Goskomstat Kazakhskoy SSR. Alma-Ata, 1990* (in Russian). National economy of Kazakhstan for 70 years. Statistical administration of the Kazakh SSR, 1990.

*Narodnoye khozyaistvo Kazakhstana za 60 let. Goskomstat Kazakhskoy SSR. Alma-Ata, 1980* (in Russian). National economy of Kazakhstan for 60 years. Statistics administration of the Kazakh SSR.

*Kazakhstan za 50 let. Goskomstat Kazakhskoy SSR. Alma-Ata, 1971* (in Russian). Kazakhstan during 50 years. Statistical administration of the Kazakh SSR. Alma-Ata, 1971.

*Kazakhstan v tsifrakh. Kratkiy statisticheskiy sbornik. Goskomstat Kazakhskoy SSR ppo statistike. Alma-Ata. 1988* (in Russian). Kazakhstan in numbers. Brief statistical report. Statistical administration of the Kazakh SSR. Alma-Ata, 1988.

### *Post-transitional period*

The main data sources for the post-transitional period were the annual statistical reports of the newly emerging state, accessible through the state libraries and official web sites of the government statistical agencies of Kazakhstan. Most of the post-transitional statistical data were obtained during visits to the Kazakhstan National Academic Library in Astana and electronic sources. As with the pre-transitional data, no other sources of post-transitional data were used in this research, mainly due to differences in methodologies between the Kazakhstan statistics and other international institutions and to preserve purity of the data.

*Sources of information for the post-transitional development*

*Regional'ny statisticheskiy ezhegodnik Kazakhstana. Respublikanskiy informatsionno-isdatel's-kiy tsentr. Almaty. 1991, 1992 ... 1999* (in Russian). Regional statistical yearbook of Kazakhstan. 1991, 1992, 1993, 1994, 1995... 1999 (nine reports).

*Trud i zanyatost' naseleniya v Kazakhstane 1991 – 2001 gody. Statisticheskiy sbornik. Almaty, 2003* (in Russian). Labour and employment in Kazakhstan in 1991–2001. Statistical report.

*Sotsial'no-ekonomicheskoye razvitiye Respubliki Kazakhstan. Agentstvo Respubliki Kazakhstan po Statistike. 1998, 1999, ... 2009, 2010* (in Russian). Socio-economic development of the Republic of Kazakhstan. 1998, ... 2010 (13 reports in Russian).

*Kazakhstan v tsifrakh. Broshura. 2001 ... 2011* (in Russian). Kazakhstan in numbers. Brief statistical report. 2001, 2002 ... 2011 (11 reports).

*Regiony Kazakhstana v 2004, 2005 ... 2009, 2010 godu* (in Russian). Regions of Kazakhstan in 2004, 2005 ..., 2009, 2010 (six reports).

*Sel'skoye, lesnoye i rybnoye khozyaistvo Kazakhstana* (in Russian). Agriculture, forestry and fishery in Kazakhstan (2003, ... 2010) (seven reports).

Online resources: http://www.stat.kz

### Regional maps

Regional maps of SD indicators for Kazakhstan were created using ArcGIS 10.2. The maps give a better graphical representation of the various regions in my case study country, and make it easier to understand the spatial distribution of indicators (e.g. infant mortality and oil production) and see detailed information for specific oblasts.

The shape files which provided the basis for my maps were downloaded from the Internet, using DIVA-GIS web-site, supported by University of California, Biodiversity International,

International Rice Research Institute, Museum of Vertebrate Zoology and International Potato Center (http://www.diva-gis.org/gdata).

Regional maps for Kazakhstan were created based on the most recent data available for my regional indicators of SD. They show the current development of the country and clearly identify potential future development paths towards SD goals of Kazakhstan.

## References


Alekseyenko, A. N. 2000. "Naseleniye Kazakhstana v 1926–1939 Godakh." [in Russian.] Population of Kazakhstan in 1926–1939. *Altay State University.*

Aleshina, N., and G. Redmond. 2005. "How High is Infant Mortality in Central and Eastern Europe and the Commonwealth of Independent States?" *Population Studies* 59 (1): 39–54. doi:10.1080/00324720520000332692

Anderson, B. A., and B. D. Silver. 1986. "Infant Mortality in the Soviet Union: Regional Differences And Measurement Issues." *Population and Development Review* 12 (4): 705–738. doi:10.2307/1973432

Anthopolos, R., and C. M. Becker. 2010. "Global Infant Mortality: Correcting For Undercounting." *World Development* 38 (4): 467–481. doi:10.1016/j.worlddev.2009.11.013

Atakhanova, Z., and P. Howie. 2007. "Electricity Demand in Kazakhstan." *Energy Policy* 35: 3729–3743. doi:10.1016/j.enpol.2007.01.005

Bendas, T. B. 2003. "Rossiya i Kazakhstan: Etnokul'turnyye i Gendernyye Razlichiya." [in Russian.] Russia and Kazakhstan: Ethnocultural and Gender Differences. *Orenburg State University.*

Bergson, A. 1947. "A Problem in Soviet Statistics." *The Review of Economics and Statistics* 29 (4): 234–242. doi:10.2307/1927821

Bergson, A. 1984. "Income Inequality under Soviet Socialism." *Journal of Economic Literature* 22 (3): 1052–1099.

Beurs, de K. M., and G. M. Henebry. 2004. "Land Surface Phenology, Climatic Variation, and Institutional Change: Analyzing Agricultural Land Cover Change in Kazakhstan." *Remote Sensing of Environment* 89: 497–509. doi:10.1016/j.rse.2003.11.006

Biekenov, M. 2006. "Modernizatsiya Politicheskogo Protsessa Kazakhstanskogo Obshchestva." [in Russian.] Modernization of Political Processes in the Kazakhstan Society. Kazakhstan *President Academy of Public Administration*. Astana: 219.

Bisekov, A. 2013. "Osnovnyye Puti Povysheniya Dokhodnosti Sel'skogo Naseleniya." [in Russian.] Main Routes of Income Growth for Rural Population. *Gumilev Eurasian National University.*

Black, B. S., and A. S. Tarassova. 2003. "Institutional Reform in Transition: A Case Study of Russia." *Supreme Court Economic Review* 10: 211–278.

Bossel, H. 2001. "Assessing Viability and Sustainability: A System-Based Approach for Deriving Comprehensive Indicator Sets." *Conservation Ecology* 5 (2): 12. http://www.ecologyandsociety.org/vol5/iss2/art12/

Brainerd, E. 2007. "Uncounted Costs of World War II: The Effect of Changing Sex Ratios on Marriage and Fertility of Russian Women." Economics Department. *Williams College.*

Buckley, C. 1998. "Rural/Urban Differentials in Demographic Processes: The Central Asian States." *Population Research and Policy Review* 17 (1): 71–89. doi:10.1023/A:1005899920710

Czarra, F. 2003. "Fresh water: Enough for You and Me?" *The American Forum for Global Education* 174: 2002–2003.

Dahl, C., and K. Kuralbayeva. 2001. "Energy and the Environment in Kazakhstan." *Energy Policy* 29: 429–440. doi:10.1016/S0301-4215(00)00137-3

Darimbetov, B. N., and M. U. Spanov. 2001. "Tenevaya Ekonomika V Kazakhstane: Istochniki i Mekhanizmy Realizatsiyi." [in Russian.] Shadow Economy in Kazakhstan: Sources and Mechanisms of Implementation. Accessed December 30, 2012. http://ecsocman.hse.ru/data/654/697/1217/008DARIMBETOV.pdf

DEFRA (Department for Environment, Food and Rural Affairs) 2011. "Sustainable development in government." National Indicators. Accessed September 03, 2012. http://sd.defra.gov.uk/progress/national/

Dutton, J. 1979. "Changes in Soviet Mortality Patterns, 1959–77. *Population and Development Review* 5 (2): 267–291. doi:10.2307/1971826

Easterly, W., and S. Fischer. 1995. The Soviet Economic Decline. *World Bank Economic Review* 9 (3): 341–371. doi:10.1093/wber/9.3.341

Ellman, M. 2002. "Soviet Repression Statistics: Some Comments." *Europe–Asia Studies* 54 (7): 1151–1172. doi:10.1080/0966813022000017177

Eshpanova, D. D., G. A. Narbekova, and N. Z. Biekenova. 2012. "Transofrmatsiya Tsennostnogo Soznaniya Sovremennogo Kazakhstanskogo Obschestva" [in Russian.] Transformation of Axiological Awareness of Contemporary Society in Kazakhstan. *Novossibirsk State University*: 66–72.

EBRD (European Bank for Reconstruction and Development). 2011. "Special Report on Climate Change: The Low Carbon Transition." Effective policies to induce mitigation.

EBRD (European Bank for Reconstruction and Development). 2013. "Forecasts, Macro Data, Transition Indicators."

Franke, A., A. Gawrich, *et al.* 2009. "Kazakhstan and Azerbaijan as Post-Soviet Rentier States: Resource Incomes and Autocracy as a Double 'Curse' in Post-Soviet Regimes." *Europe–Asia Studies,* 61 (1): 109–140. doi:10.1080/09668130802532977

Franz, J. S., and F. FitzRoy. 2006. "Child Mortality and Environment in Developing Countries." *Population and Environment* 27 (3): 263–284. doi:10.1007/s11111-006-0020-7

Giddings, B., B. Hopwood, and G. O'Brien. 2002. "Environment, Economy and Society: Fitting them Together into Sustainable Development." *Sustainable Development* 10 (4): 187–196. doi:10.1002/sd.199

Greenberg, I. 2007. "Kazakhstan and China Deadlock Over Depletion of a Major Lake." *New York Times*. Accessed September 13, 2012. http://query.nytimes.com/gst/fullpage.html?res=

Grid-Arendal. 2012. "Koshkar-Ata lake case study: The hazardous legacy of an uranium mine. Accessed July 10, 2013. http://www.grida.no/publications/vg/caspian/page/1356.aspx.

Guriev, S., and A. Rachinskiy. 2006. "The Evolution of Personal Wealth in the Former Soviet Union and Central and Eastern Europe." Accessed December 10, 2012. http://siteresources.worldbank.org/INTDECINEQ/

Granovsky, E.I. 2003. "Problems of Sustainable Development of the Atyrau City and Atyrau Region". Analytical Review. Almaty: The Kazakh State Research Institute for Scientific and Technical Information. Accessed September 21, 2012. http://www.unesco.kz/science/atyrau/index.html#_Toc50687559

Harrison, M. 2011. "Forging Success: Soviet Managers and Accounting Fraud, 1943–1962." *Journal of Comparative Economics* 39 (1): 43–64. doi:10.1016/j.jce.2010.12.002

Henry, L. A. 2009. "Thinking Globally, Limited Locally: The Russian Environmental Movement and Sustainable Development." In: *Environmental Justice and Sustainability in the Former Soviet Union*, edited by J. Agyeman and E. Ogneva-Himmelberger, 47–70. Cambridge, MA: MIT Press.

Howie, P., and Z. Atakhanova. 2014. "Resource Boom and Inequality: Kazakhstan as a Case Study." *Resources Policy* 39: 71–79. doi:10.1016/j.resourpol.2013.11.004

Ipek, P. 2007. "The Role of Oil and Gas in Kazakhstan's Foreign Policy: Looking East or West?." *Europe–Asia Studies* 59 (7): 1179–1199. doi:10.1080/09668130701607144

IUCN (International Union for Conservation of Nature). 2013. "The IUCN Red List of Threatened Species." Accessed July 12, 2013. http://www.iucnredlist.org/search/list.

Ivanovic, O., M. Golusin, S. Dodic, and J. Dodic. 2009. "Perspectives of Sustainable Development in Countries of Southeastern Europe." *Renewable and Sustainable Energy Reviews* 13 (8): 2079–2087. doi:10.1016/j.rser.2009.03.004

Jedrychowski, W. 1999. "Ambient Air Pollution and Respiratory Health in the East Baltic Region." *Scandinavian Journal of Work, Environment & Health* 25 (3): 5–16.

Jones, E., and F. W. Grupp. 1983. "Infant Mortality Trends in the Soviet Union." *Population and Development Review* 9 (2): 213–246. doi:10.2307/1973050

Jones Luong, P., and Weinthal, E. 2010. *Oil is not a Curse Ownership Structure and Institutions in Soviet Successor States*. New York: Cambridge University Press.

Josephson, P. R. 2007. "Industrial Deserts: Industry, Science and the Destruction of Nature in the Soviet Union." *The Slavonic and East European Review* 85 (2): 294–321.

Kaiser, M. J., and A. G. Pulsipher. 2007. "A Review of the Oil and Gas Sector in Kazakhstan." *Energy Policy* 35: 1300–1314. doi:10.1016/j.enpol.2006.03.020

Kalb, P. D., S. Vagin, P. W. Beall, and B. L. Levintov. 2004. "Sustainable Development in Kazakhstan: Using Oil & Gas Production By-Product Sulfur for Cost-Effective Secondary End-Use Products." *Global Symposium on Recycling, Waste Treatment and Clean Technology*. Madrid, September 2004.

Kaldybay, K. K., T. K. Abdrassilov, G. K. Abdygalieva, P. M. Suleymenov, and M. O. Nassimov. 2013. "Maintenance of Philosophical, Humanistic and Religious Values of Security of the Kazakh Nation." *International Scholarly and Scientific Research & Innovation* 7 (3): 198–204.

Karpukhin, D. N. 1978. "Minimum Zarabotnoi Platy." [in Russian.] Minimum salary. *Big Soviet Encyclopaedia*. Accessed December 15, 2012. http://bse.sci-lib.com/article076686.html

Kazpravda. 2005. "Tseny na prodovol'stvennyye tovary v iyune 2005 goda uvelichilis' na 0.4 protsenta" [Food prices in June 2005 increased by 0.4 percent]. No. 3 (8): 3.

Kazmunaygas. 2010. "Tengiz". Accessed July 09, 2013. http://www.kmg.kz/en/manufacturing/upstream/tengiz/

Kazakhstan Today. 2010. "Actual Wages in August, 2010 Increased by 10.5% in Kazakhstan." International Information Centre of the Republic of Kazakhstan. Accessed January 10, 2011. http://www.kt.kz/?lang=eng&uin=1133435497

Kiessling, K. L. 1998. "Conference on the Aral Sea: Women, Children, Health and Environment." *Ambio* 27 (7): 560–564.

Kim, G. N. 2009. "Koreans in Kazakhstan, Uzbekistan, and Russia." Accessed August 16, 2012. http://world.lib.ru/k/kim_o_i/a.shtml

Kirsanov, I., and D. Kim. 2007. "Tsentral'naya Aziya: Bitva Za Vodu." [in Russian.] Central Asia: Battle for Water. *Eurasian Heritage Fund*. Accessed April 02, 2013. http://www.fundeh.org/publications/articles/68/

Kojima, S. 2005. "Quantitative Policy Analysis for Sustainable Development in Water-Stressed Developing Countries: A Case Study of Morocco." *University of York*.

Martinez-Alier, J., U. Pascual, F.-D. Vivien, and E. Zaccai. 2010. "Sustainable De-Growth: Mapping the Context, Criticisms and Future Prospects of an Emergent Paradigm." *Ecological Economics* 69: 1741–1747. doi:10.1016/j.ecolecon.2010.04.017

Maulenova, S. 2009. "The Change of Social Structure of Kazakh Society under Market Economic Conditions."*Rzeszow University*: 198–201.

Meadows, D. H., D. L. Meadows, J. Randers, and W. Behrens. 1972. *The Limits to Growth*. New York, London, Earth Island: Universe Books.

Michaels, P. A. 2000. "Medical Propaganda and Cultural Revolution in Soviet Kazakhstan, 1928–41." *Russian Review* 59 (2): 159–178. doi:10.1111/0036-0341.00115

Minorities At Risk. 2006. "Assessment for Russians in Kazakhstan." Center for International Development and Conflict Management. University of Maryland.

Mitrofanskaya, Yu. 1999. "Privatization as an International Phenomenon: Kazakhstan." *American University International Law Review* 14 (5): 1399–1438.

Nasimova, G. 2011. "Uroven' Sotsial'noy Konfliktnosti v Kazakhstane: Riski i Potentsial'nyye Ugrozy. [in Russian.] Level of Social Proneness to Conflict in Kazakhstan: Risks and Potential Threats." *Central Asia and Caucasus* 4 (14): 105–114.

Neumayer, E. 2004. "Does the "Resource Curse" Hold for Growth in Genuine Income as Well?" *World Development* 32 (10): 1627–1640. doi:10.1016/j.worlddev.2004.05.005

New Scientist. 1989. "Soviet Cotton Threatens a Region's Sea – and its Children." *New Scientist* 124 (1691).

Nizhegorodskaya, T. 2011. "Chtob Zhit Na Odnu Zarplatu." [in Russian.] In Order to Live on One Salary. *Versiya*. Accessed December 14, 2012. http://versia.ru/articles/2011/oct/03/uvelichenie_zarplaty

Nove, A. 1966. "Wages in the Soviet Union: A Comment on Recently Published Statistics." *British Journal of Industrial Relations* 4 (1–3): 212–221. doi:10.1111/j.1467-8543.1966.tb00928.x

Nuti, D. M. 1989. "The New Soviet Cooperatives: Advances and Limitations." *Economic and Industrial Democracy* 10: 311–327.

Olcott, M. B. 1995. *The Kazakhs*. Stanford, CA: Hoover Institution Press.

Oldfield, J. 1999. "The Environmental Impact of Transition: A Case Study of Moscow City." *The Geographical Journal* 165 (2): 222–231. doi:10.2307/3060420

OECD (Organisation for Economic Cooperation and Development). 2008. "Main Economic Indicators." Accessed 07 October, 2013. http://stats.oecd.org/mei/

Oskenbayev, Ye, M. Yilmaz, and K. Abdulla. 2013. "Resource Concentration, Institutional Quality and the Natural Resource Curse." *Economic Systems* 37 (2): 254–270. doi:10.1016/j.ecosys.2012.11.001

Overy, R. 2011. "The Soviet–German War 1941–1945." Accessed January 20, 2013. http://www.bbc.co.uk/history/worldwars/wwtwo/soviet_german_war_01.shtml

Özcan, G. B. 2010. *Building States and Markets: Enterprise Development in Central Asia*. Basingstoke: Palgrave Macmillan.

Pasakarnis, G., and V. Maliene. 2010. "Towards Sustainable Rural Development in Central and Eastern Europe: Applying Land Consolidation." *Land Use Policy* 27 (2): 545–549. doi:10.1016/j.landusepol.2009.07.008

Pavlovskaya, O. 2013. "V Kazakhstane Grazhdan i Predpriyatiya Prizyvayut Ekonomit' Vodu." [in Russian.] Kazakhstan Appeals to Its Citizens and Businesses to Save Water. Accessed August 20, 2014. http://centralasiaonline.com/ru/articles/caii/features/main/2013/06/07/feature-01

Pearce, D., A. Markandya, and E. Barbier. 1989. *Blueprint for a Green Economy*. London: Earthscan.

Pianciola, N. 2001. "The Collectivization Famine in Kazakhstan, 1931–1933." *Harvard Ukrainian Studies* 25 (3/4): 237–251.

Pianciola, N. 2004. "Famine in the Steppe. The Collectivization of Agriculture and the Kazak Herdsmen, 1928–1934." *Cahiers du Monde Russe* 45 (1/2): 137–191.

Pomfret, R. 2006. *The Central Asian Economies since Independence*. Princeton: University Press.

Pravda. 2004. "Russia has Highest Salary Rate in CIS." Accessed December 10, 2012. http://english.pravda.ru/russia/economics/10-05-2004/5514-salary-0/

Prescott-Allen, R. 2001. *The Well-being of Nations: A Country-by-Country Index of Quality of Life and the Environment*. Washington, DC: Island Press.

Raloff, J. 2006. "Saving Sturgeon." *Science News* 169 (9): 138–140. doi:10.2307/3982303

Ramazanova, D. 2011. "The Soviet Legacy and the Future of Language Politics in Post-Soviet Kazakhstan." *Spanda Journal* 2 (2): 18–30.

Randers, J. (2010). "What was the message of the Limits to Growth? What did this little book from 1972 really say about the global future?" *The Club of Rome*. Version: 5 April 2010.

Redclift, M. 1987. *Sustainable Development: Exploring the contradictions*. London: Routledge.

Robinson, J. 2004. "Squaring the Circle? Some Thoughts on the Idea of Sustainable Development." *Ecological Economics* 48 (4): 369–384. doi:10.1016/j.ecolecon.2003.10.017

Sachs, J. D., and A. M. Warner. 1995. "Natural resource abundance and economic growth." *National Bureau of Economic Research*. Working Paper 5398.

Sarbassov, Ye, A. Kerimraya, D. Tokmurzin, G. C. Tosato, and R. Miglio. 2013. Electricity and Heating System in Kazakhstan: Exploring Energy Efficiency Improvement Paths. *Energy Policy* (in press) http://dx.doi.org/10.1016/j.enpol.2013.03.012i.

Sarkeyeva, R. 2007. "Kyrgyz Energy Policy In Transition: Price Reforms And Residential Electricity Demand." PhD diss. The University of Reading.

Severskiy, I. V. 2004. "Water-Related Problems of Central Asia: Some Results of the (GIWA) International Water Assessment Program." *AMBIO: A Journal of the Human Environment* 33 (1/2): 52–62. doi:10.1579/0044-7447-33.1.52

Sheretov, S. G. 2003. *Noveishaya Istoriya Kazakhstana: 1985–2002* [in Russian.] Contemporary History of Kazakhstan: 1985–2002. Almaty: 74–81.

Shubnaya, E. 2011. "Prominent Russians: Joseph Stalin." Accessed 04 June, 2012. http://russiapedia.rt.com/prominent-russians/leaders/joseph-stalin/

Shustov, A. 2010. "Kazakhstan: Suverennaya Demographiya." [in Russian.] Kazakhstan: Sovereign demography. Demographic Research Institute.

Simonenkov, D. V., D. B. Belan, G. N. Tolmachev, and V. E. Zuev. 2010. "Chemical Composition of Industrial Aerosol in Some Regions." *Chemical Engineering Transaction* 22: 197–202.

Spoor, M. 2002. "The Aral Sea Basin Crisis: Transition and Environment in Former Soviet Central Asia." *Development and Change* 29 (3): 409–435. doi:10.1111/1467-7660.00084

Stanton, E. A. 2007. "The Human Development Index: A History." Political Economy Research Institute. *University of Massachusetts Amherst*. Working paper Series Number 127.

Streimikiene, D., Z. Simanaviciene, and R. Kovaliov. 2009. "Corporate Social Responsibility for Implementation of Sustainable Energy Development in Baltic States." *Renewable and Sustainable Energy Reviews* 13 (4): 813–824. doi:10.1016/j.rser.2008.01.007

Thomas, M. 2015. "Sustainable Transitions? Historical Analysis of Sustainable Development Indicators in Russia and Kazakhstan and Their Regions". PhD diss. Birkbeck, University of London.

Treml, V. G. 1988. "Perestroyka and Soviet Statistics." *Soviet Economy* 4 (1): 65–94.

UN (United Nations). 2007. Indicators of Sustainable Development: Guidelines and Methodologies. October 2007. Third Edition.

UNDP (United Nations Development Programme). 2004. *Water Resources of Kazakhstan in the New Millennium*. Almaty, 2004.

UNDP (United Nations Development Programme). 1990. *Human Development Report. Concept and Measurement of Human Development*. New York and Oxford: Oxford University Press.

Vahovitch, I. 2008. "Methodological Basis for Establishment and Implementation of Regional Policy for Financial Provision of Sustainable Development." PhD diss. Lutsk National Technical University. Odessa, Ukraine.

Velkoff, V. A., and J. E. Miller. 1995. "Trends and Differentials in Infant Mortality in the Soviet Union, 1970–90: How much is Due to Misreporting?." *Population Studies* 49 (2): 241–258. doi:10.1080/0032472031000148496

Verbitskaya, L., N. Nosova, and L. Rodina. 2002. "Sustainable Development in Higher Education in Russia: The Case of St. Petersburg State University." *Higher Education Policy* 15 (2): 177–185. doi:10.1016/S0952-8733(02)00011-9

Wheatcroft, S. G., and R. W. Davies. 1994. *The Crooked Mirror of Soviet Economic Statistics*. Cambridge and New York: Cambridge University Press.

Williams, C. W., and A. C. Millington. 2004. "The Diverse and Contested Meanings of Sustainable Development." *The Geographical Journal* 170 (2): 99 104. doi:10.1111/j.0016-7398.2004.00111.x

WB (World Bank) 2012. *World Development Indicators 2012*. Washington, DC: World Bank Group. National Technical Information Service.

WB (World Bank) 2014. *Inflation, GDP Deflator (annual %)*. Accessed June 29, 2014. http://data.worldbank.org/indicator/NY.GDP.DEFL.KD.ZG

WCED (World Commission on Environment and Development). 1987. *Our Common Future. Chapter 2: Towards Sustainable Development*: 43.

Zhankubayev, B. 2012. "Sotsial'nyye Factory i Kachestvo Zhizni Naseleniya v Kazakhstane. [in Russian.] Social Factors and Quality of Life of Population in Kazakhstan." *Sotsial'na'ya Politika i Sotsial'noye Partnerstvo* 1: 62–66.

Zhylkybayev, S., S. Bondarenko, and T. Y. Tsun-sin. 2012. "Water Shortage Issues in Kazakhstan." KIMEP International Research Conference "Central Asia: Regionalization vs. Globalization", April 19–21, 2012.

# Uzbekistan's 'spirit' of self-reliance and the logic of appropriateness: TAPOich and interaction with Russia

Bernardo Teles Fazendeiro

*Centre for Critical Thought, University of Kent, Canterbury, UK*

The article looks at Uzbekistan's political economy from the perspective of a logic of appropriateness, an approach that takes rules to be the underlying principle of action. The rules are mostly in line with a 'spirit' of self-reliance (*mustaqillik*), which has shaped Tashkent's international engagement since independence. From the perspective of those rules, the article reveals some important features of Russian–Uzbek relations, particularly the difficult and often tense negotiations over the future of the Tashkent Aviation Production Association (TAPOich). Self-reliance and the rules by which it was comprised were not, in the end, conducive to long-term cooperation with Russia in the aviation sector, where collaboration was first and foremost necessary.

## Introduction

International political economy (IPE) 'teaches us how to think about the connections between economics and politics beyond the confines of a single state' (Cohen 2008, 1). It is a promising approach to studying Central Asia, although one hindered by political opaqueness in the region. Lack of transparency, difficult access to policy-makers and a reluctance to discuss politics do not make for an ideal environment in which to conduct research. There are, however, ways of approaching IPE despite these constraints and, as a matter of fact, Uzbekistan's direction in a post-Soviet political economy is still subject to much debate (Ruziev, Ghosh, and Dow 2007). Scholars who look at and take local rules as their starting point for enquiry suggest that the concept of *mustaqillik*, for now translated tentatively as 'self-reliance', plays 'a substantial part in shaping foreign policy and the international political economy of Uzbekistan' (Spechler and Spechler 2010, 163). Dina Spechler and Martin Spechler stipulate that, as 'one of the larger successor states of the former Soviet Union, the Republic of Uzbekistan has been especially concerned in its foreign relations to retain the new country's independence – political, economic, and military' (Spechler and Spechler 2009, 353). Likewise, Annette Bohr surmised national independence to be the basis of Tashkent's foreign economic policy (Bohr 1998, 20–21, 43); and Gregory Gleason demonstrates how Tashkent engaged with a 'structuralist' approach to economic growth by rejecting liberalism and emphasizing 'neo-mercantilism' (Gleason 2001, 177). Other scholars inferred connections between Uzbekistan's nation-building and foreign policy, including the extent to which they are constituted by Tashkent's institutional make-up (Luong 2002; Kazemi 2003; Collins 2005; Anceschi 2010).

What all these interpretations have in common is an applied logic of action, which gives meaning to events, organizes narratives and discloses the underlying dynamics of Central Asian IPE. This article seeks to build upon those contributions and reveals the importance of a logic of appropriateness, an approach that, as shown below, takes rules to be the underlying principle of action. I show how that same logic, as opposed to one of consequences, can be applied to Uzbek–Russian relations in the context of the V.P. Chkalov Tashkent Aviation Production Association (TAPOich – Tashkentskoye aviatsionnoye proizvodstvennoye ob'yedineniye imeni V. P. Chkalova). I argue, in addition, that Tashkent's self-reliant approach was not conducive to cooperating with Russia in the aviation sector, as it eschewed political–economic integration, or any form of systematic dependency for that matter.

Moscow is an especially relevant actor to consider when disentangling Uzbekistan's political economy, not least because President Islom Karimov often recognized Russia's special role in the post-Soviet space and in Uzbekistan in particular (Karimov 1992a, 54). And yet, a cursory glance at the 'special' status suffices to show that it barely guaranteed stable bilateral relations.[1] As for the focus on aviation, there are reasons why the sector warrants special attention: TAPOich has not yet been subject to scholarly enquiry,[2] and, more importantly, it played an key part in the bilateral relationship, as its chief executive officers (CEOs) participated routinely in the Russian–Uzbek inter-governmental commissions on economic cooperation (LexUz 1997a). TAPOich was also a source of prestige and was thus showcased in several inter-governmental visits. For instance, in 1999, during his first official visit to Uzbekistan, President Boris Yeltsin's prime minister, Vladimir Putin, toured TAPOich accompanied by his host, Karimov (BBC 1999b).

A study of TAPOich's transformation illustrates the extent to which *mustaqillik* affected bilateral relations. TAPOich is in fact no ordinary enterprise. It was one of the largest aircraft plants in the Soviet Union and would have strengthened Uzbek self-reliance. Headquartered on the outskirts of Tashkent, the plant had the potential to allow for a degree of self-sufficiency and ensure that Uzbekistan became a major industrial manufacturer at a time when other post-Soviet industries faced the prospect of closing permanently. Such aspirations were, nevertheless, impractical. *Mustaqillik*, or self-reliance, was hardly conducive to political–economic integration in a sector that first and foremost required systematic bilateral collaboration, for TAPOich relied heavily on Russian research, expertise and goods.

The article begins by conceptualizing the differences between the logics of appropriateness and consequences. It then shows briefly why self-reliance captures the spirit of Uzbekistan's rules and, thereafter, narrates the complex negotiating dynamics between Tashkent and Moscow in the context of TAPOich. The conclusion highlights and elaborates upon the key findings. But, before proceeding, a few words on sources and methodology are appropriate: all information on Tashkent's rules was obtained from and cross-checked with Karimov's speeches and works, Uzbekistan's laws and secondary sources, such as Russian and international media reports. In narrating bilateral interaction, Uzbekistan's laws and cabinet declarations – available in LexUz (an online database that includes all Uzbekistan's laws) – offered valuable information on TAPOich, which was then cross-checked with open-source material.[3] To plot the narrative and explain the events as they transpired, I applied a logic of appropriateness. In other words, and as developed further below, I show how the rules reveal the 'spirit of a game', provide meaning to key decisions, and disclose the reasons why bilateral relations evolved in the way they did in the context of TAPOich.

## Logics of appropriateness and consequences: why have a logic at all?

Logics of consequences and appropriateness are employed in depictions of Uzbekistan's IPE. Logics are heuristics that provide meaning to action, and are especially necessary if a political–economic system is opaque, that is, where access to decision-makers and confidential information is severely limited. In fact, with no direct communication, 'one is not in a position to verify his interpretation of the Other's experiences by checking them against the Other's own subjective interpretations' (Schutz 1964, 34). It is thus important to consider the implications of a logic before plotting a sequence of actions and events in a narrative. In any case, there are other ways of interpreting action – through logics of habit (Hopf 2010), practice (Pouliot 2008) and arguing (Sending 2002) – but I focus on appropriateness and consequences, since these are the main ways in which Uzbekistan's IPE is depicted. Below, I look at two of the more common ways of explaining action and justify why a logic of appropriateness, as opposed to one of consequences, is the more revealing starting point.

A logic of consequences is one of the more common ways of understanding action in Central Asia, and it is applied routinely – either tacitly or self-consciously – by scholars. It takes action to be a reflected, instrumental endeavour, in which rules exist only to restrict an individual's private preferences from being fulfilled. Hence, a logic of consequences may well be considered strategic, for it 'aims at making one's own preferences prevail, using all instruments available for achieving this objective; it is embedded in rational choice theory and follows its "logic of consequences"' (Müller 2004, 396). Furthermore, in order to measure those consequences, and since direct access to decision-makers is perhaps neither possible nor feasible, the logic often infers individual preferences ad hoc (Pouliot 2008, 261). To this end, when analysing Uzbekistan's IPE and foreign policy, those who apply a logic of consequences take the pursuit of 'regime survival' to be a core preference (Anceschi 2010, 144). Combinations of geopolitics and political economy also tend to include rent-seeking (Berman 2004; Smith 2009; Cooley 2012, 21–25) or the pursuit of hegemony (Deyermond 2009). Of course, the reasons why rent-seeking is taken to be relevant are not haphazard by any means, in fact they are based on substantial evidence (Marat 2006; Lewis 2008; Radnitz 2010; Cooley 2012; Cooley and Heathershaw 2014). But apart from empirical validity, how revealing is it to postulate that each and every Central Asian republic, Uzbekistan in particular, is driven by survival? A logic of consequences bestows a narrative with both purpose and direction, but it also sidelines a few of the features that make Uzbekistan's approach to IPE unique and distinguish it from other Central Asian republics. It also belies any need for unpacking the nature of local practices and ideology, inasmuch as all local elites are assumed to share the same underlying preferences. But even if preferences were good indicators of political action, they would remain difficult to access, and even more so in Uzbekistan, where the identities and aims of powerful elites are subject to ongoing scholarly dispute.[4]

A logic of appropriateness, in turn, does not stipulate such preferences. Instead of assuming rules to be restrictions, hindering privately held preferences or agendas from being enacted, a logic of appropriateness postulates that 'to act appropriately is to proceed according to the institutionalized practices of a collectivity, based on mutual, and often tacit understanding of true, reasonable, right and good' (March and Olsen 2005, 690). Where a logic of consequences is atomistic – focused on the individual – and congruent with instrumental behaviour, a logic of appropriateness takes rules to be ends in and of themselves, as well as the foundation upon which identities are based (Sending 2002, 445).

Rules, unlike preferences, are out in the open, whether in speeches, public works, laws or practices, and are either formal or informal 'models' that shape action (Jepperson, Wendt, and Katzenstein 1996, 56). They are ways of understanding the manner in which political–economic 'games' are played. By a 'game', however, I do not mean rational choice games (game theory or utility optimizing theories), rather a game as suggested by the hermeneutical philosophy of Hans-Georg Gadamer. Games, according to Gadamer, have their own 'spirit' and the 'particular nature of the game lies in the rules and regulations that prescribe the way the field of the game is filled' (Gadamer 2013, 111). In order to unpack the nature of Uzbekistan's political–economic 'game', one first has to understand the elements or rules by which that 'spirit' is constituted, as they affect how the actor is likely to 'play'. In this regard, not all rules are formal, in the sense of being written down explicitly, but they can be accessed via local practices, roles and identities

(March and Olsen 2005). At any rate, I do not go over the analytical differences between norms and rules and how they relate to each other; suffice it to say that rules are *general* prescriptions for action, whereas norms are also standards of behaviour expressed through the language of rights and obligations (Kratochwil 1989, 59). As I am more concerned with action than the latter's ethical, legal and cultural origin, I apply the term rule throughout the remainder of the article.

All in all, my goal is to locate briefly the 'spirit' of Tashkent's approach by inferring the rules of the game and applying them to TAPOich negotiations. It is important to be aware, however, that a logic of appropriateness does not provide a complete and total depiction of events as they once transpired, insofar as rules are general standards, and access to individual motives and decisions is lacking. The logic does, however, allow one to take local practices seriously without imposing homogenous preferences upon local elites.

### *Rules and the logic of appropriateness: self-reliance*

Self-reliance (*mustaqillik*) is the 'spirit' of Tashkent's approach to political economy and provides underlying coherence to the 'game'. Likewise, Gleason once suggested that Uzbekistan endorsed 'self-reliance' as an economic policy, focused on self-sufficiency and gradual economic reform (Gleason 2003, 119). Self-reliance is indeed the more apt way of understanding *mustaqillik*, the political–economic approach taken by Tashkent since the 1990s. *Mustaqillik* has more often been labelled 'national independence', but the translation, while not incorrect, evades a few relevant distinctions between *mustaqillik* and *istiqlol*. The latter can also be understood as independence, but in the more formal and legal sense, whereas *mustaqillik* implies a sort of genuine independence through legal, economic and cultural forms of non-dependency (Abdullayev et al. 2009, 148–149; Teles Fazendeiro 2015a). To that effect, several, especially post-colonial, regimes once invoked similar self-reliant labels.[5] I am aware, however, that other categories, like 'non-aligned', may also capture the 'spirit' of Tashkent's rules and that categorizing them under a single label is not without its own set of problems, as it may often over-determine explanation and the direction of a narrative (Teles Fazendeiro 2015b). But the point is merely to identify the 'spirit' and thus find a typology capable of capturing the rules that shape Uzbekistan's political economy. Furthermore, for reasons of space, my goal is to show what those general rules are and how they shape interaction, rather than explain their origin, since there are already several contributions that shed light on their history and evolution (e.g., Allworth 1990; Critchlow 1991; Sengupta 2003).

To find uncover the rules, I shall verify the key aims of Uzbekistan's legal system by cross-checking them with Karimov's speeches and written works, including the more tacit practices inferred by scholarship. Being one of the more important spokesmen of Uzbekistan's ruling elites, the focus on Karimov is aimed at pinpointing the goals and thus the basis on which the rules were justified. There are, in any case, other thorough contributions on Uzbek political–economic rules and practices (Kaser 1997; Bohr 1998; Luong and Weinthal 2001; Rosenberg and Zeeuw 2001; March 2002, 2003; Pomfret 2006; Spechler 2008; Özcan 2010). I categorize briefly those rules in what follows so as to narrate Uzbek–Russian interaction in the context of TAPOich.

### *The 'spirit' of self-reliance and its political–economic rules*

Uzbekistan's 'spirit' of self-reliance is characterized by the following core rules: pursuing economic growth via *mercantilism* and promoting the *manufacturing sector*; reaching *self-sufficiency*; securing *control* and *stability*.

*Mercantilism*

Instead of pursuing quick economic programmes dictated by the International Monetary Fund (IMF) and the World Bank, Uzbekistan chose to follow limited reforms. Self-reliance is predicated on mercantilism, to which Karimov often made reference in the 1990s:

> I said this about a thousand times, and I would like to repeat it again: a country has a future, is able to achieve progress and positive results and get stronger only if it earns more money in foreign currency than it spends buying things, that is, if exports exceed imports. (quoted in BBC 1999a)

Although the statement does not necessarily reflect an explicit endorsement of mercantilism, it does evince a certain disdain for a negative balance of trade. Moreover, as Rosenberg and Zeeuw (2001, 160–161) pointed out, a variety of local currency restrictions sought to impose import substitution in order to promote self-sufficiency and to ensure that the balance of trade tilted towards promoting exports, particularly in the manufacturing sector.

*Promoting the manufacturing sector*

The restrictions promoting mercantilism also privileged the manufacturing sector over the tertiary one. The latter, especially Uzbekistan's financial market, continues to be less open to foreigners: the banking sector is heavily regulated and the foreign exchange rate system remains tightly controlled (Rosenberg and Zeeuw 2001; Blackmon 2007). However, import substitution was not meant to result in autarky. On the contrary, Karimov stipulated that one of the reasons for cooperating with the West was for the sake of obtaining technology and developing the industrial sector:

> cooperation with the western world paves the way for high technology, investment in the basic sectors of industry and the comprehensive utilization of natural resources. Of particular significance for Uzbekistan is foreign assistance in the training of personnel (especially in banking and management). (Karimov 1992b, 32)

Of course, the emphasis on obtaining Western investment should not be over-emphasized, as that interest waned substantially in the late 1990s by virtue of complicated political–economic relations. In any case, obtaining international investment for the industrial sector never waned fully, insofar as Uzbekistan always pursued and maintained ties with several key partners, such as South Korea (Fumagalli 2012). The financial sector, by contrast, focused only on training and was barely open to international business. In addition to rhetorical appeals for investment, Tashkent demands an influx of at least US$150,000 and 30% of capital ownership if it is to qualify as foreign investment (LexUz 1996c). Such large initial sums tend to privilege industry more than the typical smaller-scale businesses of the service sector. In effect, the regulations and rhetorical demands are suited to large-scale projects, such as those of the manufacturing sector.

*Self-sufficiency*

From an economic point of view, promoting the manufacturing sector and endorsing mercantilism is compatible with a form of political–economic self-sufficiency. The focus on restricting imports also fits nicely with the persistent appeal for economic non-dependency:

> a country which only produces and sells raw materials is doomed to chronic misery. Our major task is to radically restructure the economy and introduce a structure capable of securing Uzbekistan's economic and political independence, taking into account all of our resources. (Karimov 1992b, 51)

The government disdained relying exclusively on the production of raw materials, including cotton, on which much of its exports depended, an aim that was, as shown below, easier said than done. And no doubt, from the political perspective, economic self-sufficiency ran parallel with Tashkent's pursuit of freedom from political–military entanglements, all of which is enshrined in Article 6 of Uzbekistan's foreign policy law (LexUz 1996d) and espoused in its membership of the Non-Aligned Movement.

*Control*

Self-reliance also envisioned strong central guidance and supervision. Currency restrictions (Rosenberg and Zeeuw 2001; Blackmon 2007) and laws supervising foreign workers (LexUz 1996b) were nothing other than means of ensuring control. Key exports, like cotton, remained strictly regulated by Tashkent (Kandiyoti 2002) and most foreign investments often required a substantial share of state participation. Research on local practices also reveals the strong role played by bureaucracy (Suhir and Kovach 2003), which only reinforced Tashkent's capacity to control events and the direction of the political economy. With regard to political reform, March (2002, 373) also noted that occasional praises of democracy and market economy were heavily caveated, portrayed more as an aim for a distant future than a short-term objective. Keeping control was thus a core rule, which Karimov admits openly: 'firmness, an authoritarian approach, if you wish, in realization of the chartered policy is needed in the transition period' (quoted in BBC 1993). In fact, control never ceased to be a priority and was further enforced by rejecting political pluralism:

> it would hardly be possible to describe as constructive the opposition of ambitious people who consider themselves offended not to be given cherished positions within the government, and who in pursuing clan and local interests oppose everybody and everything that happens in the country. (Karimov 1997, 108)

Pluralism is then restricted by laws that limit political associations (Fierman 1997, 374), foreign non-governmental organizations (NGOs) (Ilkhamov 2005, 298) and also by the everyday espousal of ideological monism, such as teaching *mustaqillik* and *mana'viyat* (morality) in Uzbekistan's school system.[6]

*Stability*

All these rules of the game are to be practised in accordance with stability. In fact, control and mercantilism overlap with the promotion of stability, and vice versa. By observing local practices, Gül Berna Özcan shows how entrepreneurs in Uzbekistan operate according to a stratified 'Mikado game', the stability of which is its chief characteristic (Özcan 2010, 52–53). Özcan rightly points out that the core rules are top-down, based on ensuring strict governmental control, balancing coalitions and thus maintaining stability. Rent-seeking, syndicates or mafia-like organizations may be tolerated, or even encouraged, so long as they 'do not openly clash with the political authorities and the presidential regime' (Özcan 2010, 166). For that reason, maintaining stability prevents any industry – or other economic endeavours for that matter – from tilting the balance of the Mikado game. Of course, stability, while crucial, should not be over-emphasized and does not always trump all other rules. While stability is to be maintained, the government of Uzbekistan still pursues political–economic investment from many partners, such as China and Russia in 2006, when relations with other states deteriorated. Seeking stability does not therefore imply complete isolation, though it does contribute to insulating Uzbekistan from the IPE and ensures governmental control over the country's more profitable sectors.

## TAPOich and self-reliance: Russian–Uzbek tensions and cooperation

Self-reliance consists of a core set of rules with which to interpret and then narrate Uzbekistan's international engagement. TAPOich is therefore one amongst several complex subject matters shaping Uzbek–Russian relations. In its heyday, before Perestroika, the plant employed 30,000 workers (Lembrez 2011) and was one of the largest aircraft production centres in the whole of the Soviet Union. Aviation was a major export and also a tremendous source of pride, legitimacy and prestige before the collapse of the Soviet Union (Bailes 1976), much like all other large-scale technological projects sponsored by Moscow right up to 1991 (Josephson 1995).

Named after Valerii Chkalov, one of the greatest aviation heroes of the former Soviet Union, the factory was founded originally in Moscow in 1932, moving to Uzbekistan in 1941 so as to avoid being destroyed during the Second World War. TAPOich later specialized in the production of Ilyushin-type aircraft and was one of the only plants in the former Soviet space with both the experience and the capacity to produce large cargo airplanes in scale. But, in order to improve production and promote exports, TAPOich and the airplanes it manufactured were in dire need of modernization in the early 1990s, a difficult task due to the collapse of the Soviet Union, foreign competition and the fact that Russia's renowned 'experimental design bureaus' (*Opytnoye Konstruktorskoye Buro* – OKB) were beset by political and administrative obstacles (Hendley 1998).

Despite the hurdles, aviation was congruent with self-reliance. On top of that, President Karimov is also apparently committed to aviation. Prior to his political prominence, he was an employee of TAPOich (Jo'rayev and Fayzullayev 2000, 43) and local sources suggest that he continues to be interested in the future of the sector (Aviation Week and Space Technology 1998). Personal preferences aside, the Uzbek government founded Uzbekistan Airways (UA) and bought modern passenger aircraft from Boeing right after independence. At the time, TAPOich was unable to fulfil an order of that magnitude, as its manufacturing capacity was geared toward producing large cargo airplanes and smaller passenger aircraft. And so, to what extent was TAPOich's future compatible with self-reliance? To answer this question, I concentrate on Tashkent's approach to IPE in order to highlight how it affected bilateral cooperation. In the conclusion I discuss briefly the impact of Moscow's own rules and the extent to which they also affected bilateral interaction.

### *TAPOich struggling to remain alive and to develop export capacity*

In accordance with self-reliance, TAPOich was not privatized quickly after the collapse of the Soviet Union. It was 'de-nationalized' only in April 1996 (LexUz 1996a), although most of the company remained under Tashkent's strict governmental control: 10% was allocated to workers of the company; and the National Bank for Foreign Economic Activity and the Ministry of Foreign Economic Relations were granted 6.7% each. Indeed, the importance of keeping national control over the company was stipulated in the charter, approved by Uzbekistan's Cabinet of Ministers in 1993, which required TAPOich to be a state-held enterprise (LexUz 1993).[7]

Control and stability were kept for the meantime, and so the authorities in Tashkent explored ways of promoting those exports. The Ilyushin cargo planes (Il-76), of both civilian and military varieties, in addition to smaller passenger/cargo varieties (Il-114), were promising designs. Their production consisted of research conducted at Ilyushin headquarters in Moscow and the assembly of the main components by TAPOich. Collaboration between Russia and Uzbekistan was therefore necessary if TAPOich were to survive. By 1994, the first prototype of the modified Il-76MF cargo plane was built and certified by the International Civilian Aviation Organisation (ICAO) (Komissarov and Gordon 2001, 25–27). Both parties cooperated and problematic issues were temporarily sidelined or at least not publicly discussed. To that effect, during Il-76MF's maiden flight in August 1995, the plane was designated with alternative prefixes and painted with both the flags of Uzbekistan and Russia to avoid disagreements on ownership (Gordon and Komissarov 2001). Indeed, so long as control was not questioned, cooperating with the Ilyushin complex was both necessary and congruent with Uzbekistan's self-reliance.

Thereafter, the Cabinet of Ministers routinely sent out warnings to staff in the 1990s, calling for better promotional campaigns abroad (LexUz 1999). Uzbekistan's government also created a leasing company to facilitate TAPOich exports (LexUz 1997b) and approached foreign governments and international agencies, such as the US Trade and Development Agency, to secure financial assistance (Aviation Daily, 1996).[8]

In spite of the promotional campaigns, TAPOich did not give rise to much foreign interest in the 1990s. Other challenges also gradually came to the fore after Moscow and Tashkent discussed the future of the company and its role within the Russian aviation sector. By 1997, Moscow decided to fuse all major Ilyushin production facilities and TAPOich was considered to be a natural member of that consortium. The future of the company and Uzbekistan's aviation sector was thus finally being questioned and some sort of long-term bilateral compromise was necessary (BBC 2003). Tashkent signalled, however, that it would not relinquish its commitment to self-reliance easily, thereby demanding US$300 million if it were to give up control over the facility. Negotiations stagnated thereafter, although a temporary solution was proposed in May 2001, as Putin and Karimov agreed to use TAPOich jointly (RIA 2001).

### *TAPOich gains new life: where to produce aircraft?*

With the new Il-76 and Il-114 fully modernized in the late 1990s, Tashkent remained reluctant to relinquish its control over the company, especially if Moscow was also reluctant or simply unable to offer a significant concession. In the meantime, and in accordance with self-sufficiency, Tashkent began supplying its own airline, UA, with small passenger aircraft assembled in TAPOich. In a deal worth US$21.5 million, UA procured three new Il-114–110 in 2001, and then again more aircraft in 2005.[9]

In spite of its promise as a small-scale passenger aircraft, the Il-114–100 captured little attention abroad. It was the larger transport airplanes that were potential sources of export and also the reason for increased bilateral friction between Moscow and Tashkent, especially after India agreed to import six Il-78 refuelling aircraft in December 2001. After years of stagnant orders, TAPOich was finally operating again. And yet, by 2003, bilateral disagreements over how to share royalties escalated and became public knowledge (Lantratov 2003). All things considered, Tashkent would have to negotiate the extent to which it could control Ilyushin production and its share of profits.

Later, in May 2004, Russia's foreign minister met with Uzbekistan's government with a view to discussing the future of Il-76MF production, amongst other pressing issues. Like in the late 1990s, Moscow envisaged including TAPOich in the Ilyushin production complex, but Tashkent refused to give up control over the plant (BBC 2004). The issue entered the public spotlight and was liable to increase bilateral dissent. As pressure increased, Karimov spoke on the matter in January 2005, claiming that Moscow was not seeking to relocate Ilyushin production:

> it is produced only at *our* plant. This plant has cooperative ties to 2000 enterprises in Russia, but people inexplicably choose to avoid talking about that. It is impossible for the whole production cycle of that kind of aircraft to be confined within a single country. (quoted in BBC 2005; emphasis added)

By 2005, however, Putin sought to promote the Russian aircraft sector as well as manage the transfer of technical expertise abroad. In order to fulfil those goals, Moscow decided in February 2006 to merge all major aircraft producers under one holding company: the United Aircraft Corporation (*Obyedinyonnaya Aviastroitelnaya Korporatsiya* – OAK). TAPOich was meant to be part of OAK, which further deviated from Tashkent's rules of the 'game'. In other words, Uzbekistan's authorities would probably have to give up their aim of controlling TAPOich fully if they were not to lose Ilyushin technology and the capacity to produce aircraft.

### *No compromise: TAPOich eventually ceases to be an aircraft producer*

Moscow's decision to consolidate all major aircraft plants under one company made the need for a stable long-term agreement all the more urgent. On top of that, Azerbaijan, Jordan and China showed interest in and eventually ordered the Il-76MF. China's order was by far the most promising, consisting of 38 new airplanes worth US$1.5 billion (Flight International 2005). At the time, TAPOich remained the only plant with the capacity to fulfil the order. But, for reasons that are not yet clear, Tashkent suspended the assemblage of all Il-76MF exported to China. Some public reports suggest that the price settled by Moscow barely covered Tashkent's share of the costs, although Russian officials blamed the delay on the plant's managerial incompetence (Stepanov 2007; TASS 2009). Whatever the reason, Moscow was convinced by December 2006 that all future Il-76 production was to be relocated to Ulynanovsk in Russia (BBC 2007). From Moscow's perspective, its government and companies would no longer have to depend on third parties (Evseev 2013).

With Il-76MF production transitioning away from Uzbekistan, the frailty of Tashkent's self-reliance became all the more visible. Tashkent was no longer capable of sustaining aircraft exports, maintaining the stability of the sector and controlling the direction of the industry. It would have to concede more if the sector were to remain intact. Integration was therefore one of the only promising solutions, not least because Moscow's decision to relocate Il-76MF production did not yet entail the 'death' of TAPOich. Tashkent could still make the Il-114 and thus continue to produce them locally. Of course, that brought another pressing issue to future negotiations: the level of IL-114 production would determine if any sort of compromise was to be reached (Wikileaks 2009). Karimov visited Moscow in January 2008, where he admitted that Tashkent was ready to concede. According to press reports, a settlement was agreed upon, by which Tashkent swapped 50% of its stake in TAPOich, plus one additional share, for a smaller stake in OAK (BBC 2008). Tashkent conceded and in turn obtained a small say in the Russian aviation sector. The outcome seemed promising, but Tashkent demanded more guarantees. Rather than working within the context of OAK, Tashkent's rules of the 'game', such as mercantilism, meant remaining a steady exporter of Il-114. Local authorities took that possibility seriously, and American embassy telegrams reveal the extent to which Tashkent sought to obtain a written agreement from Boeing in order to pressure Moscow (Wikileaks 2008).

In the end, however, the negotiations came to little or no avail, for no satisfactory Il-114 production quotas were settled from Tashkent's perspective. Having TAPOich relocated to OAK meant relinquishing control over the plant with no additional guarantees of sustained growth in the aircraft sector. It would in effect turn Tashkent into a junior partner and make the sector almost completely dependent on Moscow.

With no compromise, TAPOich eventually came into increasing financial difficulties, declaring bankruptcy in 2010. According to Uzbek law, the plant was to come under administrative supervision (Ferghana 2010). Moreover, once TAPOich delivered the last Il-76MF to Jordan in the summer of 2011, Deputy Prime Minister Sergei Ivanov confirmed that it would be the last ever type of aircraft to be made in Tashkent, for the Ulynanovsk plant in Russia was now ready for production (Defense and Security 2011). Self-reliance in the aviation sector all but faded with Moscow publicly transferring production elsewhere.

In the end, the TAPOich compound remained under Tashkent's control. The government began restructuring the company with a view to promoting automobile production, and thus sought investment and assistance from General Motors and Daimler Mercedes (LexUz 2010). Manufacturing and promoting exports still shaped TAPOich's future, although production was no longer to be based on aviation. With TAPOich delivering the last Il-114–100 to UA in 2013, Uzbekistan's future as a major aircraft producer was indefinitely put on hold. The company was subsequently released from bankruptcy proceedings and re-designated as the Tashkent Mechanical Plant in January 2014.

**Conclusions**

A narrative plotted initially by a logic of appropriateness reveals much about action. The events and the complex negotiating dynamics focus more on the rules than on the decision-makers without positing ad hoc preferences, like survival or rent-seeking. The logic of appropriateness also reveals that the 'spirit of the game' – keeping control, manufacturing, promoting exports and maintaining self-sufficiency – was the means by which long-term bilateral cooperation in the aviation sector was hindered. Tashkent acted according to those rules and TAPOich was, for that reason, unable to integrate fully with the Russian aviation sector. Of course, this is not to say that Moscow's position was entirely innocent, rather that Tashkent's rules and the way they influenced action were not entirely amenable to mutual cooperation. Moscow, of course, had its own rules and gradually became set on consolidating the sector in order to control exports, deliveries and technological secrets, all of which affected Tashkent's own long-term aspirations. And yet, Moscow did also make concessions, such as providing Tashkent with a stake, if only a small one, in OAK. But the authorities in Uzbekistan stuck to keeping full control over the future of the plant and to pursuing manufacturing guarantees elsewhere. What this outcome also highlights is that the focus on mercantilism, in conjunction with the reluctance to make concessions, made Tashkent more of a competitor than a partner of Moscow. Read in this way, the narrative almost amounts to a struggle over status, predicated on avoiding dependency.

While a narrative plotted by a logic of appropriateness reveals much about the key features of the bilateral relationship, it is important not to neglect the limitations of the story and the potential for further research. A logic of appropriateness neglects individual decision-makers almost by default, and so specific actions, like Tashkent suspending the multi-millionaire contract with China, are open to further empirical research: why was it interrupted at that moment in time; and what role did it play in future bilateral negotiations? That said, while there is room for applying a logic of consequences, it is important not to overstate the argument of instrumental action. The narrative could, of course, be reinterpreted by imposing ad hoc preferences upon the elites, such as survival or rent-seeking, although that would barely account for the specificity of Uzbekistan's approach to IPE. Had the narrative initially been based on a logic of consequences, whereby actions are explained through rent-seeking and survival, then there would be little, if any, need to account for self-sufficiency and mercantilism; individuals in power would fulfil their aspirations – in this case, survival – without necessarily abiding by the rules of the 'game'. But that then begs the following question: could further integration with Russia not also ensure the survival of the aviation sector? Without referring first to the spirit of the game and thus the rules on which action was predicated, the question would remain unanswered. In any case, there is always room for applying a logic of consequences. TAPOich may well have been one amongst several issues that Tashkent was negotiating at the time, and thus being adamant about keeping control could have been instrumental in obtaining concessions elsewhere. Indeed, a strong and uncompromising stance guarantees enough leeway for negotiating new business opportunities, such as repairing Russian aircraft or other potentially profitable contracts (Evseev 2013). Either way, the point is not that a logic consequences is irrelevant, rather that a logic of appropriateness remains the more compelling starting point for understanding action. There is no need to impose ad-hoc preferences to make sense of what is happening locally. The future of TAPOich was predicated on self-reliance, a compilation of political–economic rules that were not entirely in keeping with steady bilateral cooperation after the end of the Soviet Union.

Lastly, in the light of the repercussions of self-reliance, it is worth pondering whether alternatives were feasible. The thought experiment is certainly pertinent insofar as a less rigid negotiating position may have opened the way for sustainable bilateral cooperation. Of course, that alternative has its own trade-offs. Although self-reliance hindered collaboration, it did allow Tashkent to control the plant in the short run and remain self-sufficient, to a degree. Capital and some expertise were kept locally, even if only temporarily, and UA's fleet currently consists of seven Il-114 models – all assembled in Uzbekistan. Had control and stability not been priorities, Tashkent may well have been unable to supply UA with aircraft 'made in Uzbekistan' and to continue exporting technology nearly ten years after the end of the Soviet Union. So, the narrative has more than one layer of complexity. Put differently, self-reliance was not entirely unreasonable, not least because there is nothing to suggest that Moscow was initially amenable to making Uzbekistan a stakeholder in what it gradually came to see as its own aviation sector.

Counterfactuals aside, it is important to bear in mind that Uzbekistan adheres to a strict set of rules that affected and still affect its political–economic development. The emphasis on large industrial projects, coupled with both the reluctance to concede and the ambition to become a major exporter, were not entirely compatible with economic integration. That 'spirit of the game' had both costs and benefits, of course, although TAPOich could hardly avoid that it was dependent on Russian support. So, in the end, self-reliance barely fostered mutual good will, which was necessary for sustaining Uzbekistan's aviation sector.

## Acknowledgements

The author is grateful to Gül Berna Özcan and the reviewers for the invaluable feedback provided. The author is also grateful to Naomi Teles Fazendeiro for the helpful editing; as well as Rustam Navoiy, who very patiently assisted in translating key passages.

## Disclosure statement

No potential conflict of interest was reported by the author.

## Notes

1. In the mid-1990s public friction was visible between both states, followed by increasing political and economic cooperation once Vladimir Putin became Russia's president in 2000; which was then succeeded by Tashkent's decision to exit and suspend membership of Russian-sponsored organizations, such as the Eurasian Economic Community (Eurasec) in 2008 and the Collective Security Treaty Organisation (CSTO) in 2012. For more on Uzbek–Russian relations, including Russia's engagement with Central Asia more broadly, see Jonson (2001), Allison (2004), Perovic (2005); Fumagalli (2007), Spechler and Spechler (2009), Cooley (2012), and Pikalov (2014).
2. Lembrez (2011), for instance, looks into TAPOich, but focuses on anthropology rather than on political–economy.
3. The only material applied herein that was confidential at the time of those negotiations was telegrams later leaked by Wikileaks. To plot the narrative and explain the events as they happened, I applied those sources and a logic of appropriateness. Where access to the minds of the negotiators were not possible, the logic provides the narrative with a direction, including the underlying reasons why bilateral relations evolved in the way they did in the context of TAPOich.
4. Whether Karimov has been able to centralize control remains questionable. It is not entirely clear how power remains distributed among different actors, though scholarship agrees that there are 'clans' (Collins 2006), regional power (Luong 2002) or patrimonial (Ilkhamov 2005) networks, as well as a mesh of other relations (Tunçer-Kilavuz 2009), all of which form, compete or overlap with each other.
5. For more on self-reliance as a political–economic typology, see Holsti (1982, 4) and Turku (2009). For the use of the term 'self-reliance' by other states, see, for example, Michael Yahuda's account of Maoist political ideology (Yahuda 1983, 53).

6. Works on independence ideology (*Mustaqillik Mafkurasi*) – like school manuals (e.g., Ortiqov 2009) and history books (e.g., Jo'rayev and Fayzullayev 2000) – quote Karimov extensively.
7. Tashkent did eventually open 25.6% of the company's shares to foreign ownership in 1998, although it later cancelled the tender after no substantial offers were made (TASS, 24 November 2004).
8. The appeal for Western technology paid off eventually: by the mid-1990s, the newer Il-114–100 aircraft were to be equipped with Canadian Pratt and Whitney PW-127H engines (Flight International 1999, 53).
9. By 2014, UA had seven Il-114–100 in its fleet, the last of which was delivered in May 2013.

## References


Abdullayev, M. et al. 2009. *Self-Reliance: Popular-Scientific Glossary* [*Mustaqillik: Izohli ilmiy-ommabop lug'at*]. Tashkent: Sharq.

Allison, R. 2004. "Strategic Reassertion in Russia's Central Asia Policy." *International Affairs* 80 (2): 277–293. doi:10.1111/j.1468-2346.2004.00383.x

Allworth, E. 1990. *The Modern Uzbeks from the Fourteenth Century to the Present: A Cultural History*. Stanford: Hoover University Press.

Anceschi, L. 2010. "Integrating Domestic Politics and Foreign Policy Making: The cases of Turkmenistan and Uzbekistan." *Central Asian Survey* 29 (2): 143–158. doi:10.1080/02634937.2010.498231

Aviation Daily. 1996. "TDA Signs Grant to Promote Aviation Exports, June 25. Accessed April 2012. http://Lexisnexis.co.uk.

Aviation Week and Space Technology. 1998. "Uzbekistan Airways Rebuilds Its Central Asian Hub". April 1998. Accessed April 2012. http://Lexisnexis.co.uk.

Bailes, K. E. 1976. "Technology and Legitimacy: Soviet Aviation and Stalinism in the 1930s." *Technology and Culture* 17 (1): 55–81. doi:10.2307/3103253

BBC (BBC Summary of World Broadcasts). 1993. "Uzbekistan; Karimov Defends his policies against accusations of strong-arm tactics". June 12. Accessed April 2012. http://Lexisnexis.co.uk.

BBC. 1999a. "Uzbek President Sums up 1998 Economic results". February 16. Accessed April 2012. http://Lexisnexis.co.uk.

BBC. 1999b. "Russian Premier Visits Uzbek Aircraft Factory, Russian Theatre". December 11. Accessed April 2012. http://Lexisnexis.co.uk.

BBC. 2003. "Transfer of Il-76 Manufacture from Uzbekistan to Russia "Political Issue". September 12. Accessed April 2012. http://Lexisnexis.co.uk.

BBC. 2004. "Defence Minister's Visit Shows Russia Still has Role in Uzbekistan's security. May 13. Accessed April 2012. http://Lexisnexis.co.uk.

BBC. 2005. "Uzbek Gives Wide-Ranging Interview to Russian Paper". January 20. Accessed April 2012. http://Lexisnexis.co.uk. [Original in Nezavisimaya Gazeta, 14 Jan 05].

BBC. 2007. "First Russian-assembled Il-76 aircraft expected in 2010". May 14. Accessed May 2014. http://Lexisnexis.co.uk.

BBC. 2008. "Russian, Uzbek Cooperation accords signs". February 6. Accessed May 2014. http://Lexisnexis.co.uk.

Berman, I. 2004. "The New Battleground: Central Asia and the Caucasus." *Washington Quarterly* 28 (1): 59–69. doi:10.1162/0163660042518134

Blackmon, P. 2007. "Divergent Paths, Divergent Outcomes: Linking Differences In Economic Reforms to Levels of US Foreign Direct Investment and Business in Kazakhstan and Uzbekistan." *Central Asian Survey* 26 (3): 355–372. doi:10.1080/02634930701702563

Bohr, A. 1998. *Uzbekistan Politics and Foreign Policy*. London: The Royal Institute of International Affairs.

Cohen, B. J. 2008. *International Political Economy: An Intellectual History*. Princeton: Princeton University Press.

Collins, K. 2006. *Clan Politics and Regime Transition in Central Asia*. Cambridge: Cambridge University Press.

Collins, K. 2005. "Political and Institutional Constraints and Opportunities for Regional Cooperation. *UNDP: Bringing Down the Barriers: Regional Cooperation for Human Development and Human Security*. Central Asia Human Development Report.

Cooley, A. 2012. *Great Games, Locals Rules: The New Great Power Contest in Central Asia*. Oxford: Oxford University Press.

Cooley, A., and J. Heathershaw. 2014. "Dictators without Borders." *Open Democracy*. Accessed May 2014. https://www.opendemocracy.net/od-russia/john-heathershaw-alexander-cooley/dictators-without-borders.

Critchlow, J. 1991. *Nationalism in Uzbekistan: A Soviet Republic's Road to Sovereignty.* London: Westerview Press.

Defense and Security (Russia). 2011. "In Proud Solitude; Russian aircraft-building industry gave up cooperation with Uzbekistan." June 6. Accessed September 2012. http://Lexisnexis.co.uk.

Deyermond, R. 2009. "Matrioshka hegemony? Multi-levelled hegemonic competition and security in post-Soviet Central Asia." *Review of International Studies* 35: 151–173. doi:10.1017/S0260210509008365

Evseev, V. 2013. "O protivorechivosti rossi'skouzberksk otnoshenii v voennopoliticheskoi' sfere." *Mirovaia e'konomika i mezhdunarodnye otnosheniia* 6: 66–74.

Ferghana. 2010. "Uzbekistan: Tashkent Aircraft factory, named after Chkalov, goes bankrupt." October 13. Accessed November 2010. http://enews.fergananews.com/news.php?id=1878.

Fierman, W. 1997. "Political Development in Uzbekistan: Democratization?" In *Conflict, Cleavage and Change in Central Asia and the Caucasus*, edited by K. Dawish and B. Parrot, 360–408. Cambridge: Cambridge University Press.

Flight International. 1999. *Commercial Aircraft Directory*, August 25–31: 1–80.

Flight International. 2005. "Il-76 Transports and IL-78 Tankers Top $1.5bn Russia-China Arms deal", September 13. Accessed April 2012. http://Lexisnexis.co.uk.

Fumagalli, M. 2007. "Alignments and Realignments in Central Asia: The Rationale and Implications of Uzbekistan's Rapprochement with Russia." *International Political Science Review* 28 (3): 253–271. doi:10.1177/0192512107077098

Fumagalli, M. 2012. "South Korea's Engagement in Central Asia from the End of the Cold War to the 'New Asia Initiative." *The Journal of Northeast Asian History* 9 (2): 69–97.

Gadamer, H. G. 2013. *Truth and Method.* London: Bloomsbury.

Gleason, G. 2001. "Foreign Policy and Domestic Reform in Central Asia." *Central Asian Survey* 20 (2): 167–182. doi:10.1080/02634930120073488

Gleason, G. 2003. *Markets and Politics in Central Asia.* London: Routledge.

Hendley, K. 1998. "Struggling to Survive: A Case Study of Adjustment at a Russian Enterprise." *Europe-Asia Studies* 50 (1): 91–119. doi:10.1080/09668139808412525

Holsti, K. 1982. *Why Nations Realign: Foreign Policy Restructuring in the Postwar World.* London: George Allen & Uwin.

Hopf, T. 2010. "The Logic of Habit in IR." *European Journal of International Relations* 16 (4): 539–561. doi:10.1177/1354066110363502

Ilkhamov, A. 2005. "The Thorny Path of Civil Society in Uzbekistan." *Central Asian Survey* 24 (3): 297–317. doi:10.1080/02634930500310378

Jepperson, R., A. Wendt, and P. J. Katzenstein. 1996. "Norms, Identity and Culture in National Security." In *The Culture of National Security*, edited by Peter J. Katzenstein, 33–75. New York: Columbia University Press.

Jo'rayev, N., and T. Fayzullayev. 2000. *Mustaqil O'zbekiston Tarixi 3-Kitob* [The History of Independent Uzbekistan, book 3]. Tashkent: Sharq.

Jonson, L. 2001. "Russia and Central Asia." In *Central Asia Security: The New International Context*, edited by Roy Allison and Lena Jonson, 95–146. Washington: Brookings.

Josephson, P. R. 1995. "'Projects of the Century' in Soviet History: Large-Scale Technologies from Lenin to Gorbachev." *Technology and Culture* 36 (3): 519–559. doi:10.2307/3107240

Kandiyoti, D. 2002. "Agrarian Reform, Gender and Land Rights in Uzbekistan." *United Nations Social Policy and Development Programme, Paper* 11: 1–79.

Karimov, I. 1992a. "Milliy Manfaatlar Ustuvorling va Teng hukukli hamorlikka asoslangan Tashqi Siyosat [Supremacy of National Interests and Foreign Policy Based on Principle of Equal Partnership]." Vol. 1 of *O'zbekiston: Milliy Istiqlol, Iqtisod, Siyosat, Mafkura* [Uzbekistan, National Independence, Economy, Policy, Ideology]. Tashkent: O'zekiston, 1996, 50–61.

Karimov, I. 1992b. *Uzbekistan – the road of independence and progress.* Tashkent: Uzbekistan.

Karimov, I. 1997. *Uzbekistan on the Threshold of the Twenty-First Century.* London: Curzon Press.

Kaser, M. 1997. *The Economies of Kazakhstan and Uzbekistan.* London: The Royal Institute of International Affairs.

Kazemi, L. 2003. "Domestic Sources of Uzbekistan's Foreign Policy." *Journal of International Affairs* 56 (2): 205–216.

Komissarov, D., and Y. Gordon. 2001. *Ilyushin IL-76: Russia's Versatile Airlifter.* Hinkley: Midland Publishing.

Kratochwil, F. 1989. *Rules. Norms and Decisions: On the Conditions of Practical and Legal Reasoning in International Relations and Domestic Affairs*. Cambridge: Cambridge University Press.

Lantratov, K. 2003. "Russia and Uzbekistan share IL Aircraft". *Kommersant*, March 28. Accessed April 2012. http://Lexisnexis.co.uk.

Lembrez, M. 2011. "Identity and Solidarity in the Industrial District of Tashkent Aircraft Manufacturers [Identités et solidarités du quartier industriel des constructeurs aéronautiques de Tachkent]". *Cahiers d'Asie central.* Accessed September 2011. http://asiecentrale.revues.org/1466?lang=en.

Lewis, D. 2008. *The Temptations of Tyranny in Central Asia*. London: Hurst & Company.

LexUz. 1993. "Approval of the Tashkent Aviation Production Association, named after V.P. Chkalov, Charter [ОБ УТВЕРЖДЕНИИ УСТАВА ТАШКЕНТСКОГО АВИАЦИОННОГО ПРОИЗВОДСТВЕННОГО ОБЪЕДИНЕНИЯ ИМЕНИ В.П.]", August 31. Accessed May 2014. http://LexUz.uz/.

LexUz. 1996a. "On Privatising the Tashkent Aviation Production Association [ОБ АКЦИОНИРОВАНИИ ТАШКЕНТСКОГО АВИАЦИОННОГО ПРОИЗВОДСТВЕННОГО ОБЪЕДИНЕНИЯ ИМЕНИ В.П.ЧКАЛОВА]", April 18. Accessed May 2014. http://LexUz.uz/.

LexUz. 1996b. "On the Application of 'Regulations on the Employment of Foreign Labour Force in the Republic of Uzbekistan[О ПОРЯДКЕ ПРИМЕНЕНИЯ «ПОЛОЖЕНИЯ О ПОРЯДКЕ ПРИВЛЕЧЕНИЯ И ИСПОЛЬЗОВАНИЯ ИНОСТРАННОЙ РАБОЧЕЙ СИЛЫ В РЕСПУБЛИКЕ УЗБЕКИСТАН»], November 20. Accessed May 2014. http://LexUz.uz/.

LexUz. 1996c. "On Additional Incentives and Privileges Granted to Enterprises with Foreign Investments [О ДОПОЛНИТЕЛЬНЫХ СТИМУЛАХ И ЛЬГОТАХ, ПРЕДОСТАВЛЯЕМЫХ ПРЕДПРИЯТИЯМ С ИНОСТРАННЫМИ ИНВЕСТИЦИЯМИ]", November 30. Accessed May 2014. http://LexUz.uz/.

LexUz. 1996d. "On the Basic Principles of Uzbekistan's Foreign Activities [ОБ ОСНОВНЫХ ПРИНЦИПАХ ВНЕШНЕПОЛИТИЧЕСКОЙ ДЕЯТЕЛЬНОСТИ РЕСПУБЛИКИ УЗБЕКИСТАН]", December 26. Accessed April 2014. http://LexUz.uz/.

LexUz. 1997a. "On the Uzbek Part of the joint Uzbek–Russian Commission on Multilateral Cooperation [Об образовании Узбекской части совместной Узбекско-Российской комиссии по вопросам расширения многостороннего сотрудничества]", February 24. Accessed April 2014. http://LexUz.uz/.

LexUz. 1997b. "About Creating the Shareholder leasing company 'UZAVIALIZING' [О СОЗДАНИИ АКЦИОНЕРНОЙ ЛИЗИНГОВОЙ КОМПАНИИ «УЗАВИАЛИЗИНГ»], December 19. Accessed April 2014. http://LexUz.uz/.

LexUz. 1999. "On Socio-Economic Development for 1998, Appraisal of Economic Reforms and Economic Development of the main priorities in 1999 [ОБ ИТОГАХ СОЦИАЛЬНО-ЭКОНОМИЧЕСКОГО РАЗВИТИЯ РЕСПУБЛИКИ ЗА 1998 ГОД, ОЦЕНКЕ ХОДА ЭКОНОМИЧЕСКИХ РЕФОРМ И ОСНОВНЫХ ПРИОРИТЕТАХ РАЗВИТИЯ ЭКОНОМИКИ В 1999 ГОДУ]", February 23. Accessed April 2014. http://LexUz.uz/.

LexUz. 2010. "Measures to Ensure the Modernisation of Industrial Areas for Foreign Investments and the Production of 'Mercedes-Benz' buses' [О мерах по обеспечению реконструкции производственных площадей предприятия с иностранными инвестициями по производству автобусов «Мерседес-Бенц»]. June 25. Accessed April 2014. http://LexUz.uz/.

Luong, P. J. 2002. *Institutional Change and Political Continuity in Post-Soviet Central Asia: Power, Perception and Pacts*. Cambridge: Cambridge University Press.

Luong, P. J., and E. Weinthal. 2001. "Prelude to the Resource Curse: Explaining Oil and Gas Development Strategies in the Soviet Successor States and Beyond." *Comparative Political Studies* 34 (4): 367–399. doi:10.1177/0010414001034004002

Marat, E. 2006. "The State-Crime Nexus in Central Asia: State Weakeness, Organized Crime, and Corruption in Kyrgyzstan and Tajikistan." Silk Road Paper. Washington DC: Central-Asian Caucasus Institute.

March, A. 2002. "The Use and Abuse of History: 'National Ideology' as Transcendental Object in Islam Karimov's 'Ideology of National Independence'." *Central Asian Survey* 21 (4): 371–384. doi:10.1080/0263493032000053190

March, A. 2003. "From Leninism to Karimovism: Hegemony, Ideology, and Authoritarian Legitimation." *Post-Soviet Affairs* 19 (4): 307–336. doi:10.2747/1060-586X.19.4.307

March, J. G., and J. P. Olsen. 2005. "The Logic of Appropriateness." In *The Oxford Handbook of Public Policy*, edited by M. Rein, M. Moran, R. E. Godin, 689–708. Oxford: Oxford University Press.

Müller, H. 2004. "Arguing, Bargaining and All That: Communicative Action, Rationalist Theory and the Logic of Appropriateness in International Relations." *European Journal of International Relations* 10 (3): 395–435. doi:10.1177/1354066104045542

Ortiqov, M., ed. 2009. *Milliy Istiqlol G'oyasi [The Idea of National Independence]*. Tashkent: Toshkent Shahri Matbuotchilar.

Özcan, G. B. 2010. *Building States and Markets: Enterprise Development in Central Asia*. New York: Palgrave Macmillan.

Perovic, J. 2005. "From Disengagement to Active Economic Competition: Russia's Return to the South Caucasus and Central Asia." *Demokratizatsiya* 13 (1): 61–86. doi:10.3200/DEMO.13.1.61-86

Pikalov, A. 2014. "Uzbekistan between the Great Powers: A Balancing Act or a Multi-Vectorial Approach?" *Central Asian Survey* 33 (3): 297–311. doi:10.1080/02634937.2014.930580

Pomfret, R. 2006. *The Central Asian Political Economies since Independence*. Princeton: Princeton University Press.

Pouliot, V. 2008. "The Logic of Practicality: A Theory of Practice of Security Communities." *International Organization* 62: 257–288. doi:10.1017/S0020818308080090

Radnitz, S. 2010. *Weapons of the Wealthy: Predatory Regimes and Elite-led Protests in Central Asia*. Cornell University: Cornell University Press.

RIA (RIA Novosti). 2001. "Presidents of Russia and Uzbekistan Sign Joint Statement". May 4. Accessed April 2012. Retrieved from http://Lexisnexis.co.uk.

Rosenberg, C., and M. Zeeuw. 2001. "Welfare Effects of Uzbekistan's Exchange Rate Regime." *IMF Staff Papers* 48 (1): 160–178.

Ruziev, K., D. Ghosh and S. C. Dow. 2007. "The Uzbek Puzzle Revisited: An analysis of Economic Performance in Uzbekistan since 1991." *Central Asian Survey* 26 (1): 7–30. doi:10.1080/02634930701423400

Schutz, A. 1964. "The Dimensions of the Social World." In *Collected Papers II: Studies in Social Theory*, edited by A. Brodersen, 20–63. The Hague: Martinus Nijoff.

Sending, O. 2002. "Constitution, Choice and Change: Problems with the 'Logic of Appropriateness' and its Use in Constructivist Theory." *European Journal of International Relations* 8 (4): 443–470. doi:10.1177/1354066102008004001

Sengupta, A. 2003. *The Formation of the Uzbek Nation-State*. London: Lexington Books.

Smith, J. 2009. "The Great Game, Round Three." *Journal of International Security Affairs* 17. http://www.ciaonet.org/catalog/18676.

Spechler, M. 2008. *The Political Economy of Reform in Central Asia: Uzbekistan under Authoritarianism*. Abingdon: Routledge.

Spechler, D., and M. Spechler. 2009. "Uzbekistan among the Great Powers." *Communist and Post-Communist Studies* 42: 353–373. doi:10.1016/j.postcomstud.2009.07.006

Spechler, D., and M. Spechler. 2010. "The Foreign Policy of Uzbekistan: Sources, Objectives and Outcomes: 1991–2009." *Central Asian Survey* 29 (2): 159–170. doi:10.1080/02634937.2010.490679

Stepanov, V. 2007. "IR Airplanes failed to make it to China; the Contract Signed in 2005 Turned Out to be Unprofitable." *Gazeta*, May 14. Accessed April 2012. http://Lexisnexis.co.uk.

Suhir, E., and Z. Kovach. 2003, June. "Administrative Barriers to Entrepreneurship in Central Asia." *Center for International Private Enterprise*, 30: 1–8.

TASS. 2009. "Russia Once Again Accused Uzbekistan of Ruining the Contract on Supply of Aircraft to China." November 23. Accessed May 2014. http://Lexisnexis.co.uk.

Teles Fazendeiro, B. 2015a. "Keeping Face in the Public Sphere: Recognition, Discretion and Uzbekistan's Relations with the United States and Germany,1991–2006." *Central Asian Survey* 34 (3): 341–356. doi:10.1080/02634937.2015.1015229

Teles Fazendeiro, B. 2015b. "Rethinking Roles: Reflexive Role-Ascription and Performativity in International Relations." *International Studies Review* (forthcoming).

Tunçer-Kilavuz, I. 2009. "Political and Social Networks in Tajikistan and Uzbekistan: 'clan', region and beyond." *Central Asia Survey* 28 (3): 323–334. doi:10.1080/02634930903445052

Turku, H. 2009. *Isolationist States in an Interdependent World*. Farnham: Ashghate Publishing.

Wikileaks. 2008. "Cable 08TASHKENT1277_a". November 5. Accessed May 2014. http://www.wikileaks.org/plusd/cables/08TASHKENT1277_a.htm.

Wikileaks. 2009. "Cable 09TASHKENT128_a". February 2. Accessed May 2014. http://www.wikileaks.org/plusd/cables/09TASHKENT128_a.html.

Yahuda, M. 1983. *Towards the End of Isolationism: China's Foreign Policy after Mao*. London: Macmillan.

# Promoting empowerment? The World Bank's Village Investment Project in Kyrgyzstan

Babken Babajanian

*Institute of Public Affairs, London School of Economics and Poltical Science, UK*

This article examines the extent to which the World Bank's community-driven Village Investment Project empowered people to influence the choice of local investments (micro-projects) and to exact accountability from their leaders. It is based on qualitative interviews and group discussions in 16 rural communities. The research demonstrates that the project provided an effective mechanism for responsive infrastructure delivery to address local priority needs. However, it did not improve accountability either within or outside the micro-project boundaries. The project's bottom-up development model was not by itself sufficient to enable people to exercise power over local government officials and informal leaders in the absence of effective horizontal accountability institutions within the state.

## Introduction

The last two decades have seen proliferation of development programmes to promote citizen participation and empowerment. Depending on their operational modality, these initiatives are categorized under the umbrella terms 'social accountability' and 'community-driven development' (CDD). Since the early 1990s, the World Bank has supported 400 CDD projects in 94 countries, with total estimated project budgets of almost USD 30 billion (Wong 2012). CDD promotes 'bottom-up development' by devolving resources and decision-making responsibility for important infrastructure and service delivery to local community groups. Community participation in these activities is thought to improve the quality and sustainability of services, increase local self-reliance, and empower individuals (Dongier et al. 2003).

The Village Investment Project (VIP), which spanned 2003–2014 in Kyrgyzstan, was acclaimed as one of the World Bank's 'success stories'. The project was also known as ARIS, the name of its executing agency. It was established with the financial support of the World Bank, the Government of Japan and the UK's Department for International Development. The main objective of the VIP was to support local communities in the delivery of basic social and economic infrastructure and services. The second, related objective was to empower citizens to have a voice in community investment decisions and exact accountability from their leaders.

The VIP provided grant financing to community groups to undertake small projects (or micro-projects) to improve essential infrastructure and services. The amount of community grants was linked to population size. Typically, a rural community of about 6700 people was entitled to USD 95,000 over a four-year cycle, with funding increasing from USD 15,000 in the first year of participation to about USD 30,000 in the third (World Bank 2006a). VIP funded several micro-projects each year of the four-year cycle, each micro-project costing USD 500–15,000.

This article provides fieldwork evidence on the project's effects in promoting empowerment in Kyrgyzstan, focusing on three aspects. Firstly, it examines patterns of community participation in micro-project initiation and the ability to influence micro-project choice (responsiveness). Secondly, the article assesses people's ability to exact accountability from local leaders and prevent misappropriation of funds during micro-project implementation. Thirdly, it explores empowerment in the broader local governance domain, outside the narrow scope of the VIP micro-projects. The article is based on qualitative interviews and group discussions in 16 rural communities in the Chuy, Naryn, Issyk-Kyl and Osh regions (*oblasts*) in 2007–2008.

The article first reviews key findings on CDD impact in enhancing empowerment globally. It then presents VIP's operating procedures and explains the research methodology. After a brief review of the governance context in Kyrgyzstan, the article presents an analysis of the research data, including community participation in micro-project initiation; micro-project responsiveness to local preferences; accountability of local leaders during implementation; and responsiveness and accountability of formal authorities outside micro-projects. The final section discusses the findings and draws conclusions.

## Empowerment in CDD

Empowerment has been defined as 'the process of enhancing an individual's or group's capacity to make purposive choices and to transform those choices into desired actions and outcomes' (Alsop, Bertelsen, and Holland 2006, 1). Empowerment in CDD implies the ability of communities to express their voice and influence the choice of micro-projects as well as to hold their leaders accountable in relation to micro-project activities. Empowerment is an outcome of participation.[1] CDD interventions promote community participation as the key mechanism for strengthening people's capacity to express voice and influence service delivery choices and outcomes.

In addition to empowerment within micro-project boundaries, the CDD theory assumes that participation can 'spill over into broader decision-making processes at the community level' (Wong and Guggenheim 2005, 261; see also Wong 2012). It can empower people to take part in local planning and resource mobilization and engage with their leaders to demand greater accountability and transparency.

CDD is based on the notion of social accountability, which refers to the engagement of citizens in monitoring the actions and behaviour of local leaders and service providers and holding them responsible outside elections (Malena, Forster, and Singh 2004). Social accountability complements two other forms of accountability (ibid.). Vertical accountability assumes that elections serve as an instrument of citizens' control over their elected representatives. Horizontal accountability involves the ability of the administrative, legislative and judicial institutions of the state to exercise internal control over public institutions.

In assessing participation and empowerment, it is useful to distinguish between formal inclusion and substantive inclusion (Pozzoni and Kumar 2005). Most CDD evaluations measure formal inclusion, i.e. community participation in micro-project activities. For example, evidence from internationally prominent projects in Indonesia and the Philippines suggests high levels of community participation, as measured by the number of residents who took part in various procedural meetings and committees (PNPM Support Facility 2011; World Bank 2011). A review of CDD projects shows that factors limiting participation include poverty, limited education and low literacy, social marginalization, gender (being a woman), wealth inequality and remoteness of location (Mansuri and Rao 2013).

Formal participation may not necessarily translate into substantive inclusion, i.e. the ability of community members to influence decision making and hold their leaders accountable. There are concerns about elite domination and exclusion of marginalized groups from important decision making, resulting in inequitable distribution of project benefits (Wong and Guggenheim 2005; Dasgupta and Beard 2007; World Bank 2008; Mansuri and Rao 2013). A review of participatory projects (Pozzoni and Kumar 2005) points out the weakness of donor-supported initiatives in promoting participation of 'weaker social groups' as local decision making is often dominated by more powerful community members.

Elite domination can often result in 'negative' involvement of local leaders, or elite capture. 'Elite capture' refers to situations when the elites govern projects according to their own priorities, advance their narrow interests, and often misappropriate local resources (World Bank 2008). Elite capture has been differentiated from leadership involvement that facilitates broad-based positive outcomes, or 'benevolent capture' (Rao and Ibáñez 2005). Evidence suggests that the success of CDD micro-projects often depends on the commitment and ability of 'benevolent' local leaders to prepare proposals, mobilize community contributions and manage micro-project implementation (World Bank 2002a; Babajanian 2005; Rao and Ibáñez 2005; Vaija and White 2008). The skills and influence of these leaders appear to be crucial for initiating and delivering micro-projects aligned with people's preferences.

As for the broader empowerment effects outside the micro-project domain, the CDD literature often discusses these under the theme of improving local governance. In her review of CDD projects, Wong (2012) suggests that only four 'rigorous' quantitative evaluations sought to measure governance and they point to positive to mixed effects. It is difficult to generalize about governance effects as studies use different measures, including public attitudes towards different levels of government, participation in public meetings outside the project domain, and the use of participatory approaches and community-driven decision making in communal activities (Wong 2012).

Qualitative studies suggest that CDD interventions often fail to promote empowerment as they do not address deeply entrenched local power structures that perpetuate social inequalities and clientelistic and hierarchical relations. A qualitative study of PNPM-Rural[2] in Indonesia (Syukri, Mawardi, and Akhmadi 2010) found that citizen participation, transparency and accountability 'did not spill over into general local/village governance as the capacity of communities to impact elite control of decision-making was limited' (PNPM Support Facility 2011, 3, 25–26). The authors suggested that the project cycle was not long enough to promote transformative changes and that there was little incentive for the local elites to alter the existing governance system.

The CDD model has been criticized for proposing 'technical fixes' to complex problems that have structural origins (Li 2007). Li (2007) suggests that the Kecamatan Development Project (KDP)[3] in Indonesia did not contain mechanisms to tackle the root causes of the existing social inequalities. She argues that it viewed community as 'a governmental terrain' (259), which can be 'managed' and 'improved' through 'highly localized' (262) interventions based on sets of crafted rules and practices. She maintains that the project only intervened in the sphere that it 'could effectively frame in technical terms', but left out powerful elites who presented difficult subjects to 'govern' through donor interventions.

Similar criticism has been expressed with regard to CDD in the post-Soviet context. Based on his research in Armenia, Babajanian (2005) suggested that the bottom-up CDD model is not adequate for transformative governance effects. It is based on the 'cultural' view of institutional change, which assumes that poor governance is mostly a result of 'mental' predispositions of individuals and that local accountability can be nurtured through a process of 'social learning'. Thus, it overlooks the complex and unequal relationships between citizens and local leaders outside the micro-project boundaries.

## The Village Investment Project

The VIP was conceived in an attempt to address lessons learned from previous CDD projects in Central Asia. The World Bank's (2002b) review of 60 CDD projects supported by various agencies in Kyrgyzstan, Tajikistan and Uzbekistan concludes that these projects required only limited community participation and were not designed to promote empowerment. The study argues that 'these findings reflect a pattern found in CDD projects Bank-wide, that is, CDD tends to be top-down driven development when it comes to budgets, management, monitoring and evaluation, and bottom-up when it comes to the construction and maintenance phases, especially when physical labour is involved' (12). It recommends replicating the model of Indonesia's KDP as especially suitable for the governance context in Central Asia and for its potential to address corruption.

The VIP developed intricate institutional arrangements, seeking to promote genuine participation and empowerment. It aimed to 'foster and ensure sustained intra-community collaboration, to develop strong habits of inclusion, transparency and accountability in local development planning and implementation, and to instil good governance habits in LSG [local self-governance] institutions and officials' (World Bank 2006a, 11). It was envisaged that 'community cooperation and empowerment' would be institutionalized and serve 'as the basis for local development even when no further outside funding is being provided to them' (88). As the VIP's task team leader stated: 'Our hope is that people are getting used to long debates among themselves and with mayors and councils, and that this citizen involvement will be permanently institutionalized in the community' (World Bank 2006b).

The VIP's implementation brought about impressive results in delivering important social and economic infrastructure in Kyrgyzstan. The inadequate capacity of the central government to ensure operation and maintenance has led to the deterioration of the physical condition of infrastructure facilities throughout the country. This, in turn, has had negative effects with regard to the quality of the services delivered by this infrastructure and access to these services by the population. Between 2007 and 2012, the VIP's activities resulted in 442 rehabilitated or constructed community water points; 93,324 new piped household water connections; 684 piped household water connections resulting from rehabilitation works; 383 constructed, renovated and/or equipped health facilities; 676 rehabilitated rural roads; and 4288 newly built or rehabilitated classrooms (Rahim 2014).

There is limited compelling evidence about the empowerment effects of the project. In assessing the project's achievements, the World Bank project completion reports (World Bank 2006a, 83; Rahim 2014) use quantitative indicators, such as the numbers of community groups established, community meetings convened, men and women who took part in these meetings, and local governments publicizing community budgets. These output indicators do not allow inferences about how the micro-projects affected social relations, power dynamics and institutional structures in local communities.

In pursuing its empowerment objective, the VIP used a bottom-up development model. The communities themselves were expected to identify and prioritize local problems through a series of participatory consultations, and prepare, co-finance and implement micro-projects to address these problems. This was supposed to contribute to 'demand orientation' (or responsiveness), i.e. to enhance people's ability to influence micro-project choice and ensure that investments addressed their genuine priority needs. It was also expected to improve accountability, i.e. the ability to prevent corruption, for example attempts by the local elite to misappropriate micro-project funds.

The project applied a notion of 'geographic community' corresponding to the administrative boundaries of a village (*aiyl*) to define its main unit of intervention. It also used the notion of 'community of interest' for groups of citizens who share similar needs and get together to advance a micro-project within a geographic community.

To enable residents to exercise voice and influence their leaders, the project introduced a number of requirements for transparent information dissemination. Thus, it required that all micro-project budgets and actual costs be posted on public bulletin boards and that progress be regularly reported to the community. It obliged local leaders to make publicly available all the information on purchased items, including all payments and withdrawals, to allow public scrutiny of the outcome of the purchase. During the resource mobilization phase, the project required local leaders to provide community residents with receipts for their contributions of cash. The VIP viewed access to information as a key tool for community empowerment.

The project envisaged that the experience of collective engagement would bring about changes in people's norms, attitudes and expectations. Both local residents and their leaders would learn 'new ways' of solving common problems and appreciate the benefits of collaborative action. People would realize that they have a say in their own development and would engage with their leaders to claim their rights and demand accountability. In other words, the project saw the key obstacle to empowerment in the existing attitudes and limited awareness about the benefit of collective action and presumed that participation in local development could be facilitated through the learning experience that the project offered.

## Methodology

The present research used qualitative methods: in-depth (semi-structured) interviews and group discussions. I conducted interviews with two groups of residents. In the first group, I purposefully selected the individuals who were potentially most knowledgeable about the VIP micro-projects (key informants). These included village administration (*aiyl okmotu*) officials, local council (*aiyl kenesh*) members, village heads (*aiyl bashchi*), school directors, religious leaders and village elders (*aksakal*s), as well as ordinary community members involved in the micro-projects. The second group included ordinary community residents – men and women, including those who participated in the micro-projects and those who did not. I did not set an initial limit to the number of interviews, and the sample size in each location reflects the natural 'break point' after which the new evidence did not add substantially different information.

In addition to in-depth interviews, I carried out group interviews with 'natural' groups of local residents. Most typically, these were groups of up to four men and women who worked together in the field or gathered at the village centre and other public areas. The pilot assessment revealed that to pre-arrange focus groups I needed the approval of local authorities. As a result, such focus groups had a somewhat formal nature and appeared to restrict people from freely expressing their views. In contrast, the individuals in the natural groups were open, as they did not feel they were being interviewed at the command of local leaders.

The research focuses on micro-projects funded through two operations: VIP-1 (August 2003–December 2006) and the early stages of VIP-2 (January 2007–August 2008). It was conducted in 16 rural communities in the Chuy, Naryn, Issyk-Kyl and Osh *oblast*s. In designing the sample, I first grouped the VIP micro-projects according to the geographic area, type, and implementation stage and then randomly selected communities with completed micro-projects of different types, including schools, potable water supply systems, village clubs and resource centres. The sample micro-projects are listed in the Appendix. In total, I conducted 130 in-depth interviews and 18 group discussions (involving 54 respondents) in the summers of 2007 and 2008. To ensure anonymity, this article uses pseudonyms for respondents and alphabetic coding for community names.

## Governance in Kyrgyzstan in the 2000s

The VIP's objective of promoting empowerment was pertinent but also challenging, especially considering the governance environment in Kyrgyzstan in the 2000s. The introduction of political freedoms and market reforms after the collapse of the Soviet Union did not profoundly challenge the nature of institutional relations in the country. The lawlessness and pervasive corruption that thrived throughout the 1990s, during the presidency of Askar Akayev, affected all spheres of economic, social and political life in Kyrgyzstan (Anderson and Gray 2006; Engvall 2007). And the popular movement – often referred to as the Tulip Revolution – that ousted the corrupt Akayev on 24 March 2005 did not bring about greater democratization. Most analysts conclude that the new regime led by president Kurmanbek Bakiyev only served to further undermine democracy and the rule of law. The widespread inequality and the popular dissatisfaction with the governing elites led to another mass uprising, which forced President Bakiyev to flee Kyrgyzstan in April 2010.

President Bakiyev's regime further exacerbated the 'endemic' corruption and even fostered the involvement of criminal figures in the country's politics (Marat 2008, 229). In a sociological survey of 1500 citizens funded by the USAID, more than 60% of respondents considered the level of corruption in the country 'high', and one-third believed that corruption had increased after the Tulip Revolution (Nogoybaeva 2008). Another study similarly suggests that corruption and limited law enforcement 'spurred a culture of impunity and illegality' in the country (Ruget and Usmanalieva 2007, 447).

The Kyrgyz political system is dominated by informal power arrangements, traditional blood-based kinship solidarity and regional (clan) allegiance of political incumbents (Collins 2004; Juraev 2008). Collins (2009) describes the governance regime in Kyrgyzstan during the presidencies of Akayev and Bakiyev as 'patrimonial-authoritarian'. These regimes are governed by powerful leaders who rely on informal networks and patronage to promote the vested interests of narrow groups and personally benefit from public resources.

The channels of accountability at the local level are poor, and important decision making is dominated by the governing elites (Grävingholt et al. 2006). Decentralization reforms in the mid-1990s established 475 village councils, which are envisaged to manage local affairs through 'local self-governments' comprising *aiyl okmotu* and *aiyl kenesh*. The key role in governing rural communities belongs to the *aiyl okmotu* head, who is elected by the local council members for four years. The *aiyl okmotu* head is the most powerful local actor, and dominates local decision making with regard to resource allocation and the choice and implementation of local policies and projects. As a local council member in A3 remarked during this research, 'Nobody can go against the power of the *aiyl okmotu* head.'

## Community participation in micro-project initiation

This section examines patterns of community participation in micro-project initiation. Community members directly participated in the micro-project initiation processes, involving identification and prioritization through two forms of public consultation: focus group discussions and community-wide meetings. Their direct participation in micro-project preparation and implementation was mostly through the provision of physical inputs, such as mandatory cash or in-kind or labour (*ashar*) contributions, which were part of the VIP requirement.[4] The VIP established micro-project groups (MPGs), which acted on behalf of local community groups during micro-project preparation and implementation.

All the micro-projects covered in this research were identified and prioritized at the public consultations held through the focus group discussions and community-wide meetings. The village mobilizers, who were selected from local residents by the project's outreach team, first conducted focus group discussions with four diverse groups of local residents, such as men, women, the elderly and youth. These discussions revealed some of the important priorities of community members. After this, local leaders convened the first community-wide meeting, at which residents got together to discuss the problem areas identified by each of the focus groups and reached an agreement on priority needs in their village.

To satisfy the project's 'minimum participation requirement', local leaders mobilized community residents in the community-wide meetings. According to rough estimates by ARIS staff, on average 65 household representatives attended the first meeting and 55 attended the second meeting in one community. This represented 30–40% of all micro-project beneficiaries in one community. Whilst the local leaders managed to assemble the number of people required to pass the VIP's requirement, they complained about the difficulty in mobilizing ordinary residents. Participation was especially difficult to achieve during the agricultural season, when most farmers were busy working in their fields and orchards.

At these meetings, residents elected MPG committees to manage the micro-projects. Based on the priorities identified by the community groups, the MPG committees prepared preliminary micro-project proposals. At the second community-wide meeting, residents discussed and prioritized these proposals for presenting for final selection and approval to the local investment committee, which was made up of representatives of participating villages within the same village council area and local officials.

The VIP model relied heavily on the existing leadership capacity to prepare and implement micro-projects. The MPGs were dominated by the school and clinic directors, *aiyl bashchi* and other individuals who had leadership skills and experience working with donors. The local leaders were both male and female. The latter were mostly school directors, or heads of health centres. These leaders had important skills, formal authority and informal influence to fulfil the project's application requirements and successfully manage micro-projects. The VIP's micro-project application requirements and operational procedures were complex, and successful micro-project initiation and management necessitated significant skills and leadership potential. For example, during the preparation stage, the MPGs obtained the formal permits necessary to initiate construction work, prepared sustainability plans, collected cash contributions, mobilized residents for *ashar*, and prepared and submitted micro-project proposals. The local leaders also took the lead in the micro-project implementation, which included monitoring of civil works, negotiating with contractors, certifying completion of works and liaising with local authorities and ARIS. A local leader, Gislan, in A12 in Chuy described the importance of strong leadership:

> You need strong leaders who can help, residents cannot manage well by themselves. For example, the MPG leader is an entrepreneur and he even paid the community contribution on behalf of 20 residents. He runs around, he has good connections and he also helps with tractors, equipment. It is very difficult without such leaders, the residents here are quite passive and without such people it would be very difficult.

In most cases, these leaders themselves put forward micro-projects to address the community preferences identified during public consultations. During the first community-wide meeting, they made a case for a particular micro-project and obtained the support of community residents to prepare a proposal for it. Some communities found it difficult to identify suitable persons who were willing to lead on micro-projects. In the case when no community members volunteered to serve as MPG leaders, the *aiyl bashchi* or in some cases the *aiyl okmotu* representatives themselves identified and nominated capable individuals.

It is not accidental that school projects dominated the VIP micro-project portfolio. Due to their formal positions, school directors were highly motivated to raise funds to initiate improvements in their schools. They used their institutional leverage and administrative resources to prepare effective micro-project proposals and successfully mobilize parents to support them.

## Responsiveness to local preferences

Let us now consider the extent to which participation enabled community members to influence micro-project choice. The strict adherence to VIP procedures ensured that all the micro-projects in this study had strong community ownership and significance. As respondents suggest, their communities followed the needs-identification procedures prescribed by the VIP. The respondents reported that the village mobilizers conducted four focus group discussions to establish local needs. These needs were subsequently discussed and prioritized at the community-wide meetings. Community involvement in the focus group discussions and community-wide meetings contributed to the responsiveness of the VIP investments to people's preferences. Most local leaders appeared to appreciate the VIP requirements for community participation and talked positively about the importance of involving people in the prioritization of local investments.

All the respondents believed that the micro-projects helped address some of the immediate priority needs in their communities. Even respondents who were not direct beneficiaries of a specific micro-project acknowledged that it was important for a group of local residents in their broader community. For example, the residents who did not have children of school age agreed that the investments in school infrastructure were needed and justified. Similarly, the residents in A10 in Chui, who preferred a different micro-project over the chosen stadium rehabilitation, admitted that the stadium would benefit their fellow community residents.

To reduce the potential of elite capture, the project restricted the ability of local self-government units (*aiyl okmotu* and *aiyl kenesh*) to influence micro-project choice. The VIP involved local authorities in the discussions of communal priorities and formulation of local development plans. All the micro-projects were undertaken with the knowledge and endorsement of the *aiyl okmotu* heads. However, the VIP, sought to limit their discretionary power, to prevent their possible domination and interference. Thus, the *aiyl okmotu* heads did not have a formal role in the management of financial resources and organizational activities. The *aiyl okmotu* representatives interviewed in this study regarded the micro-projects as 'ARIS territory' and were not closely involved in micro-project processes. As an ARIS expert said, 'The *aiyl okmotu* does not do anything, they are used to the fact that ARIS does most of the work.'

When asked whether the VIP should give money directly to the local authorities, Kuban in A9 in Chuy commented: 'If foreign aid came … through the *aiyl okmotu*, it would not reach us.' The school MPG leader, Batma, in A3 in Naryn said, 'It is not clear what would happen if the control mechanisms and the procedural requirements of ARIS [VIP] were lifted', implying that she had little faith in the local self-government's accountability. The school MPG leader, Ayana, in A13 in Issyk-Kyl suggested:

> If this money went to the *aiyl okmotu*, it would be difficult, I would need to run around day and night [to chase after the money]. They should not give the money directly to the *aiyl okmotu*, it will be very difficult. We cannot trust the *aiyl okmotu* one hundred per cent. They may spend on things we don't really need.

### Accountability of micro-project leaders

This section examines people's ability to exact accountability from local leaders and prevent misappropriation of funds during micro-project implementation. In addition to its participatory procedures, the VIP instituted administrative control mechanisms to safeguard against misuse of power by local elites. It enforced strict monitoring and supervision to ensure that the project's key operational procedures and procurement requirements were observed. The local leaders emphasized that the ARIS project officers carried out strict supervision. For example, Batma in A3 in Naryn said, 'Their procedures help that everything is open, it is very important.' The *aiyl bashchi*, Abai, in A5 in Osh said, 'ARIS [VIP] is different from other organizations in that they do good monitoring. They check how we use the money.'

The local investment committee chair, Bashi, in A6 in Osh elaborated on the VIP's monitoring effectiveness:

> There is a big difference between projects. We built a health point [centre] with UNDP, but they don't really control. ARIS comes and checks halfway through and after the completion, and then they have a handover procedure. Once we made a mistake buying cheap furniture, and they made us take it back. They made us go to the market and sell the purchased furniture and get a new set. So you can't cheat them. They monitor the quality of materials and would not let us save by buying cheaper materials.

Whilst the residents appreciated that they could influence micro-project choices, they did not feel they could exact accountability from the micro-project leaders. The research documented deep suspicion and distrust that residents had towards their leaders. The local leaders involved in the micro-project processes were perceived by the residents as part of the elite networks, who, along with the formal authorities, benefited from existing economic and social opportunities. The prevailing perception was that they volunteered for micro-projects to take advantage of the micro-project funds. Many respondents believed that the quality of the infrastructure rehabilitation was poor, and they were convinced that the local leaders extracted part of the money allocated for the rehabilitation works by colluding with contractors and buying substandard materials.

The residents had ample opportunities to interact with their leaders and express their grievances. In fact, many community residents were not afraid to openly criticize local leaders at community-wide meetings and social gatherings. In all of the sample communities, there were residents who confronted their leaders and expressed their suspicions and discontent with regard to micro-project spending and quality of rehabilitation works. A local activist, Usen, in A16 in Issyk-Kyl expressed a view of local residents recurring in all studied communities:

> There are people who think that we have not used the money correctly, they come and say: 'What, you have eaten all the money?' They say: 'You have received a grant, so why are you collecting money from us?' They think we act in our own interest.

The situation in A10 in Chuy is typical of the sample communities. In the past three years, the school director, Zhidegul, has initiated and implemented three different VIP micro-projects. Local residents acknowledged that these micro-projects significantly improved the quality of the school building and the learning environment for their children. However, the director complained that despite her efforts to improve the school and to provide regular reports to the community, she was still confronted with distrust and suspicion:

> Here I am, writing projects for them, but people think differently, they think that I am pocketing money from these projects. Last year, we built the club, and people were saying that the village head pocketed the money. ... There were many disagreements. They told me: You have spent 45,000 som [USD 1230] for just redoing the toilet – one can build a house for that money.

A village elder, Sultan, in A10 expressed distrust of the school director:

> When they were reporting about the school toilet, they said they had spent 78,000 som [USD 2130], and I said you could have done it for 15,000 som [USD 410]. They say, these are the prices these days, but we have calculated the prices and they do not add up. They made people laugh.

These disagreements did not have any tangible consequences (for example, the commissioning of a review of the micro-project management practices), but they intensified public grievances and contributed to the widening of the divide between the elites and the citizens.

Local perceptions indicate that the VIP's information-dissemination requirements did not serve as an effective tool for promoting accountability and trust. Many residents doubted that their leaders had provided them with accurate information at community meetings. They did not believe they could effectively contest their leaders by using the information posted on the public boards. Gulzat in A1 in Chuy expressed a common view: 'It is not very important that they put up financial information. It does not benefit us in any way, as they still make deals amongst each other.' When the water micro-project in A4 in Naryn was postponed to the following year, some residents were convinced that the local leaders were 'eating' the cash collected as community contribution; others suggested that the leaders had invested it in their own business projects. These respondents considered the receipts they were given 'just a piece of paper'. In another example, when local leaders in A7 in Osh were compelled to hire skilled labourers instead of local unskilled workers, the residents accused them of corruption. Although this decision had been discussed at the community-wide meeting, it still provoked dissatisfaction. The local leaders complained that it was very difficult for them to manage the micro-project processes given the general atmosphere of distrust in the community.

Most respondents were convinced that voicing concerns would not change their leaders' behaviour. Dimira in A1 in Chuy said: 'We go to their meetings, it is interesting. It does not matter, though, big people will always do their own thing, they will not listen to a small person. I don't have anything, who will listen to me?' There were others who believed that contesting local leaders would actually do more harm. For example, Aziz in A2 in Naryn said:

> Our school received a lot of money, but they actually spent much less on the renovation. I was hired to work for the school project. I was paid 4000 som [USD 110], but the papers said it was 15,000 som [USD 410]. They said the window was broken so we had to buy it again, but we have not seen the replacement parts. I cannot go and tell them about corruption as my son studies there. The school elite got everything.

The respondents' views presented in this section may not necessarily indicate illegal activity on the part of local leaders; nevertheless, they are useful for understanding the nature of the relationship between citizens and local leaders. The VIP interventions did not address the existing social divide, which breeds distrust and perpetuates a sense of powerlessness among ordinary residents.

### Responsiveness and accountability outside micro-projects

To examine the VIP's empowerment effects in the local governance domain, outside the micro-project boundaries, the research solicited perceptions from ordinary residents of the responsiveness and accountability of local self-governments and people's ability to claim their rights and influence government officials. The responses suggest that the VIP's interventions did not affect relations of accountability between residents and local authorities.

The weak financial and administrative capacity of the state constrains its ability to reach out to the local residents and respond to their needs. Local residents were aware of the limitations that the *aiyl okmotu* experienced because of financial and administrative constraints. Dimira in A1 expressed a common view: 'And how can the *aiyl okmotu* help [if they do not have resources]?'

As well as limited capacity, poor accountability at the local level appears to be a critical problem. There was suspicion that local authorities were mostly concerned about their own interests and took advantage of their position. Many respondents complained that local officials exhibited little attention and care, even for those who had especially difficult circumstances, such as single mothers and persons with a disability. Nurai in A2 in Naryn, whose son had a disability, said, 'The *aiyl okmotu* are not really interested in how people live, they only pursue their own interests.' Kabyl in A9 in Chuy said:

> The *aiyl okmotu* do not help, they only take money for taxes, for the harvest. ... They just eat money themselves and rip your skin off. It is obvious they use all the money on themselves. We had it before [in Soviet times], too, but it has increased now. The 150 *som* [USD 4] for the grass is not going to go to the budget, but they will use it for their own needs. ... They will spend on a [Parliament] deputy, or when the *akim* [head of regional administration] comes to the village they will kill a sheep for him. ... The *aiyl okmotu* people are there only for themselves, for themselves and their relatives. ... Kyrgyzstan is not going to become developed any time soon, we are only going backwards.

The respondents alleged instances of corruption in the provision of state-funded social security benefits and humanitarian aid. In all the sample communities, the research identified poor households who did not receive their social entitlements. They did not have the money or connections to obtain the legal documents and certificates to apply for these benefits. For example, Farima in A16 in Issyk-Kyl did not apply for social assistance for her adopted daughter because she could not afford the paperwork:

> Nothing can be solved without money. We pay the *aiyl okmotu* for the certificates. Without paying them a little bit you can't receive the benefit. … If you need something or have a problem to solve, you have to bribe them, so that you can get what you want.

Some respondents found it difficult to deal with the regional agencies who determine eligibility for old-age pensions (Social Security Fund) and disability benefits (VTEK). They complained that their local authorities were not willing to facilitate their access to these benefits, for example by helping them obtain the required paperwork and mediating their issues with these agencies. Residents in A2 in Naryn alleged that the *aiyl okmotu* distributed humanitarian aid to the better-off residents and ignored some of the poorest.

Whilst many residents were not afraid to express their dissatisfaction to the authorities, they did not feel they had the power to assert their rights and influence the behaviour of local officials. Here are some examples of people's views. Jyrgal in A9 in Chuy expressed an opinion that was echoed in most interviews: 'When people want something, they will say it, but it has little benefit. People should be able to get what they want.' Bakyt in A14 in Issyk-Kyl said, 'It makes no sense to appeal to the *aiyl okmotu*. They simply would not listen. In short, it's corruption, you give money and you get what you want.' Orlan in A10 in Chuy said, 'We have stopped raising issues, as it is all useless. People don't go to meetings, they have given up, as nothing is being done. They promise and do not deliver and people do not trust them anymore.'

The respondents were concerned that in the absence of adequate law enforcement, local officials can abuse their positions of authority. As the relations between the local authorities and residents were highly personalized, people depended on the good will of their authorities to obtain necessary paperwork. Thus, they felt that voicing grievances could have negative consequences for them. This relationship narrowed the power base of citizens and weakened the impact of their demands. Emil in A2 in Naryn said:

> If you complain, they say we'll try to solve it tomorrow. If you complain again, they will be cross with you. So you stop going there next time. If you need documents or something, they will not do it for you. It is the same as in Soviet times. They do not care, they never fulfil your requests.

Baurujan in A11 in Chuy suggested that ordinary residents may feel pressured not to persist in complaining:

> We have so many problems, but we can't tell them all to the *akim* or other authorities. If we tell them, the *aiyl okmotu* head or *sovkhoz* director will reprimand us, they will say, why did you tell them all that?

His fellow community member Bek echoed this view:

> And what's the use of expressing your dissatisfaction, it will not change anything. If you complain too much, next time you go to the *aiyl okmotu* to ask for a certificate or something like that, they will tell you: You have been quite active, haven't you? And they may refuse your request. Now there is lots of fear, so the *aiyl okmotu* can pressure you through their administration, as people are dependent on them.

Several respondents linked local governance with the overall institutional environment in the country. For example, a local activist, Asan, in A4 in Naryn did not think that participation in the VIP micro-projects could improve local accountability. Instead, he believed that public institutions perpetuated corruption, thus undermining people's trust in their local leaders:

> There is only one way to improve people's trust in the government: it is important that the laws work equally for everyone, they need to improve the rule of law. The pyramid of corruption is still the same, the top was replaced and the rest is the same. Everything comes from the top, they are greedy. Why should people trust me [as a micro-project group leader], if they don't trust people at the top?

Similarly, in commenting on the impact of the VIP project, an *aiyl okmotu* official, Sultan, in A8 in Osh suggested that the massive gap in the relations between authorities and citizens reinforces people's distrust in the public sector in general:

> If a poor person steals a chicken, he will go to prison, but if a rich person kills someone, they won't touch him. This creates lots of distrust. People are detached from the state. They [the elite] have privatized everything based on corrupt methods. Maybe only 10 persons [in the civil service] are honest, the rest are not. This has impact on people's relations with the local authorities, and people these days do not trust authorities.

A local activist, Ainara, in A6 in Osh thought local authorities have limited financial incentives to be accountable, but even if they wanted to stay honest, they may not be able to circumvent the 'chain of corruption':

> Sometimes, I pity people who work with the *aiyl okmotu*. Their salary is low, so of course they will misuse their positions. If they had a better salary they would not do that. For example, people in the passport department receive 700 som [USD 19, per month], so it is not enough. They get numerous audits, which ask for bribes. So they have to pay them. And it's a chain. The main thing is to raise salaries at the *aiyl okmotu*. But it is also true that if corruption stays on top, it will not go away. They [from top] will come and say: You have a salary of 1000 dollars, so you should share it with us.

Local accountability is deeply enmeshed in the broader institutional environment of the country. It is hard to see how bottom-up projects can enable local residents to exercise power over local officials, considering the restricted ability of the state to enforce the rule of law and sanction illegal behaviour.

## Conclusion

The VIP provided an effective mechanism for participatory infrastructure delivery to address the immediate needs of local community groups. Overall, the VIP interventions were successful in opening up channels for expression of the genuine priority demands of ordinary residents. The establishment of spaces and opportunities for participatory consultation and prioritization contributed to the responsiveness of VIP investments. The micro-projects were strictly monitored and supervised, which in most cases insulated them from outside interference and ensured that community groups were able to pursue their interests.

The VIP model capitalizes on the ability of existing leaders to initiate micro-projects, prepare proposals, mobilize community contribution and manage micro-project implementation. The local leaders in this study can be regarded as benevolent, as they contributed to resolving priority needs in local communities. This finding is consistent with the evidence from other countries suggesting that local leaders play a crucial role in CDD projects. It is natural that micro-project preparation and effective management require strong leadership capacity. Community groups need skills, formal authority and informal influence to comply with CDD requirements. This, however, also implies that community groups with limited leadership capacity may not be successful in advancing their priorities and benefiting from CDD investments.

Leadership domination in the absence of effective channels for participation and accountability renders community groups vulnerable to elite capture, which can result in exclusion and resource misappropriation. As mentioned earlier, the CDD literature identifies elite capture as a serious concern, especially in highly unequal contexts with weak law enforcement. Therefore, empowerment of ordinary group members is essential to preventing capture. However, this research suggests that local residents felt powerless to influence their leaders and prevent corruption. The overwhelming perception among community members was that the local elites took advantage of the VIP micro-projects to extract cash for personal gain. Furthermore, the VIP did not translate into community empowerment in the broader governance sphere and did not affect the relations of accountability between residents and local authorities.

The project's empowerment outcomes must be understood in relation to the institutional context of Kyrgyzstan. The limited state capacity for service provision and law enforcement contributes to the emergence and strengthening of clientelistic networks and informal channels for the allocation of scarce resources at the local level. Corruption in Kyrgyzstan and some other post-Soviet countries is 'systemic' (Stefes 2006). It is firmly entrenched in the political structures and administrative institutions and has become a parallel system of governance. Systemic corruption is based on hierarchical patron–client networks that extend from top down to lower-level officials (Stefes 2006). The latter are expected to share the illicit income collected from ordinary citizens and businesses with their superiors in exchange for protection and other benefits.

The prevalence of informal 'rules of the game' restricts democratic accountability and constrains the potential for citizen empowerment. Powerful elites are unlikely to succumb to popular demands in political systems that have 'biased' law enforcement and lack 'formal remit for addressing injustices' (Jenkins 2007, 143). In this context, people's voice alone was not sufficient to challenge elite power and interests. The existing institutions not only influenced the relations between community members and formal leaders but also created a divide between ordinary residents and informal leaders, such as the micro-project leaders in the VIP communities. The pervasive corruption and clientelism generated an atmosphere of distrust in the local communities. People were suspicious of local leaders who were in the position to take advantage of economic opportunities offered by development projects.

The VIP was based on conceptual and empirical misconceptions about the causes of poor governance and disempowerment. It reflected the 'cultural' view of institutional change (Babajanian 2005), which assumes that poor governance is conditioned by 'mentality' and attitudes and that local governance can be improved as a result of 'collective learning'. This assumption was summarized by Indonesia's KDP task team leader: 'KDP's underlying premise has been that villages learn about democracy by practicing it' (Guggenheim 2006, 138). The VIP interpreted empowerment as a product of habit, attitudes, experience and capacity. Like other CDD projects, the VIP assumed that access to resources, information and knowledge can nurture a process of social learning and enable people to engage with their leaders and influence local decision making. This conceptualization of empowerment ignores the importance of institutional structures that determine the nature of local decision making, resource allocation, and inclusion or exclusion.

Citizen empowerment requires that the state itself promote or ensure the accountability of public institutions. The literature on social accountability initiatives[5] stresses the importance of horizontal accountability for supporting and sustaining collective action (Agarwal, Heltberg, and Diachok 2009; Aiyar et al. 2009; Fox 2015; Joshi 2010; Schatz 2013). State-driven (supply-side) and citizen-driven (demand-side) accountability mechanisms are thought to be 'complementary and mutually reinforcing' (McNeil and Malena 2010, 5). Horizontal accountability involves political, fiscal, administrative and legal arrangements for oversight and control within the state (ibid.). It necessitates effective arrangements for monitoring and audit as well as incentives and sanctions to influence the behaviour of government officials and service providers.

Evidence suggests that social accountability may not be effective in the absence of horizontal accountability. According to Schatz (2013), the effectiveness of social accountability in reducing corruption systemically must be understood in relation to horizontal accountability, which is essential for systemic monitoring and sanctioning within public institutions. Social accountability has a limited potential to reduce corruption if it directly substitutes for horizontal accountability functions, i.e. when citizens apply direct pressure on public officials. Schatz shows that social accountability initiatives in Mumbai and Tanzania failed to reduce corruption because they did not activate horizontal mechanisms. In contrast, systemic reduction in corruption can be achieved when social accountability activates and sustains horizontal accountability. Social accountability initiatives in Uganda and Bangalore prompted governments to strengthen internal accountability and adopt systemic monitoring as they combined public pressure with the threat of electoral accountability. This in turn reduced opportunities for corruption.

Evidence from CDD projects shows the importance of horizontal control and oversight mechanisms in promoting local accountability. In a randomized field experiment in 608 village road rehabilitation projects under the World Bank's KDP project in Indonesia, inducing direct community participation in project monitoring only marginally affected missing expenditure (Olken 2007). In contrast, increasing the probability of a government audit from 4% annually to 100% substantially reduced missing funds.

Fox (2015), in his review of 'influential' studies of social accountability and CDD, highlights the weakness of localized interventions based on the assumption that access to information can stimulate collective action and empower local communities to influence public institutions. On the contrary, he finds more 'promising' (356) the approaches that – in addition to activating citizen voice – sought to scale up collective action beyond the local domain and promote reforms to improve public-sector accountability and responsiveness. He suggests that accountability can be promoted through facilitating coalitions between 'pro-accountability actors' within the state and society. This can enable 'mutual empowerment', in which collective action exerts pressure from below, whilst government reformists provide support and political space to meet people's demands.

The VIP project did not seek to activate horizontal accountability; it mainly prioritized collective action as a means to greater participation and accountability. In the absence of effective horizontal accountability, bottom-up interventions are not sufficient to enhance people's ability to influence local decision making. Collective action cannot be effective without institutional arrangements to ensure that the ruling elites comply with legal norms and to sanction any violations of citizen rights. In order to promote empowerment, bottom-up projects must be combined with state-driven efforts to tackle corruption and enforce accountability.

## Acknowledgement

I am grateful to Gazbubu Babayarova for her research assistance, as well as Jude Howell and David Lewis at LSE for their guidance and support. Many thanks to Gül Berna Özcan, Royal Holloway, and the anonymous reviewers for helpful feedback. This work would not have been possible without the individuals in the Kyrgyz communities who shared their time, experiences, views and life stories.

## Disclosure statement

No potential conflict of interest was reported by the authors.

## Funding

This research was supported by the ESRC Non-Governmental Public Action Programme [grant number PTA-155-27-0012].

## Notes

1. The literature often uses the terms 'empowerment' and 'participation' interchangeably. For example, the term 'participation' can be used to denote a process but also an outcome, e.g. the ability to express voice and influence decision making.
2. PNPM-Rural, which is part of the broader PNPM programme, reaches over 77,000 villages in over 5000 sub-districts, including all rural districts in Indonesia (PNPM Support Facility 2011).

3. The KDP, acclaimed as one of the most successful CDD projects, was initiated in 1998 with the support of the World Bank and continued through 2007, when it was expanded into PNPM-Rural. It shares its core operational features with the VIP.
4. See Babajanian (2011) for a detailed discussion of the community-contribution requirement in the VIP project.
5. This is a broad term encompassing different bottom-up initiatives, including participatory performance monitoring (e.g. citizen report cards, community score cards, social audits) and participatory governance (e.g. public expenditure tracking surveys, participatory budgeting).

## References


Agarwal, S., R. Heltberg, and M. Diachok. 2009. *Scaling-up Social Accountability in World Bank Operations*. Washington, DC: World Bank.

Aiyar, Y., B. Posani, A. Patnaik, and M. Devasher. 2009. *Institutionalizing Social Accountability: Considerations and Policy.* Accountable Government Policy Research Paper No 2. New Delhi: Centre for Policy Research, Accountability Initiatives.

Alsop, R., M. Bertelsen, and J. Holland. 2006. *Empowerment in Practice: From Analysis to Implementation.* Poverty Reduction Group. Washington, DC: World Bank.

Anderson, J. H., and C. W. Gray. 2006. *Anticorruption in Transition 3: Who is Succeeding ... and Why?* Washington, DC: World Bank.

Babajanian, B. 2005. "Bottom Up and Top Down? Community Development in Post-Soviet Armenia: The Social Fund Model." *Social Policy and Administration* 39 (4): 448–462. doi:10.1111/j.1467-9515.2005.00449.x.

Babajanian, B. 2011. "Problematising the Community Contribution Requirement in Participatory Projects: Evidence from Kyrgyzstan." *Development in Practice* 21 (3): 317–329. doi:10.1080/09614524.2011.558068.

Collins, K. 2004. "The Logic of Clan Politics: Evidence from the Central Asian Trajectories." *World Politics* 56 (2): 224–261. doi:10.1353/wp.2004.0009.

Collins, K. 2009. "Economic and Security Regionalism among Patrimonial Authoritarian Regimes: The Case of Central Asia." *Europe-Asia Studies* 61 (2): 249–281. doi:10.1080/09668130802630854.

Dasgupta, A., and V. A. Beard. 2007. "Community Driven Development, Collective Action and Elite Capture in Indonesia." *Development and Change* 38 (2): 229-249.

Dongier, P., J. Van Domelen, E. Ostrom, A. Ryan, W. Wakeman, A. Bebbington, S. Alkire, T. Esmail, and M. Polski. 2003. "Community-Driven Development." In *The PRSP Sourcebook*, Chapter 9. Washington, DC: World Bank.

Engvall, J. 2007. "Kyrgyzstan: Anatomy of a State." *Problems of Post-Communism* 54 (4): 33–45. doi:10.2753/PPC1075-8216540403.

Fox, J. A. 2015. "Social Accountability: What Does the Evidence Really Say?" *World Development* 72: 346–361. doi:10.1016/j.worlddev.2015.03.011.

Grävingholt, J., B. Doerr, K. Meissner, S. Pletziger, L. Von Rümker, and J. Weikert. 2006. *Strengthening Participation through Decentralisation: Findings on Local Economic Development in Kyrgyzstan.* DIE Studies 16. Bonn: German Development Institute.

Guggenheim, S. E. 2006. "Crises and Contradictions: Explaining a Community Development Project in Indonesia." In *The Search for Empowerment: Social Capital as Idea and Practice at the World Bank*, edited by A. Bebbington, S. E. Guggenheim, E. Olson, and M. Woolcock, 111–145. Bloomfield, CT: Kumarian Press.

Jenkins, R. 2007. "The Role of Political Institutions in Promoting Accountability'." In *Performance Accountability and Combating Corruption*, edited by A. Shah, 135–181. Washington, DC: World Bank.

Joshi, A. 2010. "Review of Impacts and Effectiveness of Transparency and Accountability Initiatives: Service Delivery." Annex 1. Prepared for the Transparency and Accountability Imitative Workshop, October 14–15, 2010, Institute of Development Studies, Brighton.

Juraev, S. 2008. "Kyrgyz Democracy? The Tulip Revolution and Beyond." *Central Asian Survey* 27 (3–4): 253–264.

Li, T. M. 2007. *The Will to Improve. Governmentality, Development, and the Practice of Politics*. Durham and London: Duke University Press.

Malena, C., R. Forster, and J. Singh. 2004. *Social Accountability. An Introduction to the Concept and Emerging Practice.* Social Development Paper No 76. Washington, DC: World Bank.

Mansuri, G., and V. Rao. 2013. *Localizing Development: Does Participation Work?* A World Bank Policy Research Report. Washington, DC: World Bank.
Marat, E. 2008. "March and After: What Has Changed? What Has Stayed the Same?" *Central Asian Survey* 27 (3–4): 229–240.
McNeil, M., and C. Malena. 2010. *Lessons from Social Accountability: Institutions in Africa*. Washington, DC: World Bank.
Nogoybaeva, E. 2008. *Proekt 'Nastroenia Strany' 2005–2007*. Centre for Social Research Publication. Bishkek: American University of Central Asia.
Olken, B. 2007. "Monitoring Corruption: Evidence from a Field Experiment in Indonesia." *Journal of Political Economy* 115 (2): 200–249. doi:10.1086/517935.
PNPM Support Facility. 2011. *PNPM-Rural Impact Evaluation*. Accessed January 7, 2013. http://pnpm-support.org/sites/all/sites/default/files/PNPM+IE+Final+REVISED%20done.pdf.
Pozzoni, B., and N. Kumar. 2005. *A Review of the Literature on Participatory Approaches to Local Development for an Evaluation of the Effectiveness of World Bank Support for Community-Based and -Driven Development Approaches*. The World Bank Operations Evaluation Department. Washington, DC: World Bank.
Rahim, A. Z. 2014. *Kyrgyz Republic - Second Village Investment Project: P098949 - Implementation Status Results Report: Sequence 15*. Washington, DC: World Bank.
Rao, V., and A. M. Ibáñez. 2005. *The Social Impact of Social Funds in Jamaica: A Mixed-Methods Analysis of Participation, Targeting and Collective Action in Community Driven Development*. World Bank Policy Research Working Paper No 2970. Washington, DC: World Bank.
Ruget, V., and B. Usmanalieva. 2007. "The Impact of State Weakness on Citizenship a Case Study of Kyrgyzstan." *Communist and Post-Communist Studies* 40 (4): 441–458. doi:10.1016/j.postcomstud.2007.10.002.
Schatz, F. 2013. "Fighting Corruption with Social Accountability: A Comparative Analysis of Social Accountability Mechanisms' Potential to Reduce Corruption in Public Administration." *Public Administration and Development* 33: 161–174. doi:10.1002/pad.1648.
Stefes, C. 2006. *Understanding Post-Soviet Transitions: Corruption, Collusion and Clientelism*. Basingstoke: Palgrave Macmillan.
Syukri, M., S. Mawardi, and Akhmadi. 2010. *The Impact of PNPM-Rural 2010: A Qualitative Study*. Jakarta: SMERU Research Institute.
Vaija, A., and H. White. 2008. "Can the World Bank Build Social Capital? The Experience of Social Funds in Malawi and Zambia." *Journal of Development Studies* 44 (8): 1145–1168.
Wong, S. 2012. *What Have Been the Impacts of World Bank Community-Driven Development Programs? CDD Impact Evaluation Review and Operational & Research Implications*. Washington, DC: World Bank.
Wong, S., and S. Guggenheim. 2005. "Community-Driven Development: Decentralization's Accountability Challenge." In *East Asia Decentralizes: Making Local Government Work*, edited by D. Subbarao and R. White, 253–267. Washington, DC: World Bank.
World Bank. 2002a. *Social Funds: Assessing Effectiveness*. Operations Evaluation Department (OED). Washington, DC: World Bank.
World Bank. 2002b. *The Context for Community Driven Development in Central Asia: Local Institutions and Social Capital in Kyrgyz Republic, Tajikistan and Uzbekistan – First Phase Report, CDD Experience and Lessons to Date*. Washington, DC: World Bank. Accessed July 3, 2015. http://documents.worldbank.org/curated/en/2006/07/6730125/context-community-driven-development-central-asia-local-institutions-social-capital-kyrgyz-republic-tajikistan-uzbekistan-first-phase-report-cdd-experience-lessons-date.
World Bank. 2006a. *Project Appraisal Document: Second Village Investment Project*. Report 36611-KG. Washington, DC: World Bank. Accessed August 20, 2014. http://documents.worldbank.org/curated/en/2006/07/6936447/kyrgyz-republic-second-village-investment-project.
World Bank. 2006b. "Addressing Poverty at the Village Level in the Kyrgyz Republic." Accessed September 16, 2014. http://web.worldbank.org/WBSITE/EXTERNAL/NEWS/0%2c%2ccontentMDK:20976955~menuPK:141310~pagePK:34370~piPK:34424~theSitePK:4607%2c00.html.
World Bank. 2008. *CDD and Elite Capture: Reframing the Conversation*. Social Development How to Series, Vol 3. Washington, DC: World Bank.
World Bank. 2011. *Impact Evaluation KALAHI-CIDDS Final Survey*. Washington, DC: World Bank.

## Appendix: Micro-projects Studied in this Research

| Community | Micro-project type and description | Micro-project cycle stage |
|---|---|---|
| A1 | Resource centre (renovation of the building) | Completed |
| | School (renovation and purchase of furniture) | Completed |
| A2 | Club (rehabilitation of the building and purchase of equipment) | Preparation |
| | Potable water (rehabilitation of the water supply network) | Implementation |
| A3 | School (remodelling of the sports hall) | Implementation |
| A4 | Potable water (rehabilitation of the water supply network) | Preparation |
| | Potable water (rehabilitation of the water supply network) | Implementation |
| A5 | School (partial construction of the school building) | Completed |
| | Electricity supply (purchase and installation of a generator) | Completed |
| A6 | Potable water (rehabilitation of the water supply network) | Completed |
| | Cafe (renovation and purchase of furniture and supplies) | Completed |
| A7 | School (rehabilitation of the sports hall) | Completed |
| A8 | School (rehabilitation of the heating supply system) | Completed |
| A9 | Potable water (construction of a dam and rehabilitation of the water supply network) | Implementation |
| A10 | School (renovation of the building and toilets; installation of heating supply) | Completed |
| | Club (rehabilitation of the building) | Completed |
| | Stadium (fencing the area) | Preparation |
| A11 | Club (rehabilitation of the building and purchase of equipment) | Implementation |
| A12 | Potable water (rehabilitation of the water supply network) | Completed |
| A13 | School (rehabilitation of the sports hall) | Completed |
| | Health centre (renovation and purchase of equipment) | Completed |
| A14 | School (rehabilitation of the heating system) | Implementation |
| | Potable water (rehabilitation of the water supply network) | Implementation |
| A15 | School (renovation of the concert hall) | Completed |
| A16 | School (purchase of musical equipment and renovation of the dining hall) | Completed |

# 'Donors are not interested in reality': the interplay between international donors and local NGOs in Kyrgyzstan's HIV/AIDS sector

Svetlana Ancker and Bernd Rechel

*Faculty of Public Health and Policy, Department of Health Services Research and Policy, London School of Hygiene & Tropical Medicine, UK*

This article explores the interplay between international donors and local NGOs in Kyrgyzstan's HIV/AIDS sector. It argues that donors have transposed ready-made policies without sufficient consideration of the local context and that NGOs have responded strategically, adapting their proposals and reports to the expectations of donors. This complex interplay has resulted in unintended consequences that have undermined an effective response to the HIV/AIDS epidemic. It has given rise to 'virtual realities' detached from developments on the ground. The funding system has also led to corruption and misappropriation of funds and the failure of NGOs to become sustainable. Largely bypassing the state in the allocation of funds, international donors have also undermined an already weak state.

## Introduction

The dissolution of the Soviet Union in 1991 created numerous challenges for its successor states, including political instability, economic stagnation, and the breakdown of social welfare and health systems. For Kyrgyzstan, the post-Soviet transition also coincided with and, in some ways, propelled the spread of human immunodeficiency virus and acquired immunodeficiency syndrome (HIV/AIDS), a new public health challenge, among its population. As in other countries of Central Asia, HIV infections, associated with a rapid increase in the trafficking and use of drugs and commercial sex work, have increased sharply since the early 2000s. As of 1 June 2013, a total of 4747 HIV infections were officially registered in Kyrgyzstan, a prevalence (proportion of population) of less than 0.1% (CCC 2013). However, this undercounts the number of actual infections. The United Nations Joint Programme on HIV/AIDS (UNAIDS 2013a) estimated that around 12,000 people were living with HIV/AIDS in Kyrgyzstan in 2011, a prevalence of 0.4%.

HIV/AIDS has enjoyed greater prominence in the international arena than many other diseases, receiving high levels of donor funding (Shiffman 2006; UNAIDS 2013b). In many low- and middle-income countries, international agencies had a decisive influence on shaping national policy responses. This was also the case in Kyrgyzstan. However, the country was more open to external influences than its Central Asian neighbours and has received the most funding per capita (Ancker and Rechel 2015) from the Global Fund to fight HIV/AIDS, Tuberculosis and Malaria (Global Fund). It was one of the first countries in the former Soviet Union to mount a comprehensive response to the growing epidemic and adopt policies that reflected what were promoted by international agencies as 'best international practices' in HIV/AIDS prevention and management. Yet, despite its claims to progress, HIV/AIDS policy and programme efforts in Kyrgyzstan have been unsystematic and have often been created in a declarative manner to appease donors and the rest of the international community. Of crucial importance for the national response to the epidemic were local NGOs, which, unlike the state sector, received most of the international funding and training.

This article aims to unpack the resulting interplay between international donors and local NGOs. It argues that international agencies came with ready-made recipes for how to tackle the epidemic, while local NGOs responded strategically, aiming to fulfil the expectations of donors, in order to access funding. This had a number of unintended consequences that undermined the effectiveness of HIV/AIDS policies and programmes. The agendas of international donors and local NGOs have converged in the creation of 'virtual realities' detached from developments on the ground. It also gave rise to corruption and the misappropriation of funds, and led to a lack of sustainability. The focus on NGOs did not help build the weak capacity of the state to tackle health emergencies.

The article is based on a review of academic and grey literature and 54 qualitative interviews that were conducted in October–November 2011 in Bishkek. Interviewees included representatives of the major stakeholder groups involved in HIV/AIDS policy-making – state institutions (21), NGOs (11), international organizations (15) and the media (7). Interviews were semi-structured and followed a pretested topic guide, which included questions on the main HIV/AIDS actors, their interests and involvement in HIV/AIDS policy-making, the role of donors and the impact of international assistance.

## The role of international donors in national HIV/AIDS policies

Since its emergence in the 1970s and 1980s, HIV/AIDS has become one of the most politicized diseases, through which a variety of stakeholders contest their legitimacy and power. International agencies have played a particularly crucial role in shaping HIV/AIDS policies, especially in low- and middle-income countries.

International (or transnational) actors can be defined as 'actors that seek to influence policy in multiple countries through the advocacy of specific, well-elaborated policy proposals' (Beland and Orenstein 2010, 4). According to Harman (2009b), the growing number and strength of international and civil-society actors in the area of HIV/AIDS have challenged the traditional view and authority of the state, and lines of responsibility for the response to the epidemic have become blurred. International agencies have placed HIV/AIDS firmly on national and international political agendas, defining both the 'problem' and the 'solution' (Hall and Midgley 2004; Mwacalimba 2012). A powerful international norm emerged in the late 1990s, defined and promoted by multilateral bodies, industrialized countries and transnational HIV/AIDS advocacy networks. This norm defines HIV/AIDS as a threat to international peace and stability and prescribes policies to be implemented at international and national levels. The primary source of creating and diffusing this norm is UNAIDS, the UN agency charged with coordinating global action against the epidemic. It promotes normative change and 'best practices' (Vieira 2007).

In addition to this 'soft' power of norm diffusion and persuasion, international donors also exercise 'hard' power in the form of conditionality (Beland and Orenstein 2010). Using the funding at their disposal, some donors try to pressure decision makers and introduce policy changes through funding conditionalities and coercion. However, without the power of persuasion, governments rarely respond to this kind of pressure (Beland and Orenstein 2010; Eyben 2010). Apart from the few donors that possess significant funding, such as the Global Fund, most international funders rely on ideational influence by proposing ideas and shaping the preferences of key policy makers, as well as supporting and empowering other actors, such as NGOs

(Beland and Orenstein 2010). The adoption of these norms at the domestic level can then be decisive for bringing about policy change (Sjöstedt 2008).

The HIV/AIDS agenda and the concepts promoted by donor agencies are often far removed from local realities, yet carry a prescriptive character and set out the direction for a preferred course of action (Van Der Vliet 1996; Seckinelgin 2008). Such a top-down approach is often imposed by powerful international organizations, such as the Global Fund, and justified by the presumed lack of leadership, capacity and expertise on the part of national governments (Harman 2009a). Furthermore, many donor agencies implement their activities in pursuit of their own interests and agendas (Wedel 2001; Balabanova, Oliveira-Cruz, and Hanson 2008). They seek quick and visible results within a short timeframe, without taking into account the epidemiological cycle of the HIV/AIDS epidemic and its long aftermath, which would require long-term planning and commitment (Slater 2004; Balabanova et al. 2010).

By pressuring for short-term positive results, international organizations can forgo long-term planning and the development of local capacity, and create systems that can undermine already weakened state structures and their decision-making capacity (Campbell 2003). In fact, as Heald (2003) critically notes, from the very beginning international funding for HIV/AIDS skewed national health priorities and systems. In many African countries, for example, specific budgets for HIV/AIDS led to the creation of narrow vertical structures that were at odds with the wider health system, while the prescriptive manner of international funding and the growing role of international agencies undermined governments' sense of ownership and capacity to respond (Wedel 2001; Heald 2003; Brugha et al. 2004).

At the same time, national stakeholders, particularly NGOs, have strong incentives to define and organize themselves in a certain way, in order to access international HIV/AIDS resources (Theodoulou 1996). Local organizations that are more articulate, politically savvy, strategic and skilful at playing the 'funding game' (such as through good grant-writing skills and the use of particular buzzwords) are more likely to be successful in receiving funding (Van Der Vliet 1996; Wedel 2001). They need to master an 'economy of targets and grants, a language (often English) of logframes, mission statements, aims, objectives, outputs and outcomes, and social conventions such as working groups, minuted meetings, documentation of activities, emailing and applying for funding' (Cornish et al. 2012, 470). Having secured funding, these organizations protect their funding allocations with vigilance and try to prevent others from entering the competition (Van Der Vliet 1996; Wedel 2001). This leads to 'fostering competition for grants that breeds mistrust, bitterness, and secrecy within and between the organizations' (Wedel 2001, 114). Furthermore, funding practices themselves can undermine the localism and empowerment that many HIV/AIDS interventions aim to achieve (Cornish et al. 2012).

Overall, the approach of funding agencies, in often driving their own agendas and seeking quick results in environments of low state capacity and weak health systems, can lead to fragmented and unsustainable results, while priorities unaligned with local needs can produce unintended consequences, encourage fictitious data, and thus lead to a 'distortion of reality' (Collins and Rau 2000; Wedel 2001). Crucially, development projects are always the result of a complex interplay between international donors, local governments and recipient organizations. They are adaptations that can sustain credibility among their different audiences (Mosse 2005) and be used by a range of actors for their own ends (Ferguson 1990).

### Kyrgyzstan's local context

With a GDP per capita of USD 1160 in 2012, Kyrgyzstan is the poorest country in Central Asia after Tajikistan (World Bank 2013), and this situation has not changed despite its long and friendly relations with Western aid organizations. Kyrgyzstan lacks any substantial natural resources (apart from gold) and well-developed industrial infrastructure; its economy has depended heavily on external aid and investment, making it particularly vulnerable and volatile (Pomfret 2006; Radnitz 2010; Oraz 2013). Between 1992 and 2000, funding from international financial institutions, such as the World Bank, Asian Development Bank, International Monetary Fund and European Bank for Reconstruction and Development, reached USD 1.7 billion (Pomfret 2006). Most of this international aid was used for consumption and to soften the shock of transition, rather than as investment in key industries to generate subsequent income (Pomfret 2006).

Initially led by president Askar Akayev, the country managed to earn itself a reputation as a progressive state, an 'island of democracy' and the 'Switzerland of Central Asia', and attracted the praise and attention of international donors (Matveeva 2010; Radnitz 2010; Wilkinson 2010; Cummings 2012; Morozova 2013). The early 1990s were a period of political reforms and liberalization; however, by the mid-1990s the situation had already changed and was followed by prolonged periods of corrupt regimes and political instability, which undermined state capacity even further.

## International donors in Kyrgyzstan

### *Levels of funding*

Compared to some of its wealthier neighbours (e.g. Kazakhstan and Uzbekistan), Kyrgyzstan relies heavily on international donor funding for HIV/AIDS. In 2012, total spending on the HIV/AIDS response in Kyrgyzstan was almost USD 9.5 million, but only about USD 3.8 million came from the state budget, with international donors accounting for the remainder (see Table 1) (UNAIDS 2013b).

Major multilateral donors include the World Bank, United Nations agencies such as the United Nations Development Programme (UNDP), the United Nations Children's Fund and UNAIDS, and the World Health Organization, while others, such as the United States Agency for International Development, the Centers for Disease Control, and the German Society for International Cooperation (GIZ), offer technical and financial support on a bilateral basis. In addition, there are several large international NGOs, such as the Soros Foundation–Kyrgyzstan, AIDS Foundation East-West and Population Services International, that have been involved in various aspects of HIV/AIDS work. Among the donor agencies that are funding HIV/AIDS efforts in Kyrgyzstan, the Global Fund has been one of the most influential, outweighing all earlier international contributions. Since 2004 it has accounted for half of the budgeted amount for national HIV/AIDS programming, and in 2012 almost three-quarters (71%) of international

Table 1. Regional HIV/AIDS spending (in USD), according to domestic and international sources of funding (2010–2012).

| | 2010 | | 2011 | | 2012 | |
|---|---|---|---|---|---|---|
| | Domestic sources | Internat. sources | Domestic sources | Internat. sources | Domestic sources | Internat. sources |
| *Kazakhstan* | n/a | n/a | 30,346,857 | 6,540,163 | 30,352,251 | 7,457,645 |
| *Kyrgyzstan* | 1,407,901 | 9,827,360 | 1,441,565 | 4,279,280 | 3,886,526 | 9,512,763 |
| *Tajikistan* | 1,718,968 | 13,514,154 | 2,269,834 | 13,032,203 | n/a | n/a |
| *Uzbekistan* | 16,985,205 | 6,678,413 | 12,636,531 | 6,513,177 | 13,334,449 | 10,771,819 |

*Note.* n/a: no data available on the given year.
Source: UNAIDS (2013b).

funding for HIV/AIDS in Kyrgyzstan came from the Global Fund (Murzalieva et al. 2009; MOH 2012b; UNAIDS 2013b). Altogether, the Global Fund has approved about USD 58.8 million in HIV/AIDS funding for Kyrgyzstan, with USD 47.6 million disbursed in 2004–2013 (Global Fund 2013).

International aid helps cover all major projects and activities in the area of HIV/AIDS, including operational and administrative costs, the development and distribution of information resources, the procurement of expendable materials, medical equipment and supplies, and vital medications to prevent and treat HIV/AIDS, as well as social services for most-at-risk populations and people living with HIV/AIDS. International agencies are the sole funders of most NGOs, providing financial support for their daily operations, capacity building and programme activities.

### *Norm diffusion*

In the interviews, all local HIV/AIDS stakeholders agreed that international donors had a decisive influence on national HIV/AIDS policies and programmes (Ancker and Rechel 2013). This can take a variety of forms. Donors mobilized various stakeholders around HIV/AIDS, highlighted its importance for policy, helped develop an appropriate legal framework aligned with international norms and standards, and acted as a catalyst for creating formal structures and processes. A departmental head from one of the state health institutions admitted: 'I would say, the contribution of international organizations is 100%, of course [they are] invaluable, since they act both as donors and experts with great experience. ... They, of course, have great experience in, let's say, some strategic things, activities and normative documents.'

International agencies also provide technical input into policy development, offer training, support field studies, and propose recommendations in various areas of HIV/AIDS prevention, treatment and care. UNAIDS and the World Health Organization have been actively involved in both development and evaluation of Kyrgyzstan's national HIV/AIDS programmes by assisting with the evaluation of the epidemiological situation and the state response, and by offering advice and recommendations. Meanwhile, UNAIDS has helped implement an integrated and coordinated HIV/AIDS response framework. The Global Fund has been actively involved in efforts to create a strong monitoring and evaluation system, including through the development of a unified database with common indicators, data collection, and analysis mechanisms. The experience of international agencies, backed by significant financial and technical resources, gives them authority to suggest policy actions, which the state may be inclined to adopt.

International agencies also influence HIV/AIDS policy making indirectly, by showing their political support and generating political will in government agencies, through offering examples of successful international HIV/AIDS programmes, and by bringing international experts to Kyrgyzstan and taking key state decision makers on study tours abroad, where they can see 'best practices' and approaches in action. One example is a UNDP project, Support to the Government to Respond to HIV/AIDS. Since 1997 UNDP has been working with the Office of the Government and other partner organizations (NGOs, ministries, media, and later the Global Fund) on improving HIV/AIDS–related policies, incorporating HIV/AIDS within the national development agenda and other strategic documents, and increasing the capacity of local policy actors and national ownership (UNDP 2012).

Support for professional capacity in the HIV/AIDS sector has been one of the biggest contributions of international organizations. Donors have played a critical role in motivating and improving the technical capacity of state and NGO stakeholders by offering them training, sending them to conferences and seminars, and providing them with the latest information. Thanks to international agencies that supported and advanced the notion of civil society (Atlani-Duault 2007), HIV/AIDS NGOs have grown tremendously and are now able to advocate for their interests, carry out programmatic activities, offer services to different population groups, apply for other sources of funding, and argue for the legal rights of their clients. Furthermore, using various working groups as formal platforms, international organizations often act as facilitators of partner dialogue, coordinate donor and partner activities, and balance the interests of the state and NGO sectors.

Yet, a number of interviewees from the state and NGO sectors pointed out that donor agencies use a 'cookie-cutter' approach and follow their own interests, which are not always appropriate for the local context or beneficial for the country. For example, a representative of a sex workers NGO revealed that, while donors choose to fund prevention activities, such as the distribution of condoms and information, sex workers see other needs, such as physical safety from harassment by law enforcement agencies, as a priority. Many respondents mentioned that, by pouring funds into programme areas and at-risk populations that donors consider a priority (e.g. injecting drug users), they neglect other areas (e.g. youth, migrants, and the general population), despite advocacy by local experts.

### *Conditions and requirements*

International agencies get to set the HIV/AIDS agenda and place conditions on how funding will be used. They need government approval to set up their programmes in the country, but they also place requirements on the funding they offer (Wedel 2001; Atlani-Duault 2007; Seckinelgin 2008). As interviewees from local and international agencies noted, each donor agency has its own list of programmatic, procedural and funding requirements to ensure that their funding is spent in what they perceive as the most efficient and productive way, with maximum output and impact.

NGO staff felt that a lot of funding comes with stringent conditions (or 'strings attached'), thus undermining the ownership and decision-making capacity of receiving organizations and, ultimately, the country as a whole. Other respondents, however, believed that some of the donor conditions were beneficial for the country, prompting it to reform certain spheres of its HIV/AIDS work. For example, multi-sectoral collaboration with active involvement of all actors, with a specific emphasis on inclusion of most-at-risk populations and people living with HIV/AIDS, and a well-functioning Country Coordinating Committee (CCC) were some of the requirements for funding by the Global Fund. As an NGO leader explained: 'If it wasn't for the Global Fund, [the CCC] would have not happened. Because the Global Fund gives a grant under the condition that the CCC is adequate. And reluctantly, perhaps, state institutions had to do it to receive the funds.' While some of the conditions and requirements of international donors were thus accepted as beneficial, this was not the case for all of them.

### *Interests and agendas*

Donor agencies in Kyrgyzstan have a range of interests and agendas. HIV/AIDS falls under the general development agenda of providing technical and financial assistance to developing countries. According to some local respondents, in view of the gravity of the epidemiological situation and the country's geographic proximity to major drug routes, the international community wants to avert a potential spillover of HIV/AIDS from the Central Asian region into Europe. Unlike in the African continent, where much of the general population has been affected by HIV/AIDS, donors viewed Central Asia's concentrated epidemic as a chance to prevent a generalized epidemic and make a name for themselves. A staff member of a donor agency admitted: 'I think maybe one of the things that attracts donors to the region … is kind of a sexy idea of "this is a growing epidemic", "the fastest-growing epidemic", and if we can stop it, we'll be famous.'

Although in this case the motives may be noble, the quote illustrates that donors can have agendas and motivations different from those of local actors.

Driven by internal politics and the wider economic situation (e.g. change in government, or the global economic crisis), donor countries may also shift their funding to other geographical or social areas, leaving previously planned activities without funding. Among donors that have recently left Kyrgyzstan are Hivos International and the United Kingdom's Department for International Development, while large regional projects, such as the Central Asia Regional HIV/AIDS Project and the Central Asia AIDS Project, ended recently. Some local respondents believed that the departure of some donors could be explained not only by donor fatigue and a decline in international funding but also by an overall change in priorities and the dominance of such a large funder as the Global Fund in Kyrgyzstan's HIV/AIDS sector. To avoid duplication and waste, some donors have redirected their funding elsewhere.

## The Kyrgyz state

Donor agencies, originally aiming to support a weak health system unable to deal with the HIV/AIDS epidemic, have often taken over the functions of state health institutions and driven HIV/AIDS efforts according to their own vision and interests. Being financially independent and influential due to their access to large amounts of funds, donors get to choose with whom to collaborate on the ground, be it state institutions, NGOs or other stakeholders. Often they bypass the state in the delivery of projects, entrusting it instead to local NGOs. This has coincided with a wider development agenda of civil-society-building and democracy promotion in the former Soviet countries in the 1990s. Similar to the argument of Atlani-Duault (2007) that NGOs are perceived as a counter-balance to the government's authority as part of a global agenda of promoting 'good governance', some respondents thought international agencies helped develop and support the NGO sector to create a vocal and strong ally, altering the power balance and offering an alternative to the state monopoly in decision making and service delivery. As a programme manager from a donor agency explained: 'At that time [in the early 1990s] state institutions tried to dictate their conditions. But then somehow the donors arrived in the country and began to cultivate the NGO movement, alternative methods of service provision and we got a good balance [between different sectors].' Similarly, a local programme manager of an international agency observed: 'First of all, our mandate is to work with the civil society, i.e. those organizations which represent the interests of vulnerable populations; second, those [organizations] which further their interests and protect their rights. We try to give them advocacy knowledge and skills.'

These two quotes illustrate how international agencies have approached the different actors in HIV/AIDS policy making in Kyrgyzstan. The overall focus is on strengthening civil society rather than the state machinery. As a result, the government became less involved in development programmes generally than international donors and, to some degree, allowed the NGO sector to grow and take over some functions of the state (Wilkinson 2014). This is similar to other countries' experiences – the Brazilian state, generally considered as doing very well in responding to HIV/AIDS, similarly fostered civic organization and mobilization around HIV/AIDS, and civic associations are now the key drivers of national HIV/AIDS policies (Rich 2013).

However, with most of the international funding and training going to NGOs and not the state sector, public health representatives in Kyrgyzstan felt that their sector was falling behind, lacking the knowledge and training, capacity and funding necessary to lead efforts in this area. State agencies become important only when their formal stamp of approval is needed for implementation; they are not invited to participate in the planning of donor activities. Donors often choose to avoid working with state agencies, as they can derail planned activities and put the outcomes desired by donors in jeopardy. Some of the respondents in state agencies resented that most international aid goes to NGOs, while state agencies still have to report on progress in addressing the HIV/AIDS epidemic. By funding local NGOs and promoting democratic principles and concepts of good governance, it appeared to many respondents from both national and international organizations that donors are manipulating the situation to their advantage, trying to widen their sphere of influence in this region of geopolitical significance.

Yet, it would be wrong to consider the Kyrgyz state a passive bystander. It promoted the development of civil society to fill gaps in service provision and tried to portray itself in the international arena as a regional 'pioneer' (Ancker et al. 2013). The country managed to retain the 'pioneer' image it had created in the early 1990s and exploited it to its own advantage (Ancker et al. 2013). At the international level, employing publicity skills and progressive slogans, and a declared commitment to good governance, human rights, accountability and majority representation, President Akayev and his successor, President Bakiev, tried to portray their regimes as democratic. This helped them gain legitimacy for their decisions and attract the attention and financial support of international donors (Cummings 2012; Matveeva 2010; Grävingholt 2011; Ramas 2011). The narratives were created strategically, for consumption by international audiences, be they foreign governments or business investors, and not necessarily for the domestic population (Marat 2009). However, the reality behind this façade of a democratic state and visionary promoter of reforms has been quite different. This contradiction between competing formal (external) and informal (internal) norms and practices spread through various aspects of the country's functioning, including the HIV/AIDS sector, and allowed it to stay afloat (Wilkinson 2010).

The international community believed that Kyrgyzstan would eventually meet their hopes of being a democratic state – the only democratic state in the region. International agencies also had their own agenda: creating what Lewis (2008, 124) called a 'virtual' Kyrgyzstan, a regional model of democratic reforms based on international principles. Yet, they failed to take into account the intricate power dynamics and the degree of elite resistance, as well as the true needs and interests of the country (Matveeva 2010; Grävingholt 2011). Later, when Western organizations were seen as imposing their own view on what Kyrgyzstan should look like and building high expectations, resistance to their ideologies and resentment to their mounting criticisms began to grow (Heathershaw 2010; Matveeva 2010; Wilkinson 2010; Cummings 2012). However, at least on paper, Kyrgyzstan continues to accommodate and comply with the pressures and interests of donors, without endangering the power of its political regimes (Spechler and Spechler 2010; Wilkinson 2010; Grävingholt 2011).

There was also a genuine desire on the part of national stakeholders to succeed with reforms. Kyrgyzstan was one of the first in the region to embark on the path of health reforms, earning praise from the international community and attracting international health funding from donors (Ibraimova et al. 2011). The health reforms and their perceived achievements have some parallels with the political and economic reforms mentioned above. Factors that enabled implementation of health reforms include 'windows of opportunity' created by the collapse of the Soviet Union and the pragmatic necessity to restructure and revamp an outdated and fragile healthcare system (Ibraimova et al. 2011). It was also part of the overall goal of liberal reforms and openness of the country to Western approaches (Ibraimova et al. 2011).

## NGOs' strategic response: learning to play the 'funding game'

To access available donor funding, NGOs reacted strategically by learning the 'rules of the game'. In this sense, a representative of one of the donor agencies reflected on the role of the Global Fund in national policy making: 'That's what pushes the government, the NGO sector and development partners … to learn the rules of the game and follow them.' By following the priorities of donors, NGOs adjusted their focus to those areas for which funding was available and not to what they thought was needed in reality. This often created frictions between funding and recipient organizations, and contributed to a sense of fierce competition and resentment within the NGO sector.

Some NGO representatives also talked about their feeling of 'being torn' between various legal and procedural requirements of donors and state agencies, as well as programme targets and reporting. For example, one NGO interviewee said there was a conflict between the 100% coverage of a certain population group that the Global Fund expected and the 60% target expected for country progress reporting under the United Nations General Assembly Special Session on HIV/AIDS (UNGASS). Some respondents mentioned that it was hard for NGOs to simultaneously meet the legal requirements of the state and various donors, which in some cases contradicted each other and had to be harmonized before any activities could take place. Recipients often felt stressed about which requirements to give priority to and meet – national or international ones.

Furthermore, each grant agreement stipulates how and on what funds should be spent, and donors always expect grantees to be financially efficient and frugal, often at the cost of project quality. In general, funders are perceived as inflexible when it comes to adjusting funding levels to take into account inflation, including increasing prices for products and services and the rising cost of living. For example, some NGOs reported the amount of funding they had been allocated a few years ago was no longer adequate to implement all planned HIV/AIDS activities as originally envisioned. Yet, during audits, funders often questioned the financial decisions of local counterparts, such as whether the funded activity met overall programme priorities, or why they purchased more expensive but better quality supplies, or paid a certain salary rate to highly qualified employees.

As mentioned above, each funding organization has its own internal processes and guidelines, which often require much paperwork at the application, progress monitoring and final reporting stages. According to many NGO representatives, writing reports and preparing for numerous audits is taking their time away from planning and implementing activities. Without a unified system of indicators and reporting, reporting is particularly taxing on NGOs that receive funding from different organizations, all of which have their own programme cycles and indicators, complex report formats and submission requirements. In case of large NGO associations, they have to collect and process reports from all member organizations before they can be submitted to the funder. As a result, NGOs, instead of becoming more productive and efficient, turn into small bureaucracies themselves. In the case of the Brazilian HIV/AIDS sector, this development has been well captured by the term 'grassroots bureaucracy' (Rich 2013).

## Unintended consequences

The way international agencies have shaped HIV/AIDS policies in Kyrgyzstan and the complex interplay between international donors and local NGOs has given rise to a number of unintended consequences, including the emergence of 'virtual realities', corruption and misappropriation of funds, lack of sustainability and a weakening of state capacity.

### *The rise of 'virtual realities'*

Besides the heavy burden of paperwork, NGO respondents felt that donors are only interested in reporting success stories and targets that have been achieved. This can be explained by the funding hierarchy and the fact that donor agencies themselves need to report to their own funders. To ensure that they continue receiving funding from governments and other sources, international agencies themselves create and sustain a 'reality' that suits their funders. As a national expert at an international agency explained: 'And donors, they are not interested in reality, they are interested in a beautiful [image].'

Just as they have to base programmes on the priorities of their own government and not local needs, they are under pressure to deliver the desired results and may avoid reporting local problems with planning and implementation. Both sides are thus interested in maintaining the legitimacy of interventions. This is in line with Mosse's (2005) observation that discourses become the end rather than the means of development and that practitioners fashion discourses and policies that do not reflect the realities they face.

In Kyrgyzstan, the quality of reporting suffers at various levels – from the top (donors themselves) to the bottom – NGOs and their contractors. It was reported by interviewees that there have been instances when outreach workers misreported the distribution of expendable materials and NGOs manipulated target data. Chasing after the desired 'reality', NGOs adjusted accordingly and learned how to write well and produce reports that leave funding agencies pleased. For instance, following Round 7 national progress reports, the Global Fund expressed its concerns over the quality of data and the accuracy of reporting, and concluded that reported achievements should be treated with caution and may not represent the actual situation (Global Fund 2011b).

This reporting 'hypocrisy', as some NGO representatives called it, creates an unhealthy environment where those NGOs that present well-written reports, using the latest technical language accepted and promoted by the international community, are usually favoured by donors and are more likely to receive the next round of funding. A national expert working in the UN system explained that NGOs have 'already learned how to copy well, they know where to take information and how to present it correctly.' As some respondents noted, the better presented the reports were, the higher were the chances of getting more funding.

Another challenge is that donors have created an uneven system of accountability when it comes to reporting. Not only are they perceived as unaccountable through formal mechanisms, such as the CCC, due to their international status and independence, but their grantees, the local NGOs, are also unaccountable to the rest of the HIV/AIDS sector. They are monitored or evaluated by the donors, but not by the government or state agencies or the population groups they aim to benefit and provide services to. A local manager of a donor agency said:

> We often hear about these massive programmes, 20 million, 30 million. When you dig deeper, what are the results? We don't have anything at the end. That's the responsibility of donors, or there should be some kind of common accountability to the people of the country, for which the funds were allocated.

Lack of transparency, accountability and information sharing, as some respondents from state agencies indicated, lead to poor coordination, duplication of efforts, and a sense of distrust among stakeholders in the HIV/AIDS sector. Yet, some respondents believed there was also a positive effect of placing responsibility on Kyrgyzstan to report progress on its commitment to key international agreements on HIV/AIDS, such as the UN's Millennium Development Goals and UNGASS, as another source of motivation. Others felt that the country does not have the appropriate tools to collect and analyse the necessary data, and that a centralized monitoring and evaluation system is needed for accurate reporting to international bodies and to properly coordinate the efforts of all HIV/AIDS stakeholders.

### *Corruption*

Corruption has become pervasive in Kyrgyzstan's society, with the ruling elite 'leading by example' (Wilkinson 2014, 151). Administrative and political offices have become investments in a market. They are purchased through unofficial payments, offering a favourable return and effectively privatizing public goods (Engvall 2011). This development has also taken hold of development aid, which has become an important source of revenue for domestic political elites (Wilkinson 2014).

The same can be observed in the HIV/AIDS sector. Most importantly, the Global Fund changed the principal recipient of its funding in 2011, after it emerged in an audit that the National AIDS Centre had been engaged in major mismanagement of grant funding. The role of the principal recipient was transferred to an international agency, UNDP (Bashmakova et al. 2009a; Global Fund 2011a).

While some respondents complained of too much checking by donors, others thought funding agencies ought to better monitor their recipients' activities. One leader of an NGO association shared her views: 'When I started working in 2007, I was shocked by the consumerist attitude [towards donor funding]; perhaps it was driven by the fact that the international community was not monitoring the money it directed towards developing countries.'

Some respondents indicated that the lack of close financial and programmatic monitoring of the Global Fund's Programme Implementation Unit provided opportunities for fraud. The respondents mentioned techniques such as registering 'fake', one-off NGOs, inflating prices and cost estimates, reselling supplies and expendable materials, and manipulating data. This information echoes the findings of the Global Fund's audit, which revealed, among many other issues, problems in the procurement of health products based on inaccurate estimates of patients and inflated prices, lack of appropriate storage for goods and supplies, and poor coordination between HIV/AIDS stakeholders (Global Fund 2011a). Even though national stakeholders agreed that fraud and corruption in the HIV/AIDS sector were major reasons for concern, they believed that not all receiving organizations should be treated with the same degree of suspicion. Many NGO respondents believed that constant negotiations over budgets, disagreements between donor and recipient agencies, and pressure to comply often lead to friction, a sense of distrust, stress and disillusion on the part of implementing agencies.

The HIV/AIDS sector, unlike other areas of public health, has been receiving a great amount of attention and funding (Shiffman 2006). As a result, many interviewees noted, it has lost a sense of responsibility and accountability. Coupled with poor financial management, it is not surprising that some of the funding in Kyrgyzstan was misappropriated and, as more funds flowed in, corruption and consumerist behaviour blossomed. A programme manager of a donor organization described these freeloading tendencies on the part of some local agencies as follows: 'I heard such rumours that people used to say: "They give us money ... why not take it, if they give it to us?"' And while some spoke of recipient organizations manipulating donors, other respondents believed that it was the other way round – international organizations, through their funding and support, were seen as manipulating the country and its HIV/AIDS sector.

### *Donor dependency and sustainability*

Given the comparatively small proportion of state funding when compared to donor contributions, the HIV/AIDS sector is highly susceptible to any changes in donor priorities and aid flows, threatening long-term planning and sustainability. While recognizing the lack of state ownership and its weakness in the funding of HIV/AIDS activities, such great financial dependence on donors, and the funding imbalance it created in the health system, worried most of the local respondents. This is how one NGO leader felt: 'Things are imposed on us from the outside, some strange programmes that lead us nowhere, except to loans, suffocating "barriers" and so on.'

Financial dependency is linked to an unequal power distribution between international and national HIV/AIDS partners. While some, mostly state agencies, viewed donor organizations as partners to collaborate with, others, namely NGOs, spoke of a different dynamic, mainly a top-down donor–recipient relationship. Many of the local and international respondents and authors thought that NGOs, while a most vibrant and active sector, were the least independent and sustainable actors in the HIV/AIDS sector and the most vulnerable to changes in international funding. Other studies on HIV/AIDS policies in Kyrgyzstan have reached the same conclusion (Murzalieva 2009; Spicer et al. 2010). Any budget cuts, interruptions or funding delays put NGOs' planning of new activities or implementation of existing ones in jeopardy.

Furthermore, donor activities are often based on short-term goals and they therefore cannot guarantee to be committed to their target groups' long-term well-being. Often, they also fail to contribute to the institutionalization of efforts. Respondents believed that donors, by doing 'a little bit here, a little bit there', prefer short-term, quick results which they can report back to the funding governments or private bodies and may not be interested in long-term sustainability. A staff member of an international organization noted: 'Well, such a situation is everywhere, i.e. we have certain pilot schools, pilot universities, pilot organizations, pilot regions. Everything is a pilot at the moment; we all wear "pilot caps"!'

Such a pilot-based and unsystematic approach, not aligned with the overall needs and priorities of the health system, neither allows for long-term planning nor gives a sense of security and predictability about a project's future; it ultimately undermines the vitality of the HIV/AIDS sector. Many respondents believed that the responsibility for the sector's sustainability lies with both the donors and the recipient organizations. Some argued that donors have already given enough and that they should have been weaning recipient organizations off international support. There have also been efforts to improve aid effectiveness through mechanisms such as the sector-wide approach, which aims to harmonize donor funding, reduce duplication and waste, and support national health strategies.

## Conclusion

The critical development literature has long established that development efforts can undermine the development they purport to achieve. Instead, they can serve different functions, such as keeping existing elites in power and solidifying structures of ownership and clientelism (Ferguson 1990). This has shifted attention to the 'side effects' or unintended consequences of development programmes (Mosse 2005), many of which are not even recognized by participants themselves (Ferguson 1990).

This article adds to this discussion by shedding light on the situation in the HIV/AIDS sector in Kyrgyzstan. It showed that international agencies have been instrumental in shaping the national response to the HIV/AIDS epidemic. They have cultivated political will among top policy makers, provided technical, financial and policy support, and built local capacity. However, policies and programmes were not always tailored sufficiently to the local context. Donors have exerted strong pressure to adopt certain policies and guidelines, as well as to meet programmatic priorities and funding requirements, often at the expense of the authority of local stakeholders and the country's real needs. Yet, local NGOs have responded strategically, playing the 'funding game' and making sure to meet the expectations of donors, whether by adjusting their priorities or their reporting.

The result is a complex interplay. The arrival of donor funding has created a co-dependent type of donor–recipient relationship, in which donors and receiving organizations need each other to fulfil their agendas and promote their interests. This is in line with findings from many other countries in Eastern Europe, but also Africa (Wedel 2001; Heald 2003; Seckinelgin 2008; Beland and Orenstein 2010). While international agencies place stringent conditions on funding and pressure their beneficiaries to adopt certain ideas and courses of action, local NGOs often alter their mission and mode of operation to access the sought-after international funding, which is then used as a means of securing power and more funding.

A number of unintended consequences can be identified. High levels of international aid, coupled with a lack of transparency and accountability, political instability and low levels of socio-economic development, have created perverse incentives for funding mismanagement. As corruption is now deeply entrenched in all levels and sectors of Kyrgyzstan's society, it will be difficult to address this issue in the HIV/AIDS sector alone. Failure to ensure the sustainability of the response to HIV/AIDS is another unintended consequence of the current system of aid. The drive of donors for quick results and desired outcomes is at odds with the long-term sustainability and integration of HIV/AIDS programmes into the overall health system. The uneven power balance and the heavy dependence on international funding also reduce decision-making power and governance capacity, and lead to institutional fragmentation, duplication and the weakening of HIV/AIDS efforts.

Perhaps one of the most worrying side effects of HIV/AIDS policies in Kyrgyzstan is the creation of 'virtual realities'. Kyrgyzstan's political elite and top decision-makers have carefully crafted the country's external image and declared progress at the international level to secure access to vital donor aid and resources. Many NGOs are similarly involved in fashioning a reality that does not exist on the ground. The country thus continues to sustain an international image that suits the interests of donors, civil society and the government, but is disconnected from national needs and priorities. This might explain, at least partially, why donor funding for HIV/AIDS in Kyrgyzstan remains high, while HIV/AIDS rates continue to grow and true progress has been lacking in recent years.

## Disclosure statement

No potential conflict of interest was reported by the authors.

## References

Ancker, S., and B. Rechel. 2013. "HIV/AIDS Policy-Making in Kyrgyzstan: A Stakeholder Analysis." *Health Policy and Planning* 30 (1): 8–18.

Ancker, S., and B. Rechel. 2015. "Policy Responses to HIV/AIDS in Central Asia." *Global Public Health* 10 (7): 817–833. doi:10.1080/17441692.2015.1043313

Ancker, S., B. Rechel, M. McKee, and N. Spicer. 2013. "Kyrgyzstan: Still a Regional 'Pioneer' in HIV/AIDS or Living on its Reputation?" *Central Asian Survey* 32 (1): 66–84. doi:10.1080/02634937.2013.771965

Atlani-Duault, L. 2007. *Humanitarian Aid in Post-Soviet Countries: An Anthropoligical Perspective.* London: Routledge.

Bashmakova, L., M. Mamyrov, D. Sorombaeva, et al. 2009a. *Overcoming Global Healthcare Problems: National Response to HIV Infection, Tuberculosis and Malaria in the Kyrgyz Republic*. Bishkek: Ministry of Health/Macro International.

Balabanova, D., M. McKee, A. Mills, G. Walt, and A. Haines. 2010. "What Can Global Health Institutions Do to Help Strengthen Health Systems in Low Income Countries?" *Health Research Policy and Systems* 8: 1–22. doi:10.1186/1478-4505-8-22

Balabanova, D., V. Oliveira-Cruz, and K. Hanson. 2008. *Health Sector Governance and Implications for the Private Sector.* Washington, D.C.: Results for Development Institute.

Beland, D., and M. Orenstein. 2010. "Transnational Actors and Public Policy." *JSGS Working Paper Series* 5: 1–17.

Brugha, R., M. Donoghue, M. Starling, P. Ndubani, F. Benedita, F. Ssengooba, and G. Walt. 2004. "The Global Fund: Managing Great Expectations." *The Lancet* 364: 95–100. The Global Fund: managing great expectations. doi:10.1016/S0140-6736(04)16595-1

Campbell, C. 2003. *Letting Them Die: Why HIV/AIDS Prevention Programmes Fail.* Bloomington: Indiana University Press.

CCC. 2013. *Epidemiologocal situation in the Kyrgyz Republic (Эпидемиологическая ситуация в Кыргызской Республике)* [Online]. Bishkek: Country Coordinating Committee (CCC) under the Government of the Kyrgyz Republic. Accessed 5 June 2013. www.aids.gov.kg/ru/

Collins, K. 2009. *Clan Politics and Regime Transition in Central Asia*. Cambridge: Cambridge University Press.

Cornish, F., C. Campbell, A. Shukla, and R. Banerji. 2012. "From Brothel to Boardroom: Prospects for Community Leadership of HIV Interventions in the Context of Global Funding Practices." *Health and Place* 18 (3): 468–474. doi:10.1016/j.healthplace.2011.08.018

Cummings, S. 2012. *Understanding Central Asia. Politics and Contested Transformations*. Milton Park and New York, NY: Routledge.

Eyben, R. 2010. *Supporting Inclusive and Democratic Ownership: a 'How to Note' for Donors*. Brighton: Institute of Development Studies.

Engvall, J. 2011. "The State as Investment Market: An Analytical Framework for Interpreting Politics and Bureaucracy in Kyrgyzstan." Doctoral thesis, Uppsala University.

Ferguson, J. 1990. *The Anti-Politics Machine. "Development," Depoliticization and Bureaucratic Power in Lesotho*. Cambridge: Cambridge University Press.

Global Fund. 2011a. *Grant Scorecard (Kyrgyzstan) – Round 7*. Geneva: The Global Fund to fight AIDS, Tuberculosis and Malaria.

Global Fund. 2011b. *Grant Performance Report (Kyrgyzstan) – Round 7*. Geneva: Global Fund to fight HIV/AIDS, Tuberculosis and Malaria.

Global Fund. 2013. *Portfolio data: HIV/AIDS*. Geneva: Global Fund to fight HIV/AIDS, Tuberculosis and Malaria. Accessed 29 May 2011. http://portfolio.theglobalfund.org/en/Country/Index/KGZ

Grävingholt, J. 2011. "The Political Economy of Governance Reform in Central Asia." In *Institutional Reform in Central Asia: Politico-Economic Challenges*, edited by J. Ahrens and H. Hoen, 155–170. London: Routledge.

Hall, A., and J. Midgley. 2004. *Social Policy for Development*. London: Sage Publications.

Harman, S. 2009a. "The Causes, Contours, and Consequences of the Multi-Sectoral Response to HIV/AIDS." In *Governance of HIV/AIDS: Making Participation and Accountability Count*, edited by S. Harman and F. Lisk, 165–179. Abingdon: Routledge.

Harman, S. 2009b. "Introduction. Governance of the HIV/AIDS Response: Making Participation and Accountability Count." In *Governance of HIV/AIDS: Making Participation and Accountability Count*, edited by S. Harman and F. Lisk, 1–8. Abingdon: Routledge.

Heald, S. 2003. "An Absence of Anthropology: Critical Reflections on Anthropology and AIDS Policy and Practice in Africa." In *Learning from HIV and AIDS*, edited by G. Ellison, M. Parker, and C. Campbell, 191–216. Cambridge: Cambridge University Press.

Heathershaw, J. 2010. "Central Asian Statehood in Post-Colonial Perspective." In *Stable Outside, Fragile Inside? Post-Soviet Statehood in Central Asia*, edited by E. Kavalski, 87–101. Aldershot: Ashgate.

Ibraimova, A., B. Akkazieva, G. Murrzalieva, and D. Balabanova. 2011. "Kyrgyzstan: A Regional Leader in Health System Reform." In *'Good Health at Low Cost' 25 Years on. What Makes a Successful Health System?*, edited by D. Balabanova, M. McKee, and A. Mills, 117–157. London: The London School of Hygiene & Tropical Medicine.

Lewis, D. 2008. *The Temptations of Tyranny in Central Asia*. London: Hurst & Company.

Marat, E. 2010. "Nation Branding in Central Asia: A New Campaign to Present Ideas about the State and the Nation." *Europe Asia Studies* 61 (7):1123–1136.

Matveeva, A. 2010. "Legitimising Central Asian Authoritarianism: Political Manipulation and Symbolic Power." In *Symbolism and Power in Central Asia: Politics of the Spectacular*, edited by S. Cummings, 12–38. New York, NY: Routledge.

MOH. 2012b. *State Programme on Prevention of HIV Epidemic and Its Social and Economic Consequences in the Kyrgyz Republic for 2012–2016*. Bishkek: Ministry of Health (MOH).

Morozova, I. 2013. "Patterns of Elite Consolidation and Rivalry in Kyrgyzstan between 1960 and 2000." In *Politics, Identity and Education in Central Asia: Post-Soviet Kyrgyzstan*, edited by P. Akçali and C. Engin-Demir, 9–32. London: Routledge.

Mosse, D. 2005. *Cultivating Development: An Ethnography of Aid Policy and Practice*. London and Ann Arbor: Pluto Press.

Murzalieva, G., J. Aleshkina, A. Temoriv, et al. 2009. *Tracking Global HIV/AIDS Initiatives and Their Impact in the Health Systems: the Experience of the Kyrgyz Republic*. Final Report. London: The Global HIV/AIDS Initiatives Network.

Mwacalimba, K. K. 2012. "Globalised Disease Control and Response Distortion: A Case Study of Avian Influenza Pandemic Preparedness in Zambia." *Critical Public Health* 22: 391–405. doi:10.1080/09581596.2012.710739

Oraz, S. 2013. "The Impact of Askar Akayev's Political Leadership in the Process of Democratisation in Kyrgyzstan." In *Politics, Identity and Education in Central Asia: Post-Soviet Kyrgyzstan*, edited by P. Akçali and C. Engin-Demir, 35–51. London: Routledge.

Pomfret, R. 2006. *The Central Asian Economies Since Independence*. Princeton, NJ: Princeton University Press.

Radnitz, S. 2010. "A Horse of a Different Color. Revolution and Regression in Kyrgyzstan." In *Democracy and Authoritarianism in the Postcommunist World*, edited by V. Bunce, M. McFaul, and K. Stoner-Weiss, 300–324. Cambridge: Cambridge University Press.

Ramas, R. R. 2011. "The Institutional Persistence of Patrimonialism in the Kyrgyz Republic." In *Institutional Reform in Central Asia: Politic-Economic Challenges*, edited by J. Ahrens and H. Hoen, 129–151. London: Routledge.

Rich, J. 2013. "Grassroots Bureaucracy: Intergovernmental Relations and Popular Mobilization in Brazil's AIDS Policy Sector." *Latin American Politics and Society* 55 (2): 1–25. doi:10.1111/j.1548-2456.2013.00191.x

Seckinelgin, H. 2008. *International Politics of HIV/AIDS. Global Disease- Local Pain*. London: Routledge.

Shiffman, J. 2006. "HIV/AIDS and the Rest of the Global Health Agenda." *Bulletin of the World Health Organisation* 84: 923. doi:10.2471/BLT.06.036681

Sjöstedt, R. 2008. "Exploring the Construction of Threats: The Securitization of HIV/AIDS in Russia." *Security Dialogue* 39 (1): 7–29. doi:10.1177/0967010607086821

Slater, R. 2004. *The Implications of HIV/AIDS for Social Protection*. London: Department for International Development.

Spechler, M., and D. Spechler. 2010. "The International Political Economy of Central Asian Statehood." In *Stable Outside, Fragile Inside? Post-Soviet Statehood in Central Asia*, edited by E. Kavalski, 71–106. Aldershot: Ashgate.

Spicer, N., J. Aleshkina, R. Biesma, Carlos Caceres, Baltazar Chilundo, Ketevan Chkhatarashvili, Andrew Harmer et al. 2010. "National and Subnational HIV/AIDS Coordination: Are Global Health Initiatives Closing the Gap between Intent and Practice?" *Globalization and Health* 6: 1–16. doi:10.1186/1744-8603-6-3

Theodoulou, S. 1996. "AIDS Equals Politics." In *AIDS: The Politics and Policy of Disease*, edited by S. Theodoulou. London: Prentice Hall.

UNAIDS. 2013a. *Country Profile-Kyrgyzstan*. Geneva: United Nations Joint Programme on HIV/AIDS (UNAIDS). Accessed 21 June 2013. www.unaids.org/en/regionscountries/countries/kyrgyzstan/

UNAIDS. 2013b. *Global Report: UNAIDS Report on the Global Epidemic 2013*. Geneva: United Nations Joint Programme on HIV/AIDS (UNAIDS).

UNDP. 2012. *Support to the Government to respond to HIV in the Kyrgyz Republic. Annual Work Plan*. Bishkek: United Nations Development Programme (UNDP) in the Kyrgyz Republic.

Van Der Vliet, V. 1996. *The Politics of AIDS*. London: Bowerdean Publishing Company Ltd.

Vieira, M. A. 2007. "The Securitization of the HIV/AIDS Epidemic as a Norm" Braz. political sci. rev. (Online), vol. 2, no. se Rio de Janeiro.

Wedel, J. 2001. *Collision and Collusion. The Strange Case of Western Aid to Eastern Europe*. New York, NY: Palgrave Macmillan.

Wilkinson, C. 2010. "International Agency in Kyrgyzstan: Rhetoric, Revolution and Renegotiation." In *Stable Outside, Fragile Inside? Post-Soviet Statehood in Central Asia*, edited by E. Kavalski, 131–155. Aldershot: Ashgate.

Wilkinson, C. 2014. "Development in Kyrgyzstan: Failed State or Failed State-building?" In *Development in Difficult Sociopolitical Contexts*, edited by A. Ware, 137–162. Houndmills: Palgrave Macmillan.

World Bank. 2013. *World Development Indicators: Kyrgyz Republic* (online database). Washington, D.C.: World Bank. Accessed 3 October 2013. http://data.worldbank.org/country/kyrgyz-republic

# The monetization of social celebrations in rural Kyrgyzstan: on the uses of hashish money

Gulzat Botoeva*

*Sociology Department, University of Essex, Colchester, UK*

This article focuses on the embeddedness of hashish production in the local economy of Toolu, a village in Kyrgyzstan. It explores how transformations in social relationships and the monetization of gift giving put constant pressure on families to find cash in a semi-subsistence agricultural economy. Although not produced on an industrial scale in the community, hashish is used as a cash crop in times of deficit. Based on a mixed-methods study combining ethnographic fieldwork with survey data, I show how the hashish economy is intertwined with different forms of reciprocal relationships based on gift-giving practices and the monetization of social relationships. In doing so, I illustrate how the hashish economy is embedded in local livelihoods and shapes emerging forms of economic morality in Kyrgyz society.

## Introduction

This article focuses on the embeddedness of hashish production in the local economy of Toolu, a village in Kyrgyzstan.[1] I explore how transformations in social relationships and the monetization of gift giving put constant pressure on families to find cash in a semi-subsistence agricultural economy. Although not produced on an industrial scale in the community, hashish is used as a cash crop and hence not only provides a supply of cash but also facilitates the maintenance of social security networks among local residents.

My study departs from other research on drug markets in Central Asia, which mainly focus on issues of Islamic extremism and violence that undermine the security of Central Asian states (Cornell and Swanström 2006; Engvall 2006; Makarenko 2002), presenting illegal drug markets as operating within the binary terms of 'black and white' or 'good and evil', in contrast with the legitimate activities of 'law-abiding citizens'. However, in examining the case of Bolivian coca production, Sanabria (2004) argues that it is impossible to disentangle the drug war matrix from the means of production. In doing so, he claims that the war's rationale is fundamentally flawed. This is in keeping with the critique that drug markets are uniquely positioned and embedded in the local societies and economies in which they operate. The existence of small-scale private drug markets that operate according to their own internal rules, and do not necessarily follow the ways in which the industrialized type of drug markets precipitate violence, nor are linked with organized criminal groups which use drug money to fund their terrorist activities, provides the evidence for such a critique (Potter 2010; Sandberg 2012). While not seeking to justify the uniqueness of the Kyrgyz case in relation to these international studies, my findings reflect the latter examples, which claim that all drug economies should be understood in their local context

*The author is now at the Department of Social Sciences, University of Roehampton, London, UK.

and therefore do not automatically pose an external threat to law and order. In this paper, I present a nuanced analysis of how small-scale hashish production and circulation of illicit commodities in Toolu are intertwined with the practices of social support and informal crediting.

Social networks and gift-giving practices are being transformed by the prevalence of hashish as cash. My analysis will focus specifically on how social celebrations (or *toi*s) are being shaped by this new economic activity. In turn, I examine how factors such as status, prestige and an emergent sense of national identity affect the involvement of various strata of society in *toi*s.

I explore below the way in which hashish production reconfigures social networking practices and how it plays an important role in maintaining reciprocal relationships between families in Toolu. While agricultural activities do not provide adequate income, social celebrations play an important role in family lives, and many need an extra source of income to take part in such activities. In particular, increased spending on social celebrations in the last 20 years has created challenges for family budgets. *Toi*s help families play a part in the lives of their relatives and friends and celebrate important milestones. They are also used as a source of social and economic support in times of need. Here we can see that although monetized gifts create barriers of entry for some poor families, social networks still retain some forms of support for those who are able to secure their membership. Hashish, therefore, is used by some families as a means of retaining membership in social networks.

The article proceeds with a note on the fieldwork and methodology, followed by a discussion of the theoretical framework. I will also describe how hashish is produced and who is involved in this illegal activity in Toolu, before finally contextualizing this through a discussion of social celebrations and the recent transformations of social relationships due to monetization of gift-giving practices.

## Methodology

The paper draws on fieldwork conducted in Toolu, a village located in Issyk-Kul *oblast* in Kyrgyzstan. Toolu has around 4000 inhabitants, who are mainly occupied with agricultural labour, cultivating their land with wheat, barley and potatoes and breeding various livestock such as sheep, cows, goats and horses.

The research is a mixed-method study, based on 64 semi-structured in-depth interviews and ethnographic observations of livelihood strategies, as well as a survey 147 households. Overall, it took nine months to conduct my fieldwork, visiting the village on two separate occasions: July–December 2009, and July–September 2010. All interviews were conducted in the Kyrgyz language. During the fieldwork I was able to collect a diverse range of interviews with both men and women. However, due to the gendered nature of the fieldwork (here I mean my own status and positionality as a female researcher), participant observation was mainly possible with women. This is in turn affected the type of data that was collected, as my main observations of social networking happened to be among women.

In an ethnographic study, having a gatekeeper, especially one with knowledge of the illegal activities that people try to hide from outsiders, is an important aspect not only of successful entrance to the community but also in building a rapport with participants (Adler 1985; Dwyer 2009; Jacobs 1998). After two weeks in the region, to which I gained access through Ainura,[2] a local English teacher who used to be an old friend of a colleague and lived in Ak-Suu *raion*, I met her relative Aikan, who lived in Toolu. After a few successful interviews with Aikan and some of her friends, I asked Aikan if I could stay in her place to continue my study in Toolu. She agreed to give me space in her house and also assist with making introductions. She was thirty-three years old, with four children, and worked topping up mobile phones and selling gas.

My choice of location was determined by a broader set of questions. Rather than exploring an illegal act in isolation, I was attempting to understand how a community negotiated the production of a drug considered illegal by the state. The Tyup region was among two other regions in Issyk-Kul *oblast* with large areas of wild-growing cannabis plants and a high involvement of local people in the drug-making process (Zelichenko 2003). Informally, the region is also known for its potent cannabis, which grows more abundantly than in other parts of Kyrgyzstan. It was identified in 1999 as one of the regions with large fields of wild-growing cannabis plants (Zelichenko 2003). Hashish and marijuana were made for sale in this region during Soviet times, but mostly by underground groups (Djakishev 2004; Musin 1988).[3] The collapse of the Soviet Union in 1991 entailed the increased involvement of previously fully employed *kolkhoz* (collective farm) and *sovkhoz* (state collective farm) workers from Kyrgyz communities in hashish making. In the 2000s, hashish making entered everyday conversation and practice in the village. Although not all families were involved in this illegal activity, by the end of 2009 some of the local men and women in their twenties and thirties produced hashish on a regular basis.

Initially, I started going around Toolu with Aikan, and she introduced me to her friends and relatives. To meet more people and to learn about community life, I also started following Aikan to different gatherings and participating in social celebrations, which helped me in gradually becoming accepted by her network of friends and relatives. I attended many significant and informal social gatherings with her: commemoration parties, funerals, a parent-teacher association meeting, and the opening of a mosque in the village, which brought the whole village together in a formal celebration. By the second year, women who usually saw me in their *sherine*[4] gatherings started talking about including me as part of their network. I felt at the beginning that they were joking, as this was subsequently repeated at numerous gatherings I realized that they were serious. However, I could not stay permanently within their circle of *sherines* as I was supposed to finish my fieldwork in two months at that time. This acceptance into the network of friends and relatives of Aikan meant that people could trust me since there were many occasions when they discussed hashish making openly without hesitation. Such gatherings served an important role in creating a space for sharing the latest news and gossip. During the summer, the militia would make frequent visits to the villages and fields, and on many such occasions women would share warnings about their presence in the village. They would also get information on who was collecting hashish for drug dealers and for how much someone could sell hashish at that moment.

Some relationships that started with the help of Aikan grew stronger during the second fieldtrip, in 2010. For instance, our friendly relationship with Jamilya, initiated during an interview in summer 2009, was followed by many informal conversations in her and her friends' houses. Jamilya was also thirty-three, with four children. She was one of the women who regularly made hashish resin from cannabis plants and therefore was able to take me to the fields to see where and how hashish was cropped. This relationship with Jamilya, being in her network of hashish-making friends and observing them in the field, allowed me to gain even greater rapport with them, as they believed that I was not related to law enforcement.

However, gaining trust among the people in Toolu was not an easy process. As the militia tried to learn about when and where sale transactions happened and started using informants by promising to free them for full cooperation, people did not talk openly about their illegal activities with strangers or newcomers. Especially at the beginning of my fieldwork, some assumed that I worked for the militia by collecting information for them. Subsequently, I convinced my participants that I was conducting sociological research as part of my doctoral studies at a university in the UK. This helped ease the tension, as most interviewees doubted that I would be affiliated with law enforcement while studying abroad. On the other hand, the same fact made some people refuse to talk about hashish as it would create a negative image abroad, not only of the region but also of the country as a whole. In such cases I tried to explain that my goal was not to present them as criminals but rather, as a researcher, to understand the socio-cultural conditions under which hashish production became widespread in the community.

The survey was used as a follow-up to the ethnographic fieldwork and served two functions: firstly, to test some of the observations developed during fieldwork concerning the changes in reciprocal relationships between families and monetization of social relationships among rich and poor families in Toolu; and secondly, to provide a broader picture of the semi-subsistence-oriented rural economy. In the survey design, the household was taken as the unit of analysis. With the help of Aikan and Jamilya, I made a map of the village and counted all the households. To find the total number of households, based on local understandings of the term, I counted it as one household when a few generations and families were sharing not only the house but also household assets and responsibilities. The total number of households at that time was 300. In the survey I covered half of the households in the village by interviewing one adult person from each of them. The survey covered questions related to the livelihoods of households, livestock and land assets they owned, and use of formal and informal microcredits. None of the survey questions related to hashish production, as one would be unlikely to receive any answer to such questions in a formal, structured interview.

## Market and moral economies

The debates on moral and market economies and their effects on social structures provide a useful framework for analyzing the transformations of social relationships in Toolu. The mainstream academic discussion on moral and market economies suggests that they exist in a dichotomous position to each other. Although the free market economy was considered to have a civilizing effect, with the self-interest of every individual being counter-checked by other members of society (Smith 1986), the proponents of the moral economy were highly critical of market economy principles. They argued that a free and self-regulated market economy had been allowed to strip away forms of protection for the poorest and weakest that were based on ideas of justice and traditional values of support (Scott 1977, 1985; Thompson 1991a). This approach to the moral economy emphasizes the importance and endurance of relations between people which are not purely determined by self-interest but based on the values of support and reciprocity, which enable the sharing of resources within the community through reciprocal exchange (Polanyi 1944; Scott 1985; Thompson 1991a, 1991b).

In the post-Soviet space, the implementation of neoliberal policies saw a return of Polanyi's critique of the disembedding nature of market economies. Some studies revealed that with the marketization of society, the social networks of 'poor groups' shrank and included only their close relatives, who in most cases held the same social position as them (Kuehnast and Dudwick 2004; Werner 1997, 1998a, 1998c, 2000). The networks were based on how well someone invested in relationships, contributing with gifts, money and physical labour in feasts. The increasing inequality was due to the monetization of some forms of relationships among the rural population, based on the material success and economic capital of some of the families (Satybaldieva 2010).

Though influential, this dichotomous approach to market and moral economies has been questioned in more recent scholarship. It was argued that market economies are also embedded in the social structures of societies in which they exist (Granovetter 1985). Markets and moral economies can exist continually, intertwining and blending with each other (Hass 2011; Zelizer 1978, 1989, 1997, 2005). Following the view that markets can also be considered as moral (Booth 1994), instead of glorifying gift-exchange-based societies, this approach proposed that market economies are based on different but still moral grounds (Browne and Milgram 2008). In this way, the moral motivations of reciprocity and support are not always neglected in market economies, and markets can even develop further through grounding themselves in local moralities (Browne and Milgram 2008). For instance, the study conducted by Sanghera and his colleagues in Kyrgyzstan was able to show that, despite the marketization of economy and society, close family members considered it important to treat each other with respect and dignity despite their level of material well-being and inability to reciprocate. Giving to and supporting family members without the expectation that it be reciprocated still existed (Sanghera, Ablezova, and Botoeva 2011).

Some studies on illegal-drug-producing communities in developing countries also brought up discussion of how drug markets brought some changes into the way that the local communities used to operate. Some reported that drug production as part of the market economy introduced a wage-labour system into the local system of social relations based on gift giving and reciprocity among Bolivian coca producers (Sanabria 1993, 2004). However, instead of suggesting that reciprocal relationships were replaced by wage labour, Sanabria argued that both forms were present at the same time and were used interchangeably. A more recent study, conducted in Bolivia among coca growers, suggests that reciprocal relationships between drug producers become infused with market principles (Pellegrini 2013). Coca producers use reciprocal labour to help each other with harvesting, while some, more busy and wealthier farmers tend to pay someone else to fulfil their obligation to return the help.

This discussion of moral and market economies is important in capturing the transformation of social relationships between families in Toolu and locating the hashish economy within these local dynamics. In what follows, I will discuss the importance of social celebrations (*tois*) in creating and maintaining social security networks, followed by an analysis of how social networks are being transformed through the monetization of gifts.

### *Hashish production*

The neoliberal reforms of structural adjustment that took place throughout the 1990s promoted freedom of markets and the creation of entrepreneurial and competitive conditions for every individual. In reality, they had starkly different and unevenly distributed results.

Market economy reforms in the agricultural sphere in Kyrgyzstan had the opposite of the intended effect and turned most farming activities into semi-subsistence ones. In Toolu, as in other villages located in the agricultural regions of Kyrgyzstan, land and many other state assets were privatized in the mid-1990s. Five-hundred and seventy-six state and collective farms distributed their arable land and non-land assets to all farm residents and farm employees throughout the country (Abdurasulov 2009; Bloch 2004). During the privatization, the population of Toolu received 0.78 hectares of land per person. With small shares of land as their main means of production, many farmers produced agricultural products mainly for their own consumption and only a small surplus for the market, becoming more subsistence-oriented in their agricultural activities (Gleason 2003).

Only a tiny minority of well-off families, who owned large fields (30–50 hectares), full machinery and large herds of livestock (around 300 sheep, 30–40 cows and 20 horses), were able to produce a surplus and generate cash. Although also a minority in the community, the poorer members could not cultivate most of their land and so rented it out (or lost ownership completely), or did not own much livestock (no livestock or one cow and a few sheep) and had to find other ways to generate income. Even the 'average' households, as many families preferred to call themselves, were not able to produce much surplus for the market as their land, usually 3–5 hectares, was enough only to harvest mainly for their own consumption. They consumed their wheat and potatoes and sold some of their harvest on the market. Usually their livestock, around 20–30 sheep and 3–4 cows, could generate some good cash. Sheep and calves could be sold at the Kara-Kol *bazaar* (market); cow's milk could be sold to dairy factories.

A few families were able to earn money through selling petrol for cars, topping up phones and selling food and clothes in small shops opened up in their houses. A few men worked as taxi drivers. But these activities were restricted to well-off families that had some capital and most importantly cars, to be able to transport goods and people. Working as a builder on an occasional basis, a man might earn two to three thousand som (£28–42) per month, or even less. Sewing one *töshök* (a traditional mattress for sitting), which requires one or two days of labour, a woman can earn 100 som (£1.4). One formal source of employment – the local school – paid a salary of around 2600–2800 som (£37–40) per month. Salaries were similar in the local administration.

Due to the low level of local wages and earnings and the semi-subsistence-oriented agricultural economy, families in Toolu were in a permanent state of deficit. In particular, the summer months were the hardest time to find any cash, as harvests were collected only in autumn. Therefore, making hashish coincided with the time when cash was in absolute deficit in the village and took its niche in the local economy. Usually men were said to be able to make on average three to five matchboxes of hashish (a small matchbox, called *korobochka,* works as a measuring unit for hashish) in one day, which would earn them 1200–2000 som (£17–28). Although women were usually said to be able to make less hashish than men, from a half a matchbox to three maximum a day, as they would not travel far from the village so as to keep up with childcare and cooking, they could make comparatively more money with hashish than through other activities. Making hashish, women could earn at least 200 som (£2.8) in a few hours.

It is difficult to know the exact number of people involved in hashish production due to the hidden nature of production and trade. A rough estimate by some informers suggests that around 100 men (usually going around with their horses) could be involved in hashish making on a usual summer day. However, hashish makers would not usually go to the fields in big groups; they made it from wild-growing cannabis plants, by rubbing the upper leaves between their palms. This meant that they needed to search for cannabis plants and travel from one field to another. However, on some occasions when militia representatives tried to catch them, instead of hiding the men went onto the hills, which gave a good indication of roughly how many were making hashish that day. According to some interviewees, it was one of the new strategies hashish-making men developed as the militia would not want to confront such large numbers of men.

Hashish was mostly sold in the vicinity of the village, as there were dealers that came to buy. Most of the drug dealers were from outside the region but with some connections among the local population.[5] In the 1990s, drug dealers would come during the daytime and ask around about who was selling hashish. However, with tightened controls since the mid-2000s and a few arrests made by the militia during the sale of hashish, they began to visit only specific middlemen and women at a certain time, usually at night. The middlemen and women usually collected hashish for the drug dealers from the local hashish makers or asked them to bring their drugs to a certain place at a certain time. The dealers paid the middlemen and women, who in turn distributed the money to the hashish makers. For their role of connecting the two they were able to take a cut of the money, usually around 50 som from each matchbox of hashish.

Hashish making is not without risk. People who make it could be caught by militia officers in the fields, travelling on horses or walking down the hills, and during the sale to the dealers. Usually the militia used to arrive in unmarked cars and civilian clothes so that people would not be able to identify them as militia representatives. When the militia saw people near the fields they stopped them and searched for drugs. Those who were caught mostly tried to negotiate a bribe with the militia. In most cases they were successful – they were told how much money their relatives should bring to the car at a certain time, normally no more than two or three hours after they were caught. If the relatives were able and willing to pay the requested sum of cash, then the person caught and held by the militia in the car would be released. The official papers that had been filled out by the militia officers would be destroyed so that the case would no longer stand. In some rare circumstances houses and sheds could be searched for hidden drugs based on a tip provided by villagers, who had themselves been caught by the militia and promised to be released with no charges if they fully cooperated. Such cases, however, occurred rarely. Usually people were able to bribe the militia and be released with no charges. The amount of the bribe varied from a few hundred to a few thousand som, depending on how much drugs they were caught in possession of and whether they were involved in a sale at that time. This is justified by militia officers by saying that there is a difference between being caught with small amounts of drugs that could be qualified as for personal use, which is dealt with in an administrative code, and being caught with bigger amounts of drugs during a transaction, which is dealt with a criminal code. Only on the rare occasions when people were not able to make a bribe were their cases officially registered in the local militia office. Such people either did not have good connections with the militia, or could not find the money on short notice. Some would be charged administrative fines as 'hashish smokers' found with a small amount of drugs in their possession, though most hashish makers did not use their own drugs due to local social control over the use of hashish. When people were caught with larger amounts of drugs, and especially during a transaction, this would be regarded as a felony and usually would be fined, in addition to suspended sentences by courts.

Hashish making in the region is an interesting story of how an activity which had been morally condemned by local people just over 20 years ago became less stigmatized despite remaining illegal. My respondents talked about hashish making as their work and hashish money as crucial in staying afloat and tackling poverty. However, similarly to what Zelizer (1997) argued about the social meaning of money, some people in Toolu believed that hashish money was tainted. During my fieldwork I heard people say '*nashanyn tubu jaman* (hashish is bad)', meaning 'hashish does not lead to anything good', or 'what goes around comes around' in Kyrgyz. Some believed that profits from selling hashish were not 'clean'. This has some similarities to 'evil' money in Kenya, which was earned through selling cannabis, tobacco and land, as it was perceived as betrayal of ancestors, as opposed to 'good' money received from sale of other agricultural products (Shipton 1984). 'Evil' money and various implications associated with it, such as a curse laid on the entire lineage of a person, did not stop farmers from engaging in these illicit practices. When such acts became widespread, the ceremony of money cleansing was sought (Shipton 1989). Therefore we see aspects of 'bitter money' practices in Toolu, similar to those in Kenya, although not enacted as thoroughly. Even though there was a uniform belief that hashish money could not be separated from the powerful spirits of the cannabis plant, the effects of using hashish money varied. People thought that everybody should try to make hashish and see the results, as it was out of human control. For some, hashish money did not help build wealth, but for others it did. Therefore, despite the fact that hashish money had some bitterness in it, it did not require cleansing through rituals, nor it was considered dangerous to use for funding social celebrations or bridewealth as in Kenya.

Instead, neutralizing strategies were developed to normalize hashish making among the local residents. My respondents often referred to hashish making as their form of work, as opposed to crime, implying self-reliance as opposed to dependence. Another strategy was to separate hashish production from the use of hashish through informal control of community members. The local discourse was that nobody took any drugs in the community. Indeed, most of the adult men and women did not use their own hashish, apart from a small number of young men in their early twenties who smoked hashish in secret as they did not want to be condemned by the community. The majority preferred to spend their hashish earnings on vodka, which was a staple of most social occasions in Kyrgyzstan. This strategy of separating hashish making from hashish smoking allowed the community to distance themselves from hashish users. Still, making too much hashish and relying only on hashish money as the main means of income was perceived as dangerous. This money was thought to either disappear quickly or not lead to any substantive wealth, in contrast to income that someone could earn from selling livestock, wheat or potatoes. If someone is making too much hashish, people would on the contrary denounce their activity and reiterate the belief that hashish is not going to make anyone rich. It was also believed that greedy hashish makers will be punished in the end, in the form of the payment of a large bribe to police, or some other unexpected expense.

### *Social celebrations*

In addition to providing necessary cash for everyday use and sustaining their agricultural activities (Botoeva 2014), hashish money was also used by many families as a means of maintaining their participation in local celebrations. In the survey, participating in social celebrations was identified as one of the main lines of household spending, together with buying food and clothes. In my survey, buying food was mentioned by 29%, buying clothes by 24%, and taking part in social celebrations by 23% of households as their main lines of spending.

The use of hashish money in local festivities started first through its use as a substitute gift during the 1990s, when instead of bringing their contribution in the form of livestock, people gave a few *korobochka* of hashish, whispering to the host that it was their *kara-koi* (black sheep), replacing the traditional gift of sheep. Later, with greater monetization of gifts, hashish money instead of hashish itself was used for hosting the *toi,* and as a form of contribution. So, why did families in Toolu have to use an illegal drug for *toi*s?

Primarily this was because social celebrations require spending money that most average and poor families do not have readily available in their budgets. The case of Sairakul, who was preparing for a *toi* to give her daughter's dowry, is illustrative of such a situation. The family had already devoted a cow and a sheep for the purposes of this *toi,* with 50,000 som (£714) in outstanding expenses. As their harvest was not large, Sairakul's family tried to find different ways of covering all the expenses.[6] Hashish money was earmarked for her daughter's clothes, as her three sons (who were in their early and late twenties) were making hashish that summer. Money from the potato harvest was earmarked for gifts for their in-laws and food expenses. Contributions of 1000 som (£14) and clothes from her nine siblings would help complete the gifts to the in-laws. Thus, families needed extra cash not only for everyday needs but also for holding celebrations and taking part in gift-exchange practices.

On numerous occasions I heard that hashish money helped families prepare gifts and monetary contributions for big celebrations and small *sherine* gatherings. Jamilya, for instance, used her hashish money for a wedding gift and new clothes for her husband and daughter. However, the money proved not enough for her to attend the wedding herself, so it was decided that her husband should represent her. Although her family cultivated two and a half hectares of land and owned livestock (a horse, 4 bulls, 2 cows, and 15 sheep) and considered themselves an 'average' family, Jamilya tried to make hashish on an everyday basis. Her main goal in making hashish was to earn a little money that could be used for everyday needs, and for participation in social rituals. The money from livestock and wheat and potato harvests was earmarked for other, bigger expenses.

In 2010, Meerim *eje,*[7] who was a widow of several years and bringing up her six children by herself, was also preparing for her first daughter to get married. She decided that her small house needed at least some cosmetic renovations in order that she did not feel too ashamed when hosting guests. Additionally, she needed money for the small celebration when her daughter and the groom would arrive from the capital city, Bishkek. As she did not own any livestock and was cultivating a very small patch of land, hashish making had already for some years helped her earn money for food and basic necessities. Thus, despite being 'bitter', hashish money was used in gift exchanges during social celebrations in the community of Kyrgyz hashish producers.

There are many reasons families take part in gift-giving practices. Gift giving at social celebrations allows them to gain status and prestige, and develop a sense of national identity within a rural community. Gift giving usually takes place at rite-of-passage celebrations such as *beshik toi* (celebration of the birth of a baby), *tushoo toi* (a feast celebrating the first steps of an infant), *süröt* (circumcision of boys), wedding ceremonies, sixtieth, seventieth and eightieth anniversaries, funerals, *kuran okutuu* (commemoration feast for the death of a relative), and *ash* (first anniversary of a death of a close relative). These feasts may be celebrated on a small or large scale, but some almost always involve large numbers of people. Wedding celebrations (or related feasts where the dowry of a bride is given or a bride-price is paid), funerals and first-anniversary commemorations are all examples of events where large numbers of guests are invited. Although many families struggle to find the money to participate in feasts, instead of a diminishing role for social celebrations we see that they have become more widespread and lavish since the Soviet period (Werner 1998a). The Kyrgyz government has acknowledged the situation that social celebrations are impoverishing the population of the country (Muraliev 1999). In the southern region of Kyrgyzstan, *aksakals*[8] and mosques have attempted to reduce funeral expenses to 'prevent poor families incurring huge debts' (Satybaldieva 2010, 110).

Celebrations are also used as major elements in reviving traditional culture in post-Soviet times. In Central Asia many traditions have not been completely erased from the cultural milieu. In Kyrgyzstan, during the Soviet era, it was still possible to hold funerals and first-anniversary commemorations in a lavish way by slaughtering many horses, as they were used as status symbols by the new Soviet Kyrgyz elites (Jacquesson 2008).[9] Since the Soviet period, the role and symbolism of celebrations have been adapted to a state ideology of preserving tradition – which allied tradition with the new national identity throughout the 1990s in almost all Central Asian countries (Tabyshalieva 2000).

Another explanation of the importance of lavish social celebrations in the everyday life of Toolu villagers has to do with status and prestige. Gift-exchange practices are used in many societies as a way of obtaining higher status by deliberately giving gifts that cannot be reciprocated by poorer members of a community (Mauss 1970; Scott 1977). With the market economy also encouraging personal consumption, a recent trend is that some richer families have begun slaughtering more livestock during funerals, as well as for third-, seventh- and fortieth-day commemorations. In some funerals the number of large livestock slaughtered reaches three to four horses or cows. Not only the type of meat but also its quality is considered an important marker of status. Other occasions are also used as status-defining activities by many families. In the case of wedding celebrations, the families of the groom and bride exchange gifts (*kiit*) as an indicator of respect that in-laws display to each other. If a family knows that the in-laws are preparing higher-value gifts, they will try to match them so as not to be perceived as lower in status. Sairakul *eje*, a 56-year-old resident, who was planning on holding a big *toi*, described what she was supposed to prepare for her daughter's in-laws:

> We have to buy *kiit*. We have coats for the groom's parents. We should buy a golden ring for his mother. For their relatives, we should buy suits, plus shawls for women. They could cost minimum 600 som [£10] each. We will also slaughter one sheep for the guests that they can take with them.

Received gifts are also widely publicized among relatives. This helps determine and interpret the status of the giving family among those on the receiving end. Sairakul *eje* explained:

> After welcoming my daughter we will also hold a small feast [*keshik*][10] by giving the meat of the whole sheep that in-laws bring and share all details with our relatives that did not attend the feast. We will invite all the households [*tütün*] of the lineage [*uruu*].

Social networks developed by families through celebrations provide a form of assistance similar to certain Soviet-era practices. Back then, social networking facilitated access to services and goods that were not easily available in a planned economy trapped in a permanent state of shortage (Ledeneva 1998, 2006; Yang 1994). Since the Soviet period, social networks have become transformed by responding to a different set of needs. They provided 'social security in uncertain times' (Werner 1998b, 610) and helped secure work outside the country (Reeves 2012; Rubinov 2010).

Two concepts, *katysh* and *yntymak*, derived from traditional Kyrgyz customs, are central to understanding the gift-giving economy of *toi*s in Toolu. *Katysh* is expressed in relationships between households in the village. By saying '*katyshybyz bar*', people mean that they *have connections* with others based on exchanges of gifts. *Katysh* can be based on networks of close and immediate relatives, in-laws and their lineage (*uruu*), and close friends and colleagues. *Yntymak* means possessing a strong bond, similar to 'solidarity' or 'unity'. *Yntymak* with other families means that they not only have connections (*katysh*) but also are duty-bound to help each other during life-cycle events.

Close relatives are nearly always involved in all the events described above. For large celebrations they not only provide gifts and money but assist in organizing them. Younger members of an extended family are supposed to provide physical help, while older members are expected to provide financial, organizational and emotional support. Maya *eje*'s network consisted mostly of her neighbours and helped her family with painting the walls and floors of a newly built house. This type of help is known in Kyrgyz culture as *ashar*, communal support in labour-intensive projects, such as renovating old or building new houses. One of my respondents, Aikan, and her family renovated their old house using *ashar*. These cases are illustrative of the support that some of the families with extended social networks can get. Inasmuch as the exchange of gifts operates as a form of credit, physical help provided in *ashar* events is also expected to be reciprocated.

Forms of reciprocity in social networks go beyond their role of safety nets during festivities. They also serve as resources that people can use in many other areas of everyday life. In Toolu being a member of a network means that there are more chances to borrow money without interest. In the survey, 72% of respondents (106 out of 147) reported that they borrowed money without interest from their networks. Among these, 34% could borrow money from their own relatives, 21% from their spouse's relatives, approximately 20% from neighbours, 14% from shops, and 11% from friends. This kind of social reciprocity and solidarity among members is thought to create a moral economy among many communities (Scott 1977; Thompson 1991a). Solidarity through gift-giving and networking especially provided protective functions for the community members. However, market forces brought changes and weakened the social cohesion in such communities (Scott 1977).

In Toolu, although the support provided by *uruu* (lineage) had not been completely lost, as everyone traced their *uruu,* it had become weaker with marketization of economy. This happened not because some members of *uruu* got excluded but because their contributions were too small. For instance, I was always reminded that there were five different *uruu* making up one clan in the village. Members of an *uruu* were invited for festivities, funerals and commemorations. One person in each *uruu* was responsible for gathering contributions for such occasions from each household. However, the amount gathered from an *uruu* as contribution was generally very small. One of my respondents, Maksat, shared his views on this matter, explaining how difficult it is to gather enough money from an *uruu* to cover all expenses:

> We help each other in the lineage. For funerals and commemorations we give 100 som [£1.40] from each household, for good occasions among close relatives we give 2000 som [£28]. For other families in the lineage it is only 100 som. In our *uruu* we have 30 households.

This shows that assistance received from within the *uruu* is not sufficient to cover the expenses of a feast (whether joyful or commemorative). Traditional *katysh* relationships based on lineage do not cover the expenses of social celebrations; costs outweigh these contributions. In cases where *katysh* contributions were increased from 100 to 1000 som (£1.40 to £14), for instance, there was increased pressure on the families that comprised the *uruu*. People could not contribute such large amounts of money to the whole lineage. They had to differentiate between their *katysh* and *yntymak* relationships. Therefore, Cholpon and Meerim's families, who had few connections and did not develop a network of friends and relatives, apart from their parents and siblings, may have received modest support from their lineage in cases of large celebrations or funerals. This support covers minor expenses such as the cost of one sheep, while higher expenses would be on the shoulders of the family holding the gathering. As a result, without a wider, more close-knit social support network, it is a challenge for those less well-off to organize community events.

### *Monetization of social networks*

As we have seen, the mutual assistance provided by networks of friends and relatives did not erode through the proliferation of market forces. Instead, a more intricate transformation of social networks than that proposed by a classical approach to the moral economy has been occurring in Toolu. As more recent approaches to moral and market economies show, both reciprocal and market economies can intermingle and sometimes reinforce one another instead of being incompatible. On the one hand, the community support did not erode and became more pronounced among some members. On the other hand, protection provided by the community was not extended to all members of community, depending upon their participation in gift-giving practices.

For instance, *yntymak,* introduced above, was described by respondents as a pre-agreed type of contribution that families make towards each other's feasts. As Sairakul *eje*'s case suggests, her family can rely on *yntymak* for monetary contributions from her siblings, as they have agreed on a certain sum beforehand. She can expect that some parts of the family expenses will be covered by those contributions. Although it is based on the notion of gift giving, there are a few differences between pre-agreed contribution and traditional gifts.

The notion of a gift is that it is not negotiated or pre-agreed (Mauss 1990). The receiver of a gift is typically expected to reciprocate in the future. Reciprocated gifts, although generally of a similar value, can be of a different form. In the case of pre-agreed *yntymak* contributions, where gifts are monetized, it becomes difficult for receivers to improvise when reciprocating. Monetary gifts reinforce the expectation that the returned gift is of the same value, transforming the way the gift-giving economy operates.

Yang (1994) also observed how money entered the traditional gift-exchange networks during the period of market reforms in the 1970 and 1980s in China. Monetary exchanges followed the logic of commodity-based exchange (market transactions) rather than reciprocal exchange of gifts. Still, the monetization of gifts did not erase the gift-exchange relationships that helped build different support networks. Social networks, according to Yang, were maintained as a tactic for succeeding in a rapidly developing market economy. Similarly, in Toolu, the monetization of gifts, although involving some rational calculation, was not a product of a purely instrumental approach to social networks. By giving money, people did not mean to stop their reciprocal relationships as in the Chinese communities (Yang 1994). In contrast, money was given when families wanted to maintain and extend their social networks. People gave money to show support, or to commemorate or celebrate important life-cycle events.

However, this does not mean that there were no instrumental elements introduced into the gift-giving practice. For instance, although 'traditional' types of gifts such as food, clothes and livestock were still in use, cash had turned into an expected and highly valued type of gift. I observed some families' tactics to receive cash as a contribution rather than 'traditional' gifts from their *katysh* relationships. Cash is more practical, after all, and could be used to cover the expenses of the gathering. Money as a form of gift became a norm when hosts invited their guests to restaurants rather than to their house. According to Aikan, holding a *toi* in a restaurant was a new tendency in the village but one that was considered prestigious and, in addition, would yield more monetary contributions than one organized at home. She believed that the expenses of a *toi* organized in a cafe/restaurant or at home were comparable. However, more people tended to bring money to a gathering organized at a cafe, and consequently the organizing family could cover more of their expenses. Just a few months after this conversation, I heard that Aikan's family had prepared a big *toi* in one of the restaurants of Kara-Kol city. The calculation of the incurred costs and 'earnings' from money gathered at the *toi,* therefore, introduces an instrumental element into this moral process of gift giving.

Though some close family members still provided help to each other without expectation of return (as also suggested by the study by Sanghera, Ablezova, and Botoeva 2011), many families were finding themselves in a different situation in a wider network of support. Although monetized gift giving still retained some of the functions of protection and support for active members, it exerted pressures on families and in turn excluded some from mutual-support networks. The following case is illustrative of such a process. I was told by a number of my interviewees that in 2009, graduates of the local school organized a lavish celebration for their twentieth graduation anniversary. A group of classmates, who were mostly well-to-do, suggested that the contribution from each male classmate should be 5000 som (£71). Their idea was to invite all the former teachers and female classmates for this occasion. This anniversary celebration turned into a three-day event in a forest reserve outside the village. Some classmates, however, were unable to take such a large sum out of their family budgets. The event was organized in springtime, and some families were struggling to finance the cultivation of their land. As a result, seven classmates decided to organize a separate celebration with a contribution of 1000 som (£14) each. They slaughtered one sheep and celebrated at the home of one of the classmates. The two separate groups did not attend each other's celebrations. Later that summer, members of the latter group shared the view that they had felt left out. Not only were they unable to attend the bigger celebration, most importantly their nonattendance had impacted their ability to maintain their relationships with other classmates. For instance, during the big celebration, the group of classmates also agreed to begin *sherine* gatherings with their families. The second group only heard about this second-hand and were not invited.

Among those who participated in the large celebration, there were those who did it at the expense of having less money for their more immediate needs. Tolubai, for instance, who participated in the bigger celebration, took out a loan at 29% interest from a bank, which was later paid off with hashish money. People of 'average' income rely on micro-credit organizations for making contributions and for organizing various events.

Sonun, a thirty-six year-old woman with four children, revealed how hard it is to take part in social celebrations while making ends meet.[11]

> If some relatives are inviting in-laws, or there is a wedding celebration, we have our *yntymak* and we have agreed to have 1000 som [£14] as a contribution to each other's feasts. In most of the cases we can't go. If you don't find 1000 som how will you go? You will be ashamed of going and as result stay at home. If you don't contribute any money you will be left out in the future. No one will invite you. People start forgetting about you. Even close relatives would say 'Oh, they will not come, they don't

> have money.' Then you will be forgotten. If you have money you are a relative, if you don't have money you lose *katysh*. We barely have flour and just stay at home. If we get invited in spring we just can't go. We attend celebrations in autumn. When you don't have money you just pray to God that there will be no *toi*, that no one invites you to a feast. It is better not to have an invitation rather than refusing to go.

Sonun's family struggled between the social pressures of participating in *toi*s and the everyday necessities of survival. In order not to be excluded from those networks of relatives and some friends, they sometimes missed an event and made their contribution later, when they could find the money. Their main source of cash in summertime was making hashish. Sonun, her husband and their two daughters regularly made hashish until 2010. In the summer of 2010, Sonun and two of her daughters were invited by some relatives to work outside the region. This case also shows how important money was in maintaining *katysh* networks, even with close relatives.

Participation in *toi*s affected not only how families viewed their relationships but also how much money was given as contributions. This was explained to me in one of the interviews, where Kanysh *eje* admitted that her family differentiated not only between *yntymak* and *katysh* but also according to how much was paid as *yntymak* between them and their friends and relatives. According to her, more money used as *yntymak,* or just given as *katysh,* signalled close relationships, a form of respect that in turn leads to an intense and very supportive network. A small amount of money signals willingness to participate in the life of other families, but does not lead to the development of close-knit relationships. It is mostly considered a symbolic type of contribution.

This explanation then helps to understand the survey findings shown in Table 1. According to the survey, all families tried to participate in *yntymak* relationships with other families. Although this clearly shows the different patterns of *yntymak* contributions according to the perceived

Table 1. *Yntymak* (contribution money) with close relatives, by socio-economic condition.

| Perceived socio-economic condition of the family[a] | *Yntymak* contribution of 50–200 som | *Yntymak* contribution of 300–500 som | *Yntymak* contribution of 1000–2000 som | *Yntymak* contribution of 3000–5000 som |
|---|---|---|---|---|
| Don't have enough money for food (Group 1) | 14.3% | 71.4% | 14.3% | 0 |
| Have enough money for food but not for clothes (Group 2) | 41.7% | 8.3% | 50.0% | 0 |
| Have enough money for food and clothes but not for durable goods (Group 3) | 7.8% | 25.5% | 60.8% | 5.9% |
| Have enough money for durable goods but not for very expensive things such as cars (Group 4) | 5.7% | 14.3% | 54.3% | 25.7% |
| Have money for everything, we don't limit ourselves (Group 5) | 0 | 0 | 33.3% | 66.7% |

[a]These five groups refer to different categories of families according to their perceived well-being.
Source: survey of 147 households in Toolu.

Table 2. Could you borrow money without interest? – by socio-economic condition.

| Respondents' self-reported status | Yes (%) | No (%) |
|---|---|---|
| Don't have enough money for food (Group 1) | 25.0 | 75.0 |
| Have enough money for food but not for clothes (Group 2) | 52.6 | 47.4 |
| Have enough money for food and clothes but not for durable goods (Group 3) | 75.0 | 25.0 |
| Have enough money for durable goods but not for very expensive things such as cars (Group 4) | 85.7 | 14.3 |
| Have money for everything, we don't limit ourselves (Group 5) | 75.0 | 25.0 |

Source: survey of 147 households in Toolu.

well-being of families, it is noticeable that even the families that did not have enough money for their own food tried to give at least 300–500 som (£4–7). In general, poor and average families would give more than they could afford. They would try to find ways to take part in big *tois* and small gatherings, either by borrowing money, or earning it through making hashish. In other regions of Kyrgyzstan, it was more common to subsidize social celebrations through remittances from close relatives who had migrated abroad (Aitieva 2015; Kapalova 2015; Satybaldieva 2015).

The perception of social networks given by Kanysh *eje* explains why monetization of gift giving leads to difficulties that some families face in getting support. For instance, although the majority of families said that they could borrow money without interest, when differentiated according to the perception of their families' well-being, I could see that not all families enjoyed financial help from their relatives and friends. This finding was supported in in-depth interviews with some of the poor families. In most cases they were told by their relatives that no one had money during such times of hardship.

As Table 2 presents, the higher their self-reported status, the better the chances they reported having in borrowing interest-free money. When families need a large sum of money, they obtain it by selling their harvest, such as potatoes and wheat (48%). Around 20% can still rely on their close relatives, and 16.6% can obtain it through micro-credit organizations. Due to the difficulties encountered in borrowing even a small amount of cash, 31.6% of households said that they sold their harvest. The results of the survey show that although a smaller proportion of families can receive support in borrowing money, a larger number of families rely on their own resources.

The monetization of gifts was therefore a complex process that was able to combine aspects of both market and moral economies. Although still rooted in the moralities of reciprocity, this emerging and constantly transforming system incorporated some instrumental elements more associated with social differentiation of the market economy.

## Conclusion

In this paper I demonstrated how the production of hashish is interlinked with the changing dynamics of social relationships and how hashish money entered the complex system of gift-giving practices in Toolu.

The moral economy of social celebrations retains an important role in rural Kyrgyz society. However, the transition from a highly subsidized socialist agricultural economy towards a semi-subsistence-oriented one under new capitalist market conditions created increased pressures on farmers for cash spending and increased consumption. Due to the growing importance of social celebrations to develop social status, gain prestige and maintain traditions, families sought cash to sustain such cultural practices. Thus, as I have presented here, the illegal hashish economy not only supports the agricultural economy but also sustains social relationships between families. Additionally, in the case of Kyrgyz communities in Toolu, as throughout the country, the 'traditional' *tois* organized as rites of passage were used as building blocks for developing a sense of national identity after the collapse of the Soviet Union. The *tois* allowed the local people to combine 'traditional' customs with the 'modern' demands of market economies.

The problem that many families in Toolu faced was finding the resources to fund such out-of-budget celebrations. This was not only a dilemma faced by people in Toolu; many regions used different strategies to be able to hold such celebrations. Hashish production helped families sustain themselves and support the local customs without resorting to mass migration, as had happened in other regions. For instance, families from southern regions used external migration as their way of subsidizing lavish celebrations (Reeves 2012; Rubinov 2012).

The use of hashish money is associated not only with the lavishness of *tois* but also with the monetization of gift-giving practices and the transformation of social-support networks as a result. The use of money as a gift puts a lot of pressure on families holding big *tois*, as well as on those that take part in them. The fear of weakening social security networks, and in turn losing status and prestige, left people scrambling for cash. Hashish money, in such a context, becomes important not only for poor families with no security networks but also for average-income families that need continued contributions to secure their membership in reciprocal social relations. Hashish production, therefore, helps maintain this system of social relations and keeps the families within the network of relatives and friends, which provides not only status and prestige but also crucial support in times of need. For poor families, who cannot maintain social networks, hashish production helps provide money for basic needs.

However, instead of arguing that market forces were able to destroy the protective functions of society that were proposed by classical theories of moral economy, I want to offer a more complex conclusion. In line with the more recent studies on moral and market economies that view all markets as moral economies but based on different moral grounds from one other (Browne and Milgram 2008; Zelizer 1997), I argue that monetization of gift giving transforms social networks into more layered and stratified dependencies. With cash as a gift becoming a norm, social networks are shrinking and becoming limited to immediate relatives, close friends and tribe members for the less well-off families that are unable to participate in feasts and reciprocate the same amount of contribution that average and well-off families can afford. Hence, monetization of gift giving is transforming the way reciprocal networks used to work.

However, monetization of gift giving does not automatically annihilate the emotional and supportive roles of social networks. These networks still perform their roles of social rituals and security nets. But in most of the cases, only those who are able to maintain the intense forms of communication and contributions are able to reap the benefits. For others, unable to contribute at various events, their networks turn into more symbolic affiliations, with no real obligations or reciprocity of support attached to them. This analysis of the process of transformation of social relationships in Toolu reveals how the moralities of gift giving intermingle with the spread of self-interested market economy exchanges among households.

### Disclosure statement

No potential conflict of interest was reported by the author.

## Notes

1. The real name of the village is not used for ethical considerations.
2. I use pseudonyms throughout the article.
3. Hashish is a cannabis resin. Marijuana is dried cannabis leaves. Hashish has much higher potency than marijuana.

4. *Sherine* are usually small gatherings held once a month on a rotation basis, with some contribution money given to the host of the dinner each time.
5. Hashish bought from Toolu villagers was usually transported to other regions of Kyrgyzstan and to Russia.
6. As she had 10 children, her family owned eight hectares of land – three hectares were irrigated, and five non-irrigated. They had cultivated all their land the previous year and lost all the harvest. That year they had to buy seeds and were only able to cultivate three hectares. The whole year they had to buy flour and all their food from the market.
7. *Eje* is a term for addressing an older woman. Although Meerim *eje* owned two and half hectares of land, she preferred to rent it out for 1680 som (£24) per year as it was too expensive to cultivate. She cultivated her small plot, near the house, with potatoes, which they used for their own consumption and to sell. Her four children received social benefits of 1200 som (£17) per month. They did not have any livestock. In winter she used to go Kara-Kol city for a few weeks and find some manual work.
8. Elderly men who are respected in their communities.
9. At the same time, even though Central Asian countries were able to retain some of their traditions, the state actually had some control over celebrations, making sure that the *nomenklatura* (political elite) did not abuse their power and financial situation openly. For instance, *nomenklatura* in Kazakhstan were not allowed to hold big celebrations which would stand out from the celebrations held by average citizens (Werner 1998a).
10. This includes sharing food left or brought from a big celebration with people who cannot participate in it.
11. Her family cultivated only their small plot (0.1 ha) near their house with potatoes. According to her account, their previous harvest was only 2500 som (£35). The bigger land that they own they cultivated only in the first years after privatization; as they could not sustain it, they rented it out to other families for 1000 som (£14) per year. Her husband worked as a builder when there was any job available in the village or nearby villages. She usually sewed *töshök*.

## References


Abdurasulov, Y. 2009. *Sostoyanie Sel'skogo Hozayistva Kyrgyzstana*. [The situation of agriculture in Kyrgyzstan]. Accessed 12 October 2013. http://www.cawater-info.net/review/agri_kyrg.htm: CA water info

Adler, P. A. 1985. *Wheeling and Dealing: An Ethnography of An Upper-Level Drug Dealing and Smuggling Community*. New York: Columbia University Press.

Aitieva, M. 2015. "Reconstituting Transnational Families: An Ethnography of Family Practices between Kyrgyzstan and Russia." PhD Thesis, University of Manchester, UK.

Bloch, P. C. 2004. "Land Privatization and Land Market Development: The "Unsuccessful" Cases of Kyrgyzstan and Uzbekistan." In *Building Market Institutions in Post-Communist Agriculture: Land, Credit, and Assistance*, edited by David Macey, William Pyle, and Stephen K. Wegren, 15–32. Lanham; Oxford: Lexington Books.

Botoeva, G. 2014. "Hashish as Cash in a Post-Soviet Kyrgyz Village." *International Journal of Drug Policy* 25 (6): 1227–1234. doi:10.1016/j.drugpo.2014.01.016

Booth, W. J. 1994. "On The Idea of the Moral Economy." *The American Political Science Review* 88: 653–667. doi:10.2307/2944801

Browne, K. E., and B. L. Milgram, eds. 2008. *Economics and Morality: Anthropological Approaches*. Lanham: Rowman Altamira.

Cornell, S. E., and N. L. P. Swanström. 2006. "The Eurasian Drug Trade: A Challenge to Regional Security." *Problems of Post-Communism* 53 (4): 10–28. doi:10.2753/PPC1075-8216530402

Djakishev, A. 2004. "Bor'ba s Narkotismom v Kyrgyzstane (v XX veke)." *Akipress* May 12, 28–32.

Dwyer, R. 2009. "Agency and Exchange: An Ethnography of A Heroin Marketplace." PhD dissertation, Curtin University.

Engvall, J. 2006. "The State Under Siege: The Drug Trade and Organised Crime in Tajikistan." *Europe-Asia Studies* 58 (6): 827–854. doi:10.1080/09668130600830904

Gleason, G. 2003. *Markets and Politics in Central Asia: Structural Reform and Political Change*. London: Routledge.

Granovetter, M. 1985. "Economic Action and Social Structure: The Problem of Embeddedness." *American Journal of Sociology* 91 (3): 481–510. doi:10.1086/228311

Hass, J. 2011. *Rethinking The Post Soviet Experience: Markets, Moral Economies, And Cultural Contradictions Of Post-Socialist Russia*. Basingstoke: Palgrave Macmillan.

Jacobs, B. 1998. "Researching Crack Dealers: Dilemmas and Contradictions." In *Ethnography at the Edge: Crime, Deviance, and Field Research*, edited by Jeff Ferrel and Mark Hamm, 160–77. Boston: Northeastern University Press.

Jacquesson, S. 2008. "The Sore Zones of Identity: Past and Present Debates on Funerals in Kyrgyzstan." *Inner Asia* 10: 281–303. doi:10.1163/000000008793066669

Kapalova, A. 2015. "Neformal'naya Economika Na Slujbe Social'noi Zashishennosti." *Vernut' Budushee: Al'manah Shtaba*. 1. Accessed 25 June 2015. http://www.art-initiatives.org/?p=15753

Kuehnast, K. R., and N. Dudwick. 2004. *Better A Hundred Friends Than A Hundred Rubles?: Social Networks In Transition, The Kyrgyz Republic*. Washington, D.C.: World Bank.

Ledeneva, A. 1998. *Russia's Economy of Favours: Blat, Networking, and Informal Exchanges*. New York: Cambridge University Press.

Ledeneva, A. 2006. *How Russia Really Works: The Informal Practices That Shaped Post-Soviet Politics And Business*. Ithaca, NY: Cornell University Press.

Makarenko, T. 2002. "Crime, Terror and the Central Asian Drug Trade." *Harvard Asia Quarterly* 6 (3): 1–24.

Mauss, M. 1970. *The Gift: Forms and Functions of Exchange in Archaic Societies*. New York: Cohen & West.

Muraliev, A. 1999. "Eldik Jakshy Kaada-Salttar menen Ürp-Addattardy Önüktürüü Jönündö. Kyrgyz Respublikasynyn Ökmötünün Toktomu." In *Erkin Too*, 11. Bishkek.

Musin, Z. 1988. "Delo Ne V Konople." *Sovetskaya Kirgiziya*, August 10.

Pellegrini, A. 2013. "Becoming A Peasant Middle Class: Coca Growers And The Politics of Indigeinity in The Bolivian Yungas." PhD Thesis, Zurich: University of Zurich.

Polanyi, K. 1944. *The Great Transformation: The Political and Economic Origins of Our Time*. New York: Rinehart and Company Inc.

Potter, G. R. 2010. *Weed, Need and Greed: A Study of Domestic Cannabis Cultivation*. London: Free Association.

Reeves, M. 2012. "Black Work, Green Money: Remittances, Ritual and Domestic Economies in Southern Kyrgyzstan." *Slavic Review* 71: 108–134. doi:10.5612/slavicreview.71.1.0108

Rubinov, I. 2010. *Migration, Development, and the "Toi" Economy: Cultural Integration of Remittances in Northern Kyrgyzstan. Research Report*. Bishkek: American University of Central Asia.

Rubinov, I. 2012. "Kyrgyz Feasts and Migrant Dreams: Embedding Remittances in Hybrid Social Networks." In *Identities in Transition*, edited by Georgina Tsolidis, 137–146. Oxford: Inter-Disciplinary Press.

Sanabria, H. 1993. *The Coca Boom and Rural Social Change in Bolivia*. Michigan: University of Michigan Press.

Sanabria, H. 2004. "The State and the Ongoing Struggle Over Coca In Bolivia: Legitimacy, Hegemony, And The Exercise Of Power." In *Dangerous harvest: Drug plants and the transformation of indigenous landscapes*, edited by Michael K. Steinberg, Joseph John Hobbs, and Kent Mathewson, 153–166. Oxford: Oxford University Press.

Sandberg, S. 2012. "The Importance of Culture For Cannabis Markets: Towards an Economic Sociology of Illegal Drug Markets." *British Journal of Criminology* 52: 1133–1151. doi:10.1093/bjc/azs031

Sanghera, B., M. Ablezova, and A. Botoeva. 2011. "Everyday Morality in Families and A Critique of Social Capital: An Investigation into Moral Judgements, Responsibilities, and Sentiments in Kyrgyzstani Households." *Theory and Society* 40 (2): 167–190. doi:10.1007/s11186-011-9138-4

Satybaldieva, E. 2010. "The Nature of Local Politics in Rural Kyrgyzstan: A Study ofSocial Inequalities, Everyday Politics and Neo-liberalism." PhD Thesis, University of Kent.

Satybaldieva, E. 2015. "Political Capital, Everyday Politics and Moral Obligations: Understanding the Political Strategies of Various Elites and the Poor in Kyrgyzstan." *Europe-Asia Studies* 67 (3): 370–387. doi:10.1080/09668136.2015.1020003

Scott, J. C. 1977. *The Moral Economy of the Peasant: Rebellion and Subsistence in Southeast Asia*. New Haven: Yale University Press.

Scott, J. C. 1985. Weapons of the Weak: Everyday Forms of Peasant Resistance. Yale: Yale University Press.

Shipton, P. 1989. *Bitter Money: Cultural Economy and Some African Meanings of Forbidden Commodities*. Washington, DC: American Ethnological Society Monograph Series.

Smith, A. 1986. *The Wealth of Nations*. Harmondsworth: Penguin Books.

Tabyshalieva, A. 2000. "Revival of Traditions in Post-Soviet Central Asia." In *Making the Transition Work for Women in Europe and Central Asia*, edited by Marnia Lazreg, 51–58. Washington, DC: World Bank.

Thompson, E. P. 1991a. "The Moral Economy of the English Crowd in the Eighteen Century." In *Customs in Common*, edited by Edward Thompson, 185–258. New York: New Press.

Thompson, E. P. 1991b. "The Moral Economy Reviewed." In *Customs in Common*, edited by Edward Thompson, 259–351. New York: New Press.

Werner, C. 1997. "Marketing Gift: Economic change in a Kazakh Village." *Central Asia Monitor* 6: 1–7.

Werner, C. 1998a. "Gift Exchange and the Transition to a Market in a Kazakh Village." *Akhmed Yasavi University Herald* 1: 12–23.

Werner, C. 1998b. "Household Networks and the Security of Mutual Indebtedness in Rural Kazakstan." *Central Asian Survey* 17: 597–612. doi:10.1080/02634939808401058

Werner, C. 1998c. "Women and the Art of Household Networking in Rural Kazakhstan." *Islamic Quarterly* 41: 52–68.

Werner, C. 2000. "Consuming Modernity, Imagining Tradition: Transnational Processes, National Identity Formation and Wedding Feasts in Post-Soviet Kazakhstan." *Anthropology of East Europe Review: Central Europe, Eastern Europe and Eurasia* 18: 1258–134.

Yang, M. M.-H. 1994. *Gifts, Favors, and Banquets: The Art of Social Relationships in China*. Ithaca, NY: Cornell University Press.

Zelichenko, A. 2003. *Afganskaya Narko Ekspansiya 1990-kh gg*. Bishkek: KRSU.

Zelizer, V. A. 1978. "Human Values and the Market: The Case of Life Insurance and Death in 19th-Century America." *American Journal of Sociology* 84 (3): 591–610. doi:10.1086/226828

Zelizer, V. A. 1989. "The Social Meaning of Money: "Special Monies"." *American Journal of Sociology* 95 (2): 342–377. doi:10.1086/229272

Zelizer, Vivianna A. 1997. *The Social Meaning of Money*. New York: BasicBooks.

Zelizer, Vivianna A. 2005. "Circuits within Capitalism." In *The Economic Sociology of Capitalism*, edited by Richard Swedberg, 289–322. Princeton and Oxford: Princeton University Press.

# Everyday disasters, stagnation and the normalcy of non-development: Roghun Dam, a flood, and campaigns of forced taxation in southern Tajikistan

Diana Ibañez-Tirado

*School of Global Studies (Anthropology), University of Sussex, Brighton, UK; Centre of Contemporary Central Asia and the Caucasus, Department of Anthropology and Sociology, SOAS, University of London, UK.*

This article conducts a comparative analysis of a catastrophic flood that hit the Kulob region of southern Tajikistan in 2010, and the government of Tajikistan's campaign to gather money to build the Roghun dam and hydropower station. It advances the notion of 'everyday disasters' in order to explain the imprecise boundaries between major catastrophic events and more mundane dimensions of the everyday as experienced by residents of Kulob. The article seeks to shed light, firstly, on the processes that underpin both Kulob residents' experiences of stagnation and the normalization of non-development, and, secondly, on the ways in which Kulob residents joke and 'do' cunning/cheating whilst dealing with disastrous events in order to cultivate an everydayness that is worth living.

## The flood: an introduction

The sound of heavy rain and thunder made it difficult to sleep, the night of 6 May 2010 in Kulob, a city of multi-storey Soviet-era buildings and detached houses 200 km south of Dushanbe, Tajikistan's capital. Mijgona, a woman in her mid-thirties who had invited me to spend the night in her house, woke up and noticed that her husband, Mahmud, was not in their room. After waiting for half an hour for Mahmud to return from the outdoor lavatory, she got up to search for him in the house's vegetable garden. In the dark, she did not notice the flow of water invading the garden, flooding the henhouses and submerging the corpses of drowned chickens and partridges. As Mijgona stepped into the mud, she was suddenly dragged downstream several metres, eventually collapsing against the garden's wall. Earlier that night, her husband had also been dragged away by the water. That night, I had heard the noise of water flowing outside the house, but not risen from my sleep. In the morning, I found Mijgona and Mahmud both bruised and obviously upset that they had lost most of their crops and poultry. They also laughed loudly about the reason Mijgona had gone to look for her husband in the middle of the night: fearing the worst, Mijgona had walked to the garden convinced that her beloved Mahmud was secretly meeting another woman. When we stopped laughing at their jokes about Mijgona's jealousy, we concluded that we had been lucky. The house in which they hosted me, and that was located on high ground at the edge of the city, was standing. In contrast, the oldest neighbourhood of Kulob city, Charamgaro Poyon (mainly made up of detached houses), had been destroyed, and many people had perished there.

The next day, when water levels in Charamgaro finally abated, many residents started to re-enter their former neighbourhood to search for the places where their houses had once stood. With tears in her eyes, Moma Farzona, an elderly woman who was an acquaintance of my host family in Kulob, explained to me:

> Our house was just in front of the bridge – but you see? There is no bridge anymore! … We saw water and a mess coming and we ran to the roof. Everything was water, water, but it was confusing – everything was dark. … In the morning we came down. We were frozen and scared. In the door of this room [pointing with her finger] the neighbour's boy was found. They didn't manage to hold his hand or – God knows! But the boy came with the water, mud and rocks and ended up here. Half of his body was trapped under the rocks. We called the neighbours. They came and we told them not to be scared. Nobody knew how to tell them. They saw him. It was hard to pull his body out – oh my God! They pulled him out while removing some heavy boulders. Of course he was dead – dead – inside him all water – oh my God!

There were many stories similar to Moma Farzona's. Days later people in Kulob started to speak about how many of their relatives were in hospital with broken bones; others were said to have been so deeply affected by the events that they had 'gone mad' (*devona shudan*).[1] According to the data released by Tajikistan's government, the flood hit Kulob and several villages in Tajikistan's eastern Khatlon region, resulting in 22 deaths, 55 missing, 200 injured, and 4000 displaced. In the days immediately following the flood, however, the affected people who had gathered in tents in the emergency camp calculated amongst themselves that over 1000 people were dead and many hundreds more missing. According to them, the authorities had refused to make this data public. My informants also told me that, following the 'path of Islam', most people who lost relatives in the flood hurried to bury the bodies of the victims. One informant, whose brother and nephew had drowned, explained to me that the official and bureaucratic procedure required to register a death was too long and, in such circumstances, the process would have surely taken a very long time. Others told me that some people had decided not to register the deaths of relatives so that, in an act of cunning/cheating (*cholok*; *zirak*; *fireb kardan*), they could continue to receive the deceased's pensions.

This article is based on 16 months of anthropological fieldwork conducted between 2009 and 2013 in the city of Kulob and several surrounding villages in the Khatlon region of southern Tajikistan.[2] This region is better known as the homeland of Tajikistan's political elite and the country's president, Emomali Rahmon (he is from Danghara, a district within Khatlon), who came to power in 1992 and consolidated his position by fighting opposition forces during the bloody civil war that afflicted Tajikistan until 1997. Since Kulob itself was not the scene of major fighting between the rival factions during the hostilities, the city flourished in the national media as a symbol of government authority. During my fieldwork, however, most Kulob residents identified themselves as 'ordinary' (*oddi*) in order to disconnect themselves from Tajikistan's political elites: my informants and acquaintances explained to me that contrary to what many Tajiks from other regions say, Kulob residents have not benefited from the outcome of the civil war. Rather, they often highlighted that Kulob lost its previous administrative role as the region's capital (which was moved to the city of Qurghon-Teppa) and that many factories from the Soviet era (e.g. food, oil and cotton processing plants) had been shut down, leaving many workers unemployed. Kulob residents' socio-economic positions, education, and backgrounds are of course internally differentiated. Yet most of my informants were united by a number of common characteristics: they shared their homes with extended and itinerant families (with members travelling back and forth to, and sending remittances from, Dushanbe and/or Russia); earned irregular incomes (even though some, like teachers and nurses, worked in stable government positions); and they all also faced recurrent debts and other economic problems arising from their low salaries or periodic unemployment.

Focusing on apparently extraordinary events that occurred in Tajikistan in 2010, this article examines a flood that hit the Kulob region, and a government-led campaign of forced taxation which aimed to collect funds from Tajikistan's residents in order to finish the construction of a dam and hydropower station in Roghun, on the Vakhksh River. I analyse the ongoing effects that the flood and the campaign, both locally referred to as 'disasters' (*fojia*), had on the everyday lives of numerous Tajikistan residents. The ongoing effects of such disastrous events overlapped with pre-existing constant electric blackouts and shortages of water that meant that many women and children had to fetch water from far from home, or procure wood to cook on fires in outdoor kitchens. Constant debt and chronic illnesses, combined with a lack of sustainable sources of income and affordable medical care, were also cited by my informants as disasters that were not eventful but rather constant aspects of people's daily lives. Therefore, I call the ongoing effects of the flood and the campaign to build Roghun 'everyday disasters'. Rather than drawing a clear boundary between mundane daily life and unexpected/catastrophic events, my acquaintances in southern Tajikistan often told me that there were so many disasters overlapping their daily routines that the general context in which their lives evolve was experienced as stagnation (*kasodí*). *Kasodí* thus implied that the current circumstances of life in Kulob remained stationary: everyday life could not become worse than the disastrous form it already had, but it could not get better either.

*Kasodí* was described by my informants as happening more acutely in Kulob than 'in other places', such as Moscow or Dushanbe, where, according to them, there existed the possibility that people's lives would improve. Stagnation was also interpreted as evolving from structural problems such as a shortage of well-paid jobs, campaigns of forced taxation, or the failed development projects of both government ministries and NGOs operating in Kulob (e.g. futile government programmes that were launched to improve medical care, or NGO projects designed to improve the access of local populations to clean water). Importantly, however, and related to the question of why stagnation was perceived as a more pronounced feature of life in Kulob than elsewhere, *kasodí* was also seen as a product of Kulob residents' proclivity to acts of cunning/cheating (*cholok*). Cunning/cheating, as I examine in more detail below, was practiced by Kulob residents when they thoughtlessly sought to take advantage of the assistance, aid and charity offered by governmental, religious or international development institutions. Therefore, cunning/cheating was paradoxically implicated in producing stagnation, as well as being a way of dealing with stagnation. Throughout this article, I use the term 'non-development' as an analytical tool to examine the consequences of the more clearly eventful nature of the flood and the campaign to build the Roghun dam and hydropower station, and *kasodí* to convey the enduring experiences of stagnation among Kulob residents.

I will analyse firstly the ways in which disasters were not seen by the people whom I came to know in Kulob as a risk or a danger that could be avoided, administered or mitigated against. In place of such constructions of risk and danger, I argue for a more complex notion of disasters' relation to the specific circumstances in which everyday life evolves. In my informants' case, they have come to assume that stagnation, rather than improvement in their general well-being, is the norm; I refer to this process as 'the normalcy of non-development'. Secondly, I examine the importance that people in southern Tajikistan place on the capacity to endure (*toba owardan*) and to circumnavigate catastrophic events towards a more mundane and less tragic dimension of their everyday lives by tackling *ziq* (a feeling described in southern Tajikistan as world-weariness, sadness, and frustration) both individually and communally, for the sake of cultivating a socially pleasing and sophisticated daily life. I will focus here specifically on forms of joking (*shŭkhí kardan*) and cunning/cheating that, according to my informants, keep people alive in times of stagnation, trouble and suffering. In this sense, my argument builds upon what Robbins (2013, 457) refers to as 'an anthropology of the good'. For Robbins this project aims to explore 'how people living in different societies strive to create good in their lives' even if such lives are characterized by suffering in the face of diverse forms of violence and deprivation.[3]

I will conclude by suggesting that joking and cunning/cheating are aspects of my informants' lives of fundamental importance to understand how they do not simply *cope* with misfortune but *deal* with the normalcy of non-development and everyday disasters in creative, lively and morally informed ways. A recognition of these aspects of their daily lives reveals Kulob residents as not the passive victims of 'natural' and socio-economic disasters but agents endowed with the 'means' to strive for a life worth living.

**Turning a disastrous event into an ordinary routine**

In her study of the affective dimensions of everyday life, Kathleen Stewart (2007) suggests that everyday life consists of complex rhythms of 'flow and arrest'. The flow of everydayness, or 'the still', is interrupted by ordinary events that, nevertheless, disrupt the quietness of this flow: 'a still life pops out of the ordinary' (21). But what counts as an event? In his study of the moral worlds of Moscovites, Zigon (2007) suggests that events are best understood as a form of moral and ethical breakdown. He argues that people live in a comfortable, unreflective and rather embodied mode of everyday life, which is, however, often interrupted by ethical moments, or 'moments that shake one out of the everydayness of being moral' (133). Hoffman and Lubkemann (2005), in their study of 'warscapes' in Africa, remark that the boundaries delineating normal everyday life and what counts as an event are problematic. In many contexts, perhaps especially in such 'warscapes', which these authors define as places where violent events and instability have 'become the norm' (318), the distinction between the event and the everyday is difficult to clearly define (see also Das 2007 and Trentmann 2009). My ethnographic examples suggest that, similarly to Zigon's informants, Kulob residents do attempt to return to something they consider to be normality, and to navigate the event, in many cases disastrous events, towards ordinariness. However, an event is a transforming force that 'shakes' (Hoffman and Lubkemann 2005), if not fully 'erodes' (Badiou 2005; Humphrey 2008) existing knowledge: therefore, the everydayness to which Kulob residents attempt to return is also constantly shifting.

Building on these approaches to the study of the event's relationship to the everyday, I am concerned with the ways in which ordinary life is crafted out of events, and the extent to which the texture of the 'ordinary' in such circumstances also exhibits a changing quality. How are these processes accounted for in contexts where a disaster is not a singular event but instead is conceived as 'an ongoing experience' and a 'result of slow processes of deterioration, erosion and negative change' (Vigh 2008, 8–9)? For many of my informants in Kulob disastrous events (such as floods and campaigns of forced taxation) as well as the expectation of non-development (in the form, for example, of constant electricity blackouts, deficient sources of income, or the absence of resources to treat a life-threatening illness) have become the norm and are experienced as unending stagnation. I suggest that by exploring the specificities of what is considered a 'disaster' (*fojia*) by people in Kulob it is possible to examine the blurred boundaries between extraordinary events and everydayness; to analyse the general sense of stagnation among Kulob residents, and to account for joking and cunning/cheating as some of the most highly valued forms through which people in Kulob attempt to transform catastrophe into more mundane aspects of their everyday lives.

Much of the literature on disasters focuses on how environment, society and technology interplay in complicated ways to produce hazards, danger zones and finally events that, because of their destructive impact on human societies, are called disasters (Oliver-Smith and Hoffman 1999). Another strand of the literature deals with disaster risk management and resilience, or the capacity of socio-ecological systems to absorb shocks through preventive measures to avoid, minimize and cope with disaster impacts (Keck and Sakdapolrak 2013). However, as Béné et al. (2012, 12) point out, 'in much of the debate on resilience and social-ecological systems, the agency of people is often veiled, focusing instead on the ability of the "system" to recover from shocks'. Therefore, my approach to analysing the flood in Kulob, as well as the campaign to gather funds for the Roghun dam and hydropower station, begins with a different set of theories that critically engage with the social construction of notions of risk. Beck (1992) and Giddens (1991) point out that 'risk' is a calculative discourse in 'modern' societies that has been incorporated into everyday life through attitudes towards consumption, work and health, in order to avoid potentially adverse scenarios. In this calculative framework for analysing disasters, such events are depicted as emerging from natural forces and departing 'from a state of normalcy to which a society returns to on recovery' (Bankoff 2003, 11). Risk and catastrophic events, furthermore, are expected to be managed through technocratic and bureaucratic means in order to avoid, reduce and repair the potential damage to human societies. Conversely, in many countries such as Tajikistan the capacities of the government to avoid damage are insufficient, or, as Simpson (2013) suggests in his analysis of the 2001 earthquake in Gujarat, these capacities are captured by private companies and investors that aim to realize profits from projects of prevention, relief and reconstruction.

In his anthropological and historical study of disasters in the Philippines, Bankoff (2003) suggests that people's constant exposure to disastrous events has led to the normalization of threat. Vigh (2008), in his work on Guinea-Bissau, refers to this type of scenario as 'crisis as context', or places where crisis has become the norm: notions of hazard, vulnerability and disaster are, therefore, discursively constructed and culturally disparate in different societies. Vigh warns us, however, that although crisis 'may become normal' because of people's constant exposure to extreme adversities, his informants in Bissau do not remain passive or indifferent to their troubles (11). Instead, Vigh's acquaintances find 'terrains of action' to improve the harsh conditions in which their everyday lives evolve. In other words, as Jackson (2011, ix) suggests in a discussion of the concept of 'well-being', the process of normalizing the occurrence of disasters is 'a field of struggle' rather than a 'settled state'. Building on the work of these authors, I suggest that Kulob residents do not see disastrous events and stagnation as ruptures, risks or circumstances that they can prevent and administer. Instead, disasters are often referred to by Kulob residents as 'normal'. These events are expected to be endured without great complaint, and thus be quickly incorporated into less tragic dimensions of their everyday lives, a process to which creative forms of joking and cunning/cheating are of considerable importance.

## The Roghun hydropower station, shortages, debt and other everyday disasters

'We do not have gas, electricity, [running] water, money or a job – but we have fresh air and clean water!' This was one of the phrases most commonly repeated to me during my stay in Kulob, often in a tone that mixed joking, pride, and desperation. Tajikistan, the so-called 'water country', lacks energy resources, such as oil and gas, that neighbouring countries in Central Asia (Turkmenistan, Uzbekistan and Kazakhstan) possess.[4] Therefore, people throughout the country, including those in the Kulob region, are subjected to daily and seasonal rationing of gas (in the very few areas of the country where it is available), electricity and pumped water. The politics of the provision of utilities was a matter of everyday life, and underpinned people's routines, especially when they struggled to secure water and to take advantage of the available hours of electricity to fulfil their daily domestic tasks.

In 2010 especially, water was evoked by Tajikistan's government as 'the body of the nation' (Suyarkulova 2014, 376) and the resource that would guarantee Tajikistan's development. Water would transform the country into a 'progressive' nation with a permanent supply of water and electricity to every house and workplace. As Suyarkulova and Féaux de la Croix (forthcoming) suggest, projects concerning energy and hydropower infrastructure were already at the core of the previous Soviet government. Soviet officials treated such engineering projects as a form of symbolic power that celebrated the conquest of nature by collective human labour, and thus an important step on the road to progress and modernization. The Soviet 'hydraulic mission' in Central Asia aimed to increase irrigation for cotton production, as well as generate affordable hydroenergy. It was according to this logic that Tajikistan's president publicly announced that it was necessary to construct a gigantic dam and hydropower station (HPS) in Roghun.[5]

A Roghun HPS on the Vakhsh River was first proposed by the Soviet regime in 1956, but only started to take shape in 1976, when Soviet engineers intended Roghun to be the highest dam in the world (335 m). However, the dam was never finished, due to a lack of funds, and was abandoned in the late 1970s despite the already relatively advanced state of works that had been undertaken there.[6] Prior to 2008, the year in which the Tajik government reactivated the project, Tajikistan had already searched for international partners, principally Russia, to assist with the final completion of the dam. However, several Russian investors declined the offer of further involvement in Roghun, since according to the terms of their participation they would not be permitted to hold the majority of shares. According to Hoji Akbar Turajonzoda (an influential former leader of Tajikistan's Islamic Opposition in the civil war), Pakistan was also interested in investing in the Roghun HPS as early as 1992, yet this plan was opposed by both Russia and Uzbekistan. According to Turajonzoda, the possible involvement of Pakistan in the project and the increasing Pakistani presence and influence in Tajikistan was one of the reasons behind the onset of civil war in 1992 (Canfield and Rasuly-Paleczek 2010). In 1993, the remaining foundations for the dam were destroyed by a flood.

Short of both investors and funds, in 2010 Rahmon launched a large-scale campaign across the country that, as I explore below, theoretically invited (but in practice compelled) most of Tajikistan's population to buy stock (*sahmiaho*) and thus to invest in the project. In exchange for investing in the construction of the dam, the buyers were issued certificates for their stock in quantities of TJS 100, 200 and 500 (equivalent to USD 21, 42 and 105). The official media played an important role in the campaign to raise funds for the Roghun HPS. The authorizing discourse of the campaign was based on depictions of Tajikistan's present as unsustainable because its existing hydropower stations are insufficient for the country's present energy needs; therefore Tajikistan's people suffer daily and seasonal electricity rationing and constant blackouts. Images of the building site in Roghun, decorated with the national flag, the words 'nation' and 'motherland', and the serious and resolute face of the president beneath a helmet were commonly displayed, not just on television but also on advertising hoardings across the country.[7] Rahmon argued that the Roghun HPS was vital to Tajikistan's strivings to become self-sufficient in energy terms. He even conjectured that, in the future, Roghun would make the country an exporter of electricity; the profits would bring astounding prosperity to the nation.

The economic impacts of the campaign, however, were felt by many individuals and families for several years. At the time of my research, the average pension and monthly salary in Kulob ranged from TJS 70 to 120 (USD 14.70 to 25.20). Aka Daler was a man in his sixties who was about to retire from his 'well-paid' job in the local council. Aka Daler's monthly income was TJS 300 TJS (USD 64), and although he was the only person earning an income in his family, he was 'invited' by state officials, or as Aka Daler himself put it, 'compelled' (*majbur*), to buy TJS 4000 (USD 840.60) in stock. The full impact of this financial outlay on the well-being of Aka Daler's family is more clearly recognized when considered in relation to his annual salary of TJS 3600 (USD 756.50). Aka Daler had to take a high-interest loan from a national bank to pay for the stock, and he remained in debt for more than two years as a direct result of the campaign to build Roghun. Furthermore, it delayed his plans of becoming a pensioner. All of Aka Daler's work colleagues (*hamkorho*) faced the same or similar conditions: if they did not buy stock, their superiors told them, they would lose their job. Another worker, also employed in a relatively stable job in a respectable government office, made the following remarks to me:

> We were told that if we want to have Tajikistan with electricity and running water in the future, and working industries and productive factories for our children, we have to make an effort to buy that stock. I agree. We have to do something good for our country. We cannot live eternally on remittances and our youngsters cannot live eternally in Russia.

Although the majority of the working people with whom I spoke shared this man's point of view, they also argued that the price of the stock, the pressure that the government placed on people to buy it, and their general degree of impoverishment did not logically meld with the Roghun HPS project.

In a comparative analysis of building dams and roads in Jimma, Ethiopia, Mains (2012) argues that it is through these projects that his informants keep believing in 'progressive narratives and a developmentalist state' even though in many cases such projects are never completed. Similarly, Kulob residents, especially students in college and university, expressed to me a feeling of being enchanted by the future realization of the dam, or, as Ferguson (1999) puts it, by the 'expectations of modernity'. However, the great majority of my informants, including such youngsters, were less enthusiastic than people in Jimma appear to have been about donating their money to the Roghun cause. In contrast to youngsters in Jimma, Kulob residents were not given jobs by the companies in charge of building Roghun. Actually, most Tajik citizens and non-approved local and foreign journalists were banned from the Roghun region and the specific building site; my informants told me that although the campaign to gather money was national and public, the details of the whole project were a well-kept 'secret' (*mahfī*; Rus. *taína*).[8]

The pervasive secrecy also applied to information about how personal liabilities were calculated and by whom, as well as the actual rules about how many shares an individual should buy and how many times the campaign would be repeated. Seemingly, the shares that workers had to buy correlated to their salaries, but in some workplaces (e.g. universities and schools) students were compelled by their teachers to buy stock to cover the stock of the academic and administrative staff. I also heard reports of nurses and doctors who in addition to the expected fees for their services gave medical attention in exchange for stock. Superiors in each company or workplace were in charge of checking the acquisition of stock by their subordinates, and to report such stock to their superiors. The general means of coercion to force people to buy stock was the threat of losing their jobs, or in the case of independent entrepreneurs, the closure by state officials of their company, shop, or business. Each of the shopkeepers in the bazaar was 'asked' to buy between TJS 200 and 1000 in stock (between USD 42 and 210). Doing so, officials told them, would ensure that their shop remained open. Students were told by their teachers that if they did not buy stock they would not be able to sit their exams, or would be refused enrolment in the following academic year. A woman explained to me that, in this way, teachers 'did cunning':

> My son, only eight years old, was requested TJS 10 for stock. He will not receive a certificate, though, because the money is actually for his teacher to buy her own stock. How will my husband manage to buy his own stock, requested by the cotton factory, and then our children's stock for the teacher?

In Kulob, as in the rest of the country, many workers (*korgar*) acquired bank loans (*qarz*) and requested urgent remittances from their relatives working in Russia to help pay for the stock. Some people I spoke to, who largely worked in factories (e.g. Kulob's milk factory) and companies (e.g. mobile phone companies), told me that a proportion of their monthly salary was being deducted to pay for stock, in addition to the loans taken from banks and relatives.

During the campaign to gather funds for Roghun, the economic challenges posed by the construction of such a colossal venture, the levels of indebtedness that Tajikistan's people faced as a result, and the potential failure of the project were entirely absent from official discourses.[9]

However, Tajikistan's government emphasized that if Tajikistan did not become energy self-sufficient, then neighbouring countries would soon begin to take advantage of its vulnerability. Indeed, according to such politicians, Tajikistan's greatest foe, Uzbekistan, was already acting in such a manner. As the Roghun project was being launched, the Uzbek government placed pressure on Tajikistan to stop building the dam. They argued that by blocking the Vakhsh River, which flows through Uzbekistan to the Aral Sea, Tajikistan was almost certain to damage the environment, desiccate important Uzbek agricultural lands, and therefore threaten the 'security' of Uzbekistan's people.[10] Strong measures were taken by Uzbekistan against Tajikistan: Uzbek air space was closed to Tajik aircraft, and the borders through which many basic imported goods (including flour, rice, medicines and cooking oils) arrived in Tajikistan from both Uzbekistan and beyond were sealed to commercial traffic.[11] As a direct consequence, prices for petrol (and transport) and basic food products increased in Tajikistan: petrol prices, for example, rose by 40% during the political crisis, eventually reaching TJS 6 (USD 1.20) per litre.

In these difficult economic and political conditions, many of my Kulobi informants remarked to me that they felt 'inspired' by their love for the motherland (*vatan*) and the bright future that Roghun offered Tajikistan. Yet, most of my acquaintances were more concerned with their daily struggle to gather the money to pay for the stock, which people I knew did by cutting back on already insufficient household expenditures. In Kulob, this period of fluctuating prices for basic goods was characterized by a reduction in wedding celebrations (*tŭiho*) – the major and most valued form of entertainment and sociality in the region. In those days, many of my informants also told me that they believed that the project would never be completed and the money they had 'invested' in the stock would never be returned to them. In addition, all of this economic uncertainty coincided with the floodwaters that hit and devastated Charamgharo. My informants often explained to me that the reason the flood that hit Kulob should not be called a disaster (*fojia*) was because there were many such events, but that, most importantly, 'The whole situation is a disaster.'

## The camp: a spatial model of the blurred boundaries between the disastrous event and everyday life

Three days after the flood, and as the campaign to collect funds for the Roghun HPS continued, an area for those affected by the flood was erected by a variety of organizations in Kulob's stadium, chosen because of its location on higher ground. Tents marked with the symbols of the Red Cross, Oxfam and the UN mushroomed quickly within the stadium. People in areas not directly affected by the flood but whose homes lay near the camp told me that this was the correct procedure to help those in the camp who were left homeless. As days passed, however, my acquaintances from these parts of Kulob began to complain that some of the victims they knew had started to 'do cunning' and to 'invite' their relatives to live in the tents with them. People in the camp had running water, free food (including 'eggs and milk on a daily basis', a standard of nutrition that was seen by many as a luxury), access to instant medical services, free medicines and vaccinations, and even a nursery for their children – the last being an unheard-of marker of opulence that the vast majority of families in Kulob could never afford. On seeing the facilities offered to the camp-dwellers, many concluded that life in the camp was of a higher standard than that outside it: basic services on the outside, they said, were next to nonexistent.

Furthermore, in the unaffected neighbourhoods the everyday shortages of water and electricity I discussed above were being experienced more frequently than before the flood; many pipes and cables had been damaged or destroyed by the floodwaters. Those living inside the camp, however, complained that their situation was in fact no better than ordinary life; many sat inside their tents and lamented the loss of their relatives, their crops or/and animals, and their houses. Soon afterwards, Tajikistan's president visited the city of Kulob and announced that all victims of the flood in the region would receive a brand-new house for free (*bepul*).

On a daily basis, however, receiving government and international aid was interpreted by many as something that dehumanized those affected by the flood, in the sense that they were fed, enumerated, ordered, registered, watched, rushed and patrolled within the camp by nurses, doctors, police officers and all kind of volunteers. The lack of privacy engendered by this routine became a daily concern for the victims in the stadium. Several people remarked to me, however, that experiencing such forms of surveillance was not such an abnormal aspect of life for them. They said that the movements of all Tajik citizens, with or without a flood or camp, were closely watched and recorded by state officials, on the grounds that doing so kept peace and stability in the country (Heathershaw 2009). At the same time, those outside the camp repeatedly told me that the situation inside the camp was better because those affected by the flood were entitled to donations from NGOs and the gifts of aid and support. After expressing these concerns, I heard on many occasions the phrase, 'We became like animals!' This phrase pointed at the paradoxes of people being fed and looked after, yet also being carefully observed and patrolled by NGO workers and state officials. It was uttered both by those in the tent-camp and those living outside it: the boundaries between what constituted disaster/camp and normalcy/outside-the-camp were far from being straightforward.

### Normalizing the disaster: joking and cunning/cheating as involvement

In addition to the debates about the quality of life within and outside the camp, the ways in which many Kulob residents thought about the flood evoked the type of general attitudes they held about everyday life: as a friend of mine told me, life was full of suffering (*azob*), but there was also plenty of time for jolly talking (*chak-chak kardan*). One of my closest friends in Kulob, Shirin, was a young mother of three children who suffered a painful and life-threatening illness. In addition to all her misfortunes, Shirin's cows and chickens had drowned in the flood waters. On the days following the flood, people called her 'poor you' (*bechora*, lit. 'without means'). Emphasizing her agency and resourcefulness, Shirin responded to such people: 'No! [Do not call me] "poor you" [*be-chora*, 'without-means']. We have means! [*chora dorem*]!'

While many in Kulob spoke about the ways in which both their everyday life and experiences in the camp were 'full' of suffering and stagnation, projects of non-development and everyday disasters, Shirin, as well as many others of my friends and informants, were also reluctant to have their personal and collective situation described in one-dimensionally pessimistic terms; indeed, they would often emphasize the high levels of resourcefulness, patience and endurance that Kulob residents demonstrated as they dealt with the recurrent situations they faced. By emphasizing that they had means (*chora*) they also tended to highlight their creativity and wit when dealing with misfortune, and the necessity of being recognized and valued as agentive in the processes affecting their lives.

Despite the loss of human lives, houses and cattle, people living inside the camp rapidly began to reorganize their 'normal' daily activities, such as visiting each other, chatting, jolly talking, sharing experiences of suffering, and, importantly, also joking and cunning/cheating. Joking, I found out during my fieldwork, is one of the most important ways in which people in southern Tajikistan socialize and also deal with misfortune. As the work of Goldstein (2003) on *favelas* in Rio de Janeiro demonstrates, laughing is not only about hilarity or escape but also about displaying resilience and dignity in the face of poverty and hopelessness. Building on Goldstein I suggest that joking and *cholok* (cunning/cheating) were modes through which Kulob residents 'normalized' disastrous events, or, as Das (2007) puts it, a way in which the 'big' events entered into the realm of the ordinary. Moreover, joking and cunning/cheating also constituted means through which Kulob residents sought to acknowledge their involvement in shaping the conditions of their daily lives. In order to understand the importance of such collective self-reflection, I borrow the term 'involvement' from Anderson's (2013) discussion of everyday narratives that lament or scorn the self among entrepreneurs in Aleppo, Syria. Involvement occurs when the narrator directs ridicule not simply at others but also at the self in order to both criticize adverse circumstances and acknowledge his or her own involvement in such scenarios. Being involved is moving beyond being acknowledged as a powerless victim or as located in a social sphere separated from the state. Rather, involvement implies that narrators are 'critical and complicit', and are agents who put themselves on display to laugh and be laughed at. Involvement is significant, Anderson suggests, because 'it becomes a way of sustaining political life and possibility under authoritarianism or any hegemonic structure' (476).

In Kulob, many of my informants, including some of those who expressed feelings of sadness and world-weariness (*ziq*) and said they had been destroyed (*vaíron*) by the flood, could be found from time to time laughing at events and turns of phrase that they found humorous and that had been uttered by people in a similar situation to their own. For example, shortly after the flood had destroyed her house, I sat with a woman who was crying in her tent, which was in the camp. Soon afterwards, her relatives arrived to visit and comfort her. She sobbed: 'I lost all my teeth! The water took them away! What a disgrace!' The other women worried: 'How? Did a rock hit you? Are you bleeding?' The woman stopped crying and began laughing loudly: 'No! I kept my gold teeth in a little box. The water took them away! Can you imagine how many teeth and how much gold were lost with the flood?' The story made the women roar with laughter, especially because some of them had entertained the idea of imitating their 'greedy' (*khasis*) neighbours in their endeavours of searching for gold in the flooded courtyards of other people's houses. One of these women eventually recognized her involvement: in such a context of misfortune and tragedy, and knowing that corpses of animals and people were still being recovered from the stinking mud, she had gone, with her husband, searching for 'treasures' (gems, gold, documents), and had found none. These women then laughed even louder until, with tears in their eyes, one of them told me: 'I swear to God! Here we laugh a lot about some stories. We laugh, and then we cry.' Indeed, people in the camp could be found joking and laughing, and minutes afterwards sobbing, as they narrated the tragedies the flood had brought about. Yet, as in the ordinary life of Kulob and the forms of sociality that are important to it, joking in the tents became popular as a daily strategy to cheer oneself and others up and render dramatic misfortune, an unexpected event, into a normal and worthy everyday life.

The other way in which people in Kulob tended to deal with misfortune, to navigate disastrous events towards everydayness and to acknowledge their involvement in experiences of stagnation was 'cheating' or 'cunning' – actions described to me as *cholok, zirak* and *fireb kardan,* all terms that might refer to astuteness or cheating, or a mixture of both.

A builder who volunteered to distribute aid to those affected by the flood bitterly complained to me that:

> There are people who were not affected and are not suffering any loss. Nevertheless, they take lots of the parcels of aid. One day I saw one of them and told him: 'You are not afraid of God! I swear to God that I saw your house and not even a drop of water entered it!' But people who are *cholok* and want to take advantage of the situation just do it.

Another man, who had worked as a volunteer during the height of the 'disaster', told me that people in Tajikistan were 'cheaters' (Rus. *moshenniki*) and that it was not difficult to realize that everybody, including him, wanted to cheat the government, the 'uncles' (patrons) and whomever else could be cheated in order to take advantage of this situation and many others that they faced on a daily basis. He illustrated his point with this story:

> People cheat! We went to deliver aid from my local mosque to the [affected] neighbourhood. One young man requested two parcels of aid from us, so he could deliver one to his father, who lived next door but who was not present at that moment. Later on his father arrived and angrily told us: 'Why did you give my parcel to my son? The bastard will never give it to me!' You see? People cheat even their own father.

These stories demonstrate that people think everyday social relations are fully implicated in the context of disaster: networks of trust and kinship are seen not only as a source of support to be called upon in times of good and bad but also as potential founts of danger. It is important to emphasize here that my argument is not that Kulob residents or government officials are 'liars' or 'cheaters' but that this is an ironic self-recognition similar to what Hertzfeld (2004) calls 'cultural intimacy' and defines as 'those aspects of a cultural identity that are considered a source of external embarrassment but that nevertheless provide insiders with their assurance of common sociality' (3).

In addition, these stories reveal aspects of people's agency, wit and creativity in dealing with disasters and the normalcy of non-development in Tajikistan, a state that is characterized by a narrow elite who hold overwhelming political and economic power and who are also currently seeking, with considerable success, to control a vast range of the country's resources, as well as to order, discipline and determine the forms of knowledge that are publicly acceptable. Rasanayagam, Beyer, and Reeves (2014, 11) advance the question of 'How is the state being done' in Central Asia, and highlight the importance of 'contingency, ambiguity and indeterminacy' as well as the capacity of reflection of those involved in performing politics in the region. By acknowledging that the experience of *kasodí* or stagnation and the actual normalcy of non-development are also manifested as cunning/cheating, and that Kulob residents as narrators are involved in such practices, I suggest that my informants in Kulob are bringing these topics to 'public discussion' in a manner that enacts 'involvement' and demands 'witnessing', regardless of the fact that their involvement can be evaluated as greedy or helpless practices that replicate 'economic and political marginalisation' (Anderson 2013, 477).

The evaluations of good and bad forms of cunning are made by Kulob residents in terms of empathy towards others, piety and religion, and also in more pragmatic ways: cunning/cheating is regarded, given the circumstances of daily life, as being, at times, a morally neutral way of achieving goals. The campaigns of forced taxation to invest in the Roghun HPS or to build the promised new houses for those affected by the flood in Kulob (as I will discuss below) were also seen as 'cunning' by many of my informants, insofar as they were convinced that some of the 'donated' money would end up in the pockets of corrupt officials. However, this cunning/cheating was reflected not only in the mischievousness (*fasod*) of the government's officials but also in the ways in which 'everybody' (*hama*), as they put it, is part of a society where cunning/cheating, even towards one's own father, is one of the ways people deal with everyday disasters and misfortune whilst attempting to be recognized as social and moral persons who are 'not simply oppressed by circumstances, but tainted or changed by them' (Anderson 2013, 477). In this sense, cunning/cheating was also evaluated as an aspect that perpetuated experiences of *kasodí* or stagnation. Many people in Kulob were aware that the distinction between an appropriating elite and a class of marginalized subalterns did little to illuminate the complexity of their daily struggles. After all, in these stories, the victims of cunning/cheating include one's own father, a government that pretends to provide aid parcels and worthy 'free' houses for those affected by the flood, and the 'astute' people who were not affected by the flood yet who attempted by all means available to them to take one of the aid parcels or even one of the promised new houses, and by doing so, cheat the government.

## Kulob's reconstruction and the future of Roghun: disaster as context

In other areas of Tajikistan people experienced the pressure of having 'to help Kulob' after the flood. The so-called ordinary people (who never appeared publicly as 'donors') were also 'requested' (compelled) to bring money to their local councils to help build the promised new houses for those affected by the flood. Newspapers reported that government officials were busy collecting these 'donations', but at the same time, the governor (*rais*) of one of Khatlon's districts told me that the money to build these new houses was forcibly taken, in the form of 'charity' or 'voluntary aid', from private companies, banks, governmental offices and ministers. The money taken from institutions such as these was then deducted directly in many cases (though not in all) from the wages of the workers; and this deduction was in addition to the one taken for the Roghun HPS. In this respect, the frequent 'donations' became to be seen by the great majority of people to whom I spoke in Tajikistan as everyday disasters and as a direct cause of their non-development, rather than as an investment in projects that would assure Tajikistan's progress and simultaneously some improvement in their general well-being.

By the end of 2010, the delays that the Roghun project had encountered added to the general sense of *kasodí* or stagnation among my informants in Kulob. The dam will not be finished unless an international techno-economic assessment requested by the IMF and the World Bank brings positive results. This was supposed to be completed in 2013, but its completion has been delayed. Meanwhile, the money gathered in the campaign apparently remains in a Tajik bank controlled by the government. In January 2013 and in August 2015, people in Kulob told me that they had been informed that the Roghun HPS was in the process of being built – this time with Russian companies as major investors and stakeholders.[12] However, when I asked them what had happened to their stock, they replied that it was 'useless' (*befoida*) and that all the people in Tajikistan who invested in the project have been cheated. Some of my friends even gave me up to USD 400 of their printed shares as 'souvenirs', describing them, in an ironic tone, as useless 'rubbish'. The previous statement, that Tajikistan was not self-sufficient in energy terms, was also contested by many of my acquaintances. Some of my informants told me that, as far as they knew, Tajikistan was already exporting electricity to China and Afghanistan. While still laughing at a joke concerning blackouts, one of my informants told me: 'We sit in the dark, while *they* export electricity to Afghanistan.' Although the Roghun HPS has not been completed, Tajikistan began to export electricity to Afghanistan in 2011 from the Sangtuda HPS on the Vakhsh River.[13]

## Conclusion

In this article, I have sought to advance the notion of 'everyday disasters' to explain firstly, the imprecise boundaries between catastrophic events and daily lives as reported by Kulob residents; and secondly, the ways these events' negative effects were experienced by them as a form of stagnation. Instead of assuming the Roghun HPS or Kulob's reconstruction as projects that would assure Tajikistan's development or an improvement in people's well-being, the flood, the campaigns of forced taxation and the constant exposure to 'everyday disasters' were seen by Kulob residents as direct causes of non-development of life in their hometown.

From this point of view, 'everyday disasters' are seen as buttressed not only by so-called natural disasters but also, as Farmer (2005) puts it, by a combination of social, political and institutional arrangements that cause injury to individuals and societies, or the structural violence in which my informants' daily lives are encompassed. In theory, policies of social development focus on improving the well-being of every individual in society, so they are treated with dignity and justice, with the aim of facilitating their full potential as citizens and human beings. My informants in southern Tajikistan explained to me that they expected the contrary:

non-development amid structural violence. They conveyed to me a common sense of stagnation in the already deprived conditions surrounding their everyday lives.

I have also sought to demonstrate the importance that Kulob residents place on joking and cunning/cheating as means to endure and circumnavigate disastrous events towards everydayness even if cunning/cheating is, at times, evaluated as a factor replicating experiences of stagnation. The everydayness to which they aim to return has also been transformed by the occurrence of disasters such as floods and constant campaigns of forced taxation, yet, through displaying humour and wit, Kulob residents attempt to be recognized and valued, and to create a dimension of individual and communal routines that are less hectic and painful, and thus to render daily life more pleasant. Furthermore, joking and cunning/cheating emphasize Kulob residents' acknowledgement of their involvement in the disaster as the context in which their everyday lives evolve, and bring these topics to public discussion. Thus, my informants aim to present themselves not straightforwardly as either moral champions or amoral cheaters, pitiful victims of floods or of structural violence, or passive objects of the state or the economic crisis that are beyond the scope of their agency.

Finally, it is important that we do not understand Kulob residents' daily struggles as coping or survival strategies that would simply come to an end once the tragedy has passed. Precisely because the context of *fojia* or disaster is a 'field of struggle' (Jackson 2011) spoken about as constant, my informants put their struggles not in terms of 'surviving' but in terms of 'living' (*zindagi kardan*) with whatever means (*chora*) they have at hand – those being a disposition towards piety, patience and endurance, the creativity of joking, the venture of cunning/cheating, or even all these means at the same time, regardless of the fact that cunning/cheating and embracing acts of piety such as delivering aid to others seem to lie at opposite ends of the spectrum of moral possibilities. Thus, although Kulob residents seemed overwhelmed by their adverse circumstances, by the unwanted outcomes of their courses of action and by the paradoxical combination of expected stagnation and the contingency of catastrophic events that underpinned their daily lives, through joking and cunning they displayed their endurance and wit, which also allowed them to create and sustain their humanity and to pursue a life worthy of being lived. After all, as my friend Shirin often told me until her death: 'We do have means.'


## Acknowledgements

I thank Trevor Marchand, Mathijs Pelkmans and Oskar Verkaaik, who provided feedback on earlier versions of this work, and Gül Berna Özcan, Magnus Marsden, Jeanne Féaux de la Croix and two anonymous reviewers, who provided feedback on this article. Following anthropological convention I have used pseudonyms for all people and small places referred to in this text.

## Disclosure statement

No potential conflict of interest was reported by the author.

## Funding

This work was supported by Consejo Nacional de Ciencia y Tecnología (CONACYT-México) under PhD scholarship 209417; and by the University of London Central Research Fund 2008–2009. Earlier versions of this article were presented at the Cambridge Central Asian Forum (2014) and the Postgraduate Seminar of the Anthropology Department at SOAS, University of London (2012).


## Notes

1. In Kulob, most people communicated with me in Tajik and/or Russian. In this text, most transliterations in brackets are in Tajik. When Russian was deployed by my informants, the abbreviation 'Rus.' precedes the transliteration.

2. The main method to gather data for this article was participant observation (2009–2013). In the aftermath of the flood, I also carried out unstructured and open-ended interviews with families affected by the flood. Some of these families were temporarily living in the emergency tent-camp. I also interviewed people who had not been directly affected by the flood but were struggling to collect funds for the Roghun HPS.
3. Robbins (2013, 457) clarifies that the anthropology of the good does not seek 'to define what universally counts as "good", but to explore the different ways people organize their personal and collective lives in order to foster what they think of as good, and to study what it is like to live at least some of the time in light of such a project'.
4. In 2010, 'Tajikistan is a water country' was one of the slogans used by the Tajik government to present the country internationally. Tajikistan hosts nearly 1300 lakes, occupying 705 $km^2$.
5. Similarly to Tajikistan's case, in her work on Kyrgyzstan, Féaux de La Croix (2011) suggests that water and dams are two of the most powerful representations of cleanliness, modernity and progress.
6. For an analysis of technical data on major dams in Central Asia, including Roghun, see Wegerich (2011).
7. Ferry and Mandana (2008) link state-led representations and management of resources (including water to produce electricity) to the project of building a nation-state insofar as this relation concerns notions of sovereignty, economic and social hardship, and achievement.
8. The villages surrounding Roghun were relocated, and access to the site and the wider region was banned, even for journalists (Ergasheva 2012; Suyarkulova 2014).
9. Some analysts consider that the construction of Roghun might 'take over 50% of Tajikistan's GDP' (Marat 2010). To provide a clearer notion of how unviable the Roghun project was (not only because it could take 50% of the country's GDP) it is important to note that, according to Danzer and Oleksiy (2010) and Kumo (2012), remittances constituted nearly 50% of Tajikistan's GDP in 2008.
10. For a detailed analysis of water resources in Central Asia and multilateral agreements on water allocation, see Laldjebaev (2010) and Wegerich (2011).
11. For a more detailed analysis of the ways in which Central Asia is exposed to price fluctuations, see Özcan (2010). For an analysis of trade routes of basic goods to Tajikistan from abroad, see Marsden (2015).
12. For a summary of the latest assessment of the Roghun project by the World Bank (July 2014), see Bisenov (2014).
13. Tajikistan's Ministry of Economic Development reported in February 2014 that the country exported 41 million kWh to Afghanistan. For more details about electricity exports from and blackouts within Tajikistan and Kyrgyzstan, see 'Tajikistan exporting electricity during winter blackouts' (2014).

## References

Anderson, P. 2013. "The Politics of Scorn in Syria and the Agency of Narrated Involvement." *Journal of the Royal Anthropological Institute* 19 (3): 463–481. doi:10.1111/1467-9655.12045

Badiou, A. 2005. *Being and Event*. London: Continuum.

Bankoff, G. 2003. *Cultures of Disaster. Society and Natural Hazard in the PHILIPPINES*. London: Routledge.

Beck, U. 1992. *Risk Society: Towards a New Modernity*. London: Sage.

Béné, C., R. Godfrey Wood, A. Newsham, and M. Davies. 2012. "Resilience: New Utopia or New Tyranny? Reflection about the Potentials and Limits of the Concepts of Resilience in Relationship to Vulnerability Reduction Programmes." IDS working paper 405, London: Institute of Development Studies.

Bisenov, N. 2014. "Roghun Dosh Remains a Problem, Says World Bank." *Business New Europe*. Accessed July 10, 2014. http://www.bne.eu/content/rogun-dosh-remains-problem-says-world-bank.

Canfield, R., and G. Rasuly-Paleczek, eds. 2010. *Ethnicity, Authority and Power in Central Asia. New Games Great and Small*. London and New York: Routlege.

Danzer, A., and I. Oleksiy. 2010. "Migration Patterns in a Remittances Dependent Economy: Evidence from Tajikistan During the Global Financial Crisis." *Migration Letters* 7 (2): 190–202.

Das, V. 2007. *Life and Words: Violence and the Descent into the Ordinary*. Berkeley: University of California Press.

Ergasheva, Z. 2012. "Human Rights Activists about Problems Facing Persons Moved from Roghun Dam Flooding Zone." *Asia-Plus*. Accessed July 10, 2014. http://news.tj/en/news/human-rights-activists-about-problems-facing-persons-moved-roghun-dam-flooding-zone.

Farmer, P. 2005. *Pathologies of Power: Health, Human Rights, and the New War on the Poor: With a New Preface by the Author*. London: University of California Press.

Féaux de La Croix, J. 2011. "Moving Metaphors we Live by: Water and Flow in the Social Sciences and Around Hydroelectric Dams in Kyrgyzstan." *Central Asian Survey* 30 (3/4): 487–502. doi:10.1080/02634937.2011.614097

Ferguson, J. 1999. *Expectations of Modernity: Myths and Meanings of Urban Life on Zambian Copperbelt*. Berkey, California; London: University of California Press.

Ferry, E., and L. Mandana. 2008. "Introduction." In *Timely Assets. The Politics of Resources and Their Temporalities*, edited by E. E. Ferry and M. Limbert, 3–24. Santa Fe: School for Advanced Research Press.

Giddens, A. 1991. *Modernity and Self-identity: Self and Society in the Late Modern Age*. Cambridge: Polity.

Goldstein, D. 2003. *Laughter out of Place: race, Class, Violence and Sexuality in a Rio Shantytown*. Berkely: University of California Press.

Heathershaw, J. 2009. *Post-conflict Tajikistan*. London: Routledge.

Hertzfeld, M. 2004. *Cultural Intimacy: Social Poetics in the Nation-state*. New York: Routledge.

Hoffman, D., and S. Lubkemann. 2005. "Warscape Ethnography in West Africa and the Anthropology of 'Events'." *Anthropological Quarterly* 78 (2): 315–327. doi:10.1353/anq.2005.0024

Humphrey, C. 2008. "Reassembling Individual Subjects: EVENTS And Decisions in Troubled Times." *Anthropological Theory* 8 (4): 357–380. doi:10.1177/1463499608096644

Jackson, M. 2011. *Life Within Limits: Well-being in a World of Want*. Durham: Duke University Press.

Keck, M., and P. Sakdapolrak. 2013. "What is Social Resilience? Lessons Learned and Ways Forwards." *Erdkunde* 67 (1): 5–19. doi:10.3112/erdkunde.2013.01.02

Kumo, K. 2012. "Tajik Labour Migrants and Their Remittances: Is Tajik Migration Pro-poor?" *Post-Communist Economies* 24 (1): 87–109. doi:10.1080/14631377.2012.647630

Laldjebaev, M. 2010. "The Water-energy puzzle in Central Asia: the Tajikistan Perspective." *International Journal of Water Resources Development* 26 (1): 23–36. doi:10.1080/07900620903391812

Mains, D. 2012. "Blackouts and Progress: Privatization, Infrastructure and a Developmentalist State in Jimma, Ethiopia." *Cultural Anthropology* 27 (1): 3–27. doi:10.1111/j.1548-1360.2012.01124.x

Marat, E. 2010. "Will Tajikistan Successfully Construct Roghun?" *Eurasia Daily Monitor* 7 (17). www.jamestown.org/single/?no_cache=1&tx_ttnews[tt_news]=35955&tx_ttnews[backPid]=7&cHash=53f9274652#.U76PSkDN58E.

Marsden, M. 2015. *Trading Worlds: Afghan Merchants Across Modern Frontiers*. London and New York: Hurst and Co; Oxford University Press.

Oliver-Smith, A., and S. Hoffman. 1999. "Anthropology and the Angry Earth: An Overview." In *The Angry Earth: Disaster in Anthropological Perspective*, edited by A. Oliver-Smith and S. Hoffman, 1–16. New York: Routledge.

Özcan, G. B. 2010. *Building States and Markets. Enterprise Development in Central Asia*. Basingstoke: Palgrave Macmillan.

Rasanayagam, J., J. Beyer, and M. Reeves. 2014. "Introduction: Performances, Possibilities and Practices of the Political in Central Asia." In *Ethnographies of the State in Central Asia: performing politics*, edited by M. Reeves, J. Rasanayagam, and J. Beyer, 1–26. Bloomington: Indiana University Press.

Robbins, J. 2013. "Beyond the Suffering Subject: Toward an Anthropology of the Good." *Journal of the Royal Anthropological Institute* 19 (3): 447–462.

Simpson, E. 2013. *The Political biography of an Earthquake: Aftermath and amnesia in Gujarat, India*. London: Hurst.

Stewart, K. 2007. *Ordinary affects*. Duke; London: Duke University Press.

Suyarkulova, M. 2014. "Between National Idea and International Conflict: The Roghun HHP as an Anti-colonial Endeavor, Body of the Nation, and National Wealth." *Water History* 6: 367–383. doi:10.1007/s12685-014-0113-7

Suyarkulova, M., and J. Féaux de la Croix. forthcoming. "Building Big Dams in Tajikistan and Kyrgyzstan: Shaping State-society Relations Through Water Infrastructure Projects".

"Tajikistan Exporting Electricity During Winter Blackouts." 2014. *Central Asia Today*, April 4. http://www.eurasianet.org/node/68237.

Trentmann, F. 2009. "Disruption is Normal. Blackouts, Breakdowns and the Elasticity of Everyday Life." In *Time, Consumption and Everyday Life. Practice, Materiality and Culture*, edited by E. Shove, F. Trentmann, and R. Wilk, 67–84. Oxford: Berg.

Vigh, H. 2008. "Crisis and Chronicity: Anthropological Perspectives on Continuous Conflict and Decline." *Ethnos* 73 (1): 5–24. doi:10.1080/00141840801927509

Wegerich, K. 2011. "Water Resources in Central Asia: Regional Stability or Patchy Make-up?" *Central Asian Survey* 30 (2): 275–290. doi:10.1080/02634937.2011.565231

Zigon, J. 2007. "Moral Breakdown and the Ethical Demand: A Theoretical Framework for an Anthropology of Moralities." *Anthropological Theory* 7 (2): 131–150. doi:10.1177/1463499607077295

# Index

For Product Safety Concerns and Information please contact our
EU representative GPSR@taylorandfrancis.com Taylor & Francis
Verlag GmbH, Kaufingerstraße 24, 80331 München, Germany